Down The Line

A Collection of Poetry, Tall Tales, 'Significant Others' and More

Becky Williams Buckman

Copyright © 2014 Becky Williams Buckman
All rights reserved.

ISBN: 1494233045
ISBN-13: 978-1494233044

For Jim

'My Love, My Soulmate'
for all Eternity

And to my Sister,

Ruth

"To love and be loved is the greatest joy on earth"

INSIDE THE LINES...

Within the covers of *'this collection'* you will find my writings: my poetry, and some of my 'tall tales' - experiences and 'miracles' of my life. It also includes works written by other members of my Johnson heritage and 'tidbits' of wisdom I've learned through my journey in life.

My Grandfather Johnson began writing sermons and preaching in the late 1800's and early 1900's. He wrote his sermons 'longhand' at first, and later on he used an old black typewriter, probably using the hunt and peck method. His lack of formal education did not hinder him in the least. Almost one hundred years later his typewriter was sold at a yard sale. I still regret not keeping the antique in my collection. What a legacy was within those old keys! I'm sure it could have 'talked' for hours. I know it had been bathed with his tears of joy and pain as he labored for his Master. Several of his sermons are in this collection of writings.

I never knew my Grandfather Johnson. That was my loss, but those who knew and *walked with him* on his journey were blessed beyond belief. I am one of the recipients of his gift of journalism that has been passed *down the line* to his descendents. I have been richly blessed with a gift that can never be taken away from me.

Several of the Johnson granddaughters have written poetry during the last two centuries. When my first cousin, Martha Johnson died, we were cleaning out her house; we found a little old 3-ring black binder with poems she'd written during her young adult years. It had been tucked away in the far corner of her closet. We had no idea she was a

Many a line was written 'down the line'

poet! We also discovered one of the poems had been published in the early 1940's. Those poems are included in this collection.

I began scribbling *my thoughts* on Blue Horse Notebook paper anytime I could find a pencil; then my head and hands went to work. I got my first portable typewriter when I went off to college; now the computer has become my *'right hand man.'* When it crashes, I am not far behind - I crash too!

I have been writing all my life. I found things in the attic that I had written as soon as I learned to spell. Well. . .maybe it was just in my *childhood diary* but thanks to my journalism background in high school and college, I have graduated past those primitive writings. I still have some of those diaries where I recounted my daily life, and dreams! They have 'revealed' a lot about who I was back then. . .and as I read through them now, I realize I have graduated past *that person*. That is a good thing!

That happened because I was mentored by many excellent journalists through the years; they helped me polish up my newspaper articles, short stories, prose and poetry. As George Eliot said: *"It is never too late to be what you might have been."* So here I go, becoming what I might have been: 'the author and editor' of my first book, DOWN THE LINE.

Becky pecking away on the Annual Staff Yearbook for Cherokee High School, Canton, Georgia, 1957

I've learned and grown on this writing journey. It has taken a lot more than just penning my thoughts. It has taken many cups of coffee, thousands of hours of discipline, diligence, patience, prayer and the 'pursuit of happiness!' I've been richly rewarded, so now I want to pass it on. My prayer is that you will reap the same abundance of blessings I've inherited.

SPECIAL THANKS

To my parents, Gordon and Leila Mae Williams, who made sure I had multiple opportunities for learning and growing, in all areas of life! I would not be where I am today if it had not been for their faith, love and support. My whole being absorbed their character, and their philosophy of life and death. They gave me their *all!*

To my husband, Jim, who taught me even more about God, life, love, laughter, dying and death. He was truly my best friend! I owe him my soul for giving me something *no one else could have given me!*

To my children, who taught me things that I did not learn in Kindergarten, in college, or in Dr. Spock's books! I'm *'still learning'* from them.

To Dr. G. Ross Freeman, my mentor, and dear friend for over sixty years. First, as my Pastor in Woodstock, Georgia, and later as he guided me in my career as a Christian educator. An author and widely known leader in the United Methodist Church, he has given me constant love and support, encouraging me to *'write, write, write.'*

To Joyce Nutt Turrentine, my Home Room and English teacher in High School. Even now, she continues to encourage the 'creative' spark within me. I treasure her friendship. A Spelling Book/Dictionary is always within my reach, thanks to all of my teachers!

DOWN THE LINE

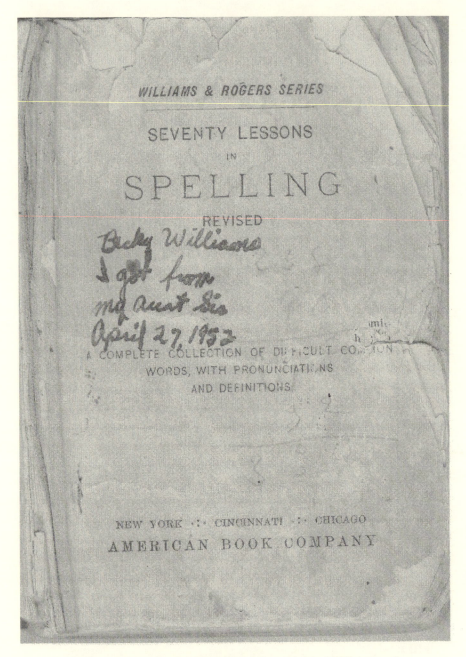

"Seventy Lessons in Spelling" Copyright, 1885, a book given to me by by Aunt Sis on my twelfth birthday in 1952.

SPECIAL THANKS

To my friends who have held me up in all kinds of weather. They are my *rainbows* every day – they reach all around our world, literally. 'The Golden Girls of Cherokee High School' have been with me since 1954. They deserve flags being flown in their honor.

To the seasoned journalists, and published authors of the Summerville Writer's Guild who have opened windows, letting in the 'light' to guide my path; they have led me down avenues I might not have found on my own.

To all the professionals in my career who let me 'fly' and soar in new directions, all the while waving me across the finish line.

Because of these people, I have wind beneath my wings!

CREDITS AND ACKNOWLEDGEMENTS

Permission has been granted by my sister, *Ruth W. Pyle,* for the printing of the poetry written by our cousin, Martha Mae Johnson, and for the Sermons written and delivered by our maternal Grandfather, The Reverend Robert Ithamar Johnson, of Woodstock, Georgia.

Permission has been granted by *Timothy M. Buckman* for the inclusion of his poetry and song lyrics.

Heidi Ruska Krone permitted the use of the lyrics of 'The Wedding Song.' Permission was granted *by Timothy Buckman* for the score.

Images and Photos: *Becky Williams Buckman*

TABLE OF CONTENTS

I. *My Poems. . . for all time*
Becky Williams Buckman (1940 -)
1

II. *Martha's Poems... In her time*
Martha Mae Johnson (1919-1998)
61

III. *'Circuit Rider' Sermons in my time*
The Rev. Robert Ithamar Johnson (1870...1934)
95

IV. *Tall Tales*
Becky Williams Buckman
115

V. *"Significant Others..."*
By various authors, and lyricists
325

VI. *Sign Language. . .*
Becky Williams Buckman
387

VII. This and 'That...'
415

VIII. Contributing Authors
423

My Poems...
for all time

Becky Williams Buckman
(1940 -)

"Poetry begins with a lump in the throat."
Robert Frost

"All good poetry is the spontaneous overflow of powerful feelings. It takes its origin from emotion recollected in tranquility."

William Wordsworth

TABLE OF CONTENTS

Down the Line 5
A Mother Knows. 7
There Will Come a Time 8
Bars and More 10
Dancing With You. 12
Shadows. 14
Mother Takes Wings. 16
I've Known Many Men 18
When I Got Wings 21
Love Hurts Love Heals. 23
I Did Not Know. 25
I'm Not A Quitter. 27
Mom's Old Rocker 28
You Have Been There 31
For Coming My Way. 33
He's The Way He Is 35
I Danced 36
I'm All Here 38
A Mother's Day 39
A Broken Heart 41
Sow Your Oats. 42
The Heart That Cries. 44
What's A Mother To Do? 46
When I Look Down 48
Don't Take Me There. 49
Put It All to Bed 51
I Am Where I Am 52
Too Many Friends. 53
Don't Slow Me Down 55
Life After Death 56
True Love Never Ends 58
My Call 60

I. MY POEMS...FOR ALL TIME

DOWN THE LINE

It came to me
Down the line
Was it just 'there?'
From out of 'where?'

Back up the road
And down the line
A far piece back,
Was writing just my knack?

I never asked
Or even wondered why.
My writing was just 'there'
But from which 'starry sky?'

Now it is just me and my pen -
And now is my time.
All from good genes,
My writing came down the line.

It was just there
All the long while -
Dormant sometimes, yet still
Coming to me down the line.

The lines came so freely
Flooding my thoughts -
More every day, deep into the night...
I know I will always write.

DOWN THE LINE

Write as I will, wherever I am.
Write as I may, but
Just what will I say?
'Random thoughts,' just for today.

Thanks be to God for giving
So many lines, every time.
I pray…Lord, keep them coming
On down the line!

Becky Williams Buckman
Oct. 19, 2009

I. MY POEMS...FOR ALL TIME

A MOTHER KNOWS

A Mother knows when you are on a cloud.
A Mother knows when you hit ground.
She knows your heart, your soul -
They are forever bound.

A Mother knows the pain you feel;
The ache that makes your heart break.
It makes walking on, and on,
Almost more than you can take.

She's standing by, just holding on
With faith and love to see you through.
To hold you up, once again,
Until all your skies are blue.

She was there with you from the start -
Nine long months...now so many years.
Your heartbeat is still tied to her heart
Through all your dreams, and your fears.

A Mother knows them all...she just does!

Becky Williams Buckman
June 16, 2011

* * * Previously published in *"Famous Poets of the American People"* and in *"Stars in Our Hearts'/ World Poetry Movement."*

DOWN THE LINE

THERE WILL COME A TIME

There will come a time -
I won't know when.
I won't bring him home.
Is it now, or is it then?

I've seen him on *'good'* days,
I've seen him on *'bad'*
I've seen him *very 'happy'*
But more often, he was *'sad.'*

There will come a time -
I've often wondered when.
It had crossed my mind…
Will it be now, or will it be then?

I've seen him *'high.'*
I've seen him down 'low'
I've seen him tossed all
About - *to and fro.*

The *call* came quick
And quite late that night.
He was more than just sick!
And we were all filled with fright.

His *time* had now come -
Nothing more could be done.
He just slipped away into heaven
His battle was now won!

Becky Williams Buckman
July 25, 2007

I. MY POEMS... FOR ALL TIME

*** Written *In memory* of my husband, Jim Buckman, within weeks after his death, June 16, 2007; first published on POETRY.COM in the Fall, 2007, in IMMORTAL VERSES, The International Library of Poetry, Fall 2007 and in GREAT POETS ACROSS AMERICA – April, 2012

DOWN THE LINE

BARS AND MORE

You had your bars -
What a *night life!*
You had your drinks:
Maybe more than wine.

The *first time around,* back then
We were so much in love but so far apart.
You found your place in life
While I found my career.

We walked away from each other -
We each chose a different road.
With many miles apart it became
Come what may. *'Just let it be. . .'*

Then one day you took a new road -
Turning your back on your old ways
You began to search for *daylight*
And for a brand new start.

You found me and 'my place,'
For the *second time around.*
You walked right in and saw my heart
Just waiting to be found!

I. MY POEMS...FOR ALL TIME

This time we could walk the same road
Together now - with a *new kind of wine*.
With love and laughter we danced through life -
Those were *the best of all times!*

*** *To honor what would have been our 42nd anniversary.*

Becky Williams Buckman
June 19, 2013

DANCING WITH YOU

The light in your eyes
Dances all around.
The smile on your face
Puts a dance in my step.

The light in my eyes
Meets with your sight.
The smile on my face
Puts a dance in your step.

The dance has begun -
Together we embrace,
Facing the moon just now -
Much later, facing the sun.

Our dance goes on forever.
Around the world we go,
Sharing our love and our smiles -
Sharing *'our dance'* as we go.

This dance of our lives
Gives light to our souls.
The glow in our hearts
Lightens our way - our goals!

What is a dance?
What is a glow?
What is a smile?
Does anyone know?

I. MY POEMS...FOR ALL TIME

We know how to dance.
We know how to show
Our own special love.
'Our dance' is forever - we know!

Dancing the Night Away in Charleston, South Carolina, Christmas 2004

Becky Williams Buckman
February 16, 2007

*** This was written especially for *'my love' Jim,* and was included in his Eulogy at his Memorial Service on June 30, 2007 in Canton Georgia.

SHADOWS

"I have a little shadow
That goes in and out with me,"
Just like the poem* says,
It is more than I can see!

There's more of me
Way out ahead -
Looming in the distance,
Who knows where it leads?

Where does my shadow go?
Lord, will I ever see just
How it 'falls' on others?
Does it bring them glee?

Or do I throw out *darkness*
To cast upon their side,
To make them look *downward*
Or even want to hide?

Lord, I pray my shadow
Brings glory in each day
To *everyone* who sees me,
As I walk along their way!

*Poem by Robert Louis Stevenson *"I Have A Little Shadow"*

I. MY POEMS...FOR ALL TIME

Becky Williams Buckman
Dec. 8, 2008

DOWN THE LINE

MOTHER TAKES WINGS

Sitting at the table,
Everyone is there.
Mom is always the last one
To take her special chair.

She is the first to get up,
To pour more coffee and tea.
It's just my mother's nature -
With her smile, don't you see?

She checks all the bowls;
The platters are all full
But not for very long before I wonder
'Who will get *the bone* to pull?'

Pulley bones, legs - all on the plate -
Dad always gets the breast; we get the rest.
Now, there is just *one wing left:*
Mom takes it and says: "It's the best!"

Dinner is done, most everyone is gone,
But she's still not done. . .
She is always in the kitchen with
Piles of dirty dishes - she's doing her best!

She's so very tired and hot -
Yet, she knows she is quite blessed.
Mom really does have wings,
And some day she will rest!

I. MY POEMS...FOR ALL TIME

She's gone now and has *new wings* -
So very happy and blessed is she.
She was a beautiful blessing to me!
Now she is flying - Oh, *so free!*

Becky Williams Buckman
May 2, 2008

Mother was always 'flying high'

*** Written in memory of my mother, *Leila Mae Johnson Williams.* (1898-1993)

DOWN THE LINE

I'VE KNOWN MANY MEN

I've known many strong men
Who walked in my path,
Giving me their hand to steady my pace -
To show me life's road and what to face.

My *Daddy* was the first to hold my hand
Guiding my steps 'til I could turn loose.
He let me go when the time was right
He turned me loose - just like a kite!

John Gordon Williams *'turning loose'* of his *'baby'* in 1971

I. MY POEMS...FOR ALL TIME

My *Pastors* were strong and gave me advice
Showing me things I'd never 'thought.'
I took in new goals that I hadn't sought
Robing myself in 'garments' that I had not bought!

I was showered with blessings from above
I received gifts of truth, compassion and love.
I sewed them into the pattern I was weaving
For my life and its goals – by *just simply believing!*

Then into my life came one special man - *'My love'*
He saw in *me* something he wanted to know.
He had *'a love'* for me, unlike any I had known.
It was God's gracious *'gift'* to me – it was mine to own!

I couldn't fathom a love quite that great
I couldn't believe or *'see'* what he saw in me but
I saw something *in him* that he had not seen
It was the *'love of God'* - made just for *his queen!*

He opened his arms and I fell in -
An innocent young woman,
Now turned into *his* queen!
Our love grew... it was a dream.

We kept on dreaming,
Moment by moment, day by day
Oh, what *a miracle!*
What more can I say?

We now were *a team,* bound by God's love
Each rather weak, but together quite strong.
Now, more than one, much more than just two -
Three strands wrapped in *one love* all day long!

> Becky Williams Buckman
> August 30, 2010

James Floyd Buckman and Carolyn Rebecca (Becky) Williams began their 'family tree' June 19, 1971, at Haygood Memorial United Methodist Church, Atlanta, Ga.

I. MY POEMS...FOR ALL TIME

WHEN I GOT WINGS

When I got my wings to fly
I didn't look back
To see who was standing by.
I looked ahead
As far as I could see
There was no one there - just me!

I was on my own,
Or so I thought...
With these new wings
I'd fly high to places unknown.
Reaching new heights,
I now was *'in flight.'*

Once, I did look back,
And standing by, there was
My precious mother.
She'd given me my wings
To watch me fly, all on my own.
She let me go, and begged me to sing!

The other time when I looked back
Mother was no longer *standing* by
But down *on her knees* rejoicing in prayer
She was smiling and laughing
Just watching me fly.

"let 'er fly!"

Becky Williams Buckman
January, 2009

*** In memory of my mother, Leila Mae Johnson Williams who gave birth to me 'late in life' but still gave me her all, and really loved every minute of it! She truly was 'my angel on earth' and 'prayed me through' many difficult times in my life!

I. MY POEMS...FOR ALL TIME

LOVE HURTS - LOVE HEALS

I walked right into beauty -
I was the beholder of his love
My eyes were so full of stars
Yet the doors of my heart opened wide.

He reached out to take me in
With open arms I held him.
His eyes beheld my being -
My being looked into his, with a grin!

Love walked right into our lives
To take us from *here* to eternity.
We were *new* every day
Growing in love's sweet sway.

With our love that ran so deep
At the altar we made those *promises*
We thought we could keep, yet
Some days the climb was much too steep.

Beyond love's hurt and awkward pain
What love would now remain?
A healing touch, a listening ear, a warm embrace
Could take us from *there* to a new plain.

When hearts and souls had been so tossed
It seemed our love was dying but
We looked for that stronger bond and
Got a tighter grip on God - we were not lost!

DOWN THE LINE

We had to let old hurts and pain fade away
So a new and stronger love could take their place.
God's higher love walked in and
He healed us with *Amazing Grace!*

Becky Williams Buckman,
December 2007

I. MY POEMS...FOR ALL TIME

I DID NOT KNOW

Those many days so long ago
I did not know I would know you so well
I did not know I could love you
The way I learned to do

Strangers back then
How long has it been?
The years rolled by, one by one
From dawn til setting sun

We fought many battles
They were all up hill
Some were lost, many were won
Our souls were fulfilled

You left us too soon
You took your wings to fly!
My God, how can this be?
I can not imagine why...

Now there is a gaping hole
Where you once belonged and
Life is so lonely without your song
Something terrible went wrong!

Many dark clouds and heavy rains
Pour into my heart -
Burdened with grief and pain
I am broken apart.

DOWN THE LINE

A part of me died when you ran ahead
Leaving ugly raw layers of hurt
That won't go away - they just stay,
Surrounding my soul for all it is worth!

But you have your own new mansion
With the crown you have won
You are singing with the angels and
Your work on earth is done!

Your colors are shining like
A rainbow in the sky
You brighten every corner up there -
We all know why!

Just know that I loved you, dear friend
From *'day one'* until the very end
The love you poured out on all of us
Was like iron and steel - it did not bend.

Until we meet again, dear Bob,
Enjoy your new home, sing in the choir,
Pass out your smiles and your hugs
Just like you did the first day we met.

Soon and very soon, I'll join you
Inside those heavenly gates and I know
You will be there to greet me -
Some days, I just can't wait!

Becky Williams Buckman
August, 2010

*** In memory of Robert (Bob) Ruska, a dear family friend

I. MY POEMS...FOR ALL TIME

I'M NOT A QUITTER

I'm not a quitter -
There were many roadblocks.
I ran into hard times
So I climbed steep rocks.

I wouldn't give up
'Til I reached my one goal.
I just wouldn't quit,
Almost losing my soul.

I kept climbing higher
I found things unseen.
I'm not a quitter -not then,
Not now, nor anywhere in between!

Quitting would never be easy
And stopping wouldn't do.
I just kept on climbing
Until I was through!

Becky Williams Buckman
Christmas Eve, 2009

DOWN THE LINE

MOM'S OLD ROCKER

Supper was done, dishes were clean;
Mom's apron now hung on its old nail.
'Twas torn ragged, and old, from days gone by.
It had been worn through many a meal
And her old recipe book knew why!

She left her hot kitchen - to the front porch she went
She'd been cooking all day - her energy was spent;
She flopped down in her favorite old rocker.
For more than an hour she 'fanned' to keep cool.
Those summer evenings, how quickly time went!

We each took our place, on those hot summer nights
Mom in her chair, Dad on his lounge, with me in the swing
Everyone knew that old rocker was hers...
There she would rest until darkness fell down.
At last, *her long day* was through.

That old rocker held Mom's 'pretty' frame
She rocked back and forth, always the same
Fanning the breeze, swatting at flies.
Her rocker had a long history - just like her years.
It had heard laughter, and rocked away many tears.

It's old wooden frame painted white by my dad,
Had seen better days but really, who cared?
Mom was still there, rocking away
In her old cane-bottom rocker, with its
Old pillow, now dingy and gray.

I. MY POEMS...FOR ALL TIME

The old cane bottom of her rocker was *sinking* quite low.
She too was sinking, *but did we really know?*
Family and friends came by - what did they say?
They talked of their *'olden days'* and
Where they soon would go.

That often went on 'til long after dark.
Their old 'church fans' waved back and forth
To keep the air moving – but what was *that* worth?
It was worth many a memory to me -
More precious than gold, and so full of mirth!

Mom's old rocker - it's story has now been told.
Now it is gone, it rotted with age.
Mom is now gone to *her new rocking chair*
Maybe even rocking on streets of gold
Lifting her voice as she sings in the air.

'Precious memories, how they linger
How they ever flood my soul...'

Mom and her rocker - they were one of a kind!

Becky Williams Buckman
January 12, 2007

***In Memory of my Mother, *Leila Mae Hawkins Johnson,* born and raised on a farm on Rope Mill Road, in Woodstock, Georgia. She was the daughter of the Rev. Robert Ithamar Johnson, some of whose sermons are included in this book.

I. MY POEMS...FOR ALL TIME

YOU HAVE BEEN THERE

You've been there for me
In the good times
And the bad.

You've held me up
Many days when
I was so very sad.

You've been a bright light
During those lonely days
And sleepless nights.

You've been a beautiful 'bloom'
Whose petals reached out
To take away my gloom.

What more can I say?
Words cannot pen my thoughts.
You have made my day!

You've seen me through
So much of life's 'stuff' -
My *thanks* is never enough!

You gave so much to
Your brother and me -
More than any eye can see!

From the depths of my heart:
"My hat is off to you -
You've played a great part."

DOWN THE LINE

You've helped me *move on;*
You have helped me heal
Now that *my love* is gone,

He has not really gone far.
He has just slipped away - he is
Waiting for me, just across the bar!

Becky Williams Buckman
April, 2008

***In memory of Margaret Buckman, the sister of my husband.

I. MY POEMS...FOR ALL TIME

FOR COMING MY WAY

I met you once
That's all it took.
I knew right then
You would be my friend.

You found the keys
I didn't know I'd lost
When I was so *undone,*
You were my friend.

You spoke each day
As you came and went
Making life more bearable -
Not quite so *'unspent!'*

You did not know then
What you did for me
But the light in your eyes
Kept me from *walking in the dark*

Back then, my days were long -
So very lonely and cold.
Some days were good – I could get through.
Yet, too many nights were boring and *'old.'*

I had traveled for so long
With my family by my side.
I had seen the good, bad and ugly
With all kinds of *banners unfurled.*

DOWN THE LINE

It was different now -
I was left alone, in *a different world*
With people I did not know.
All of *my banners hung very low.*

Youth is on your side now -
It will be yours for quite a while.
Keep sharing your smile
As you walk every mile!

While spreading your joy,
Keep sharing your light.
Thank you, *Melissa,* for coming my way -
The love you shared made everything bright.

Becky Williams Buckman
July, 2007

Dedicated to a 'new friend' in Summerville, SC

I. MY POEMS. . .FOR ALL TIME

HE'S THE WAY HE IS. . .

He's the way he is
because his parents
were the way they were.

His parents were
the way they were
because their parents were
who they were.

So, *'down the line'*
as the record goes…
Where will *'this way'* stop?
GOD only knows!

                                    Becky Williams Buckman
                                    June 19, 2012

I DANCED

Life is a Dance
You Learn As You Go

For a while I danced
Through life single file
I loved every minute
But not every mile.

I danced through life
Sometimes on my heels
One day, I fell on my face
But I got up, and I danced again.

Then I met 'my true love'
Once again, and he found his -
Then I danced through life
As a mother and his wife.

I danced through life
Some days without shoes
I danced through life
Some days on my toes.

I danced in the sun
I danced in the dark
I danced high in the air
Always on a lark.

I danced through life
Tapping out each step
Yet some days of my life
There were times of strife!

I. MY POEMS...FOR ALL TIME

Some days I danced on
Rocky ground and shifting sand -
I danced through hurt,
Along with its dirt.

I keep dancing
This time, alone
I am dancing as 'one'
But I have to go on.

I keep dancing, still looking up
And smiling, without a frown.
I will keep dancing til the day I die,
Loving each step just like a clown!

Becky Williams Buckman
August 11, 2009

I'M ALL HERE...

I'm all here, and there -
One body, to be given away
One head, to hold me together
One mind, to create.
One nose, to smell the aroma of life
One mouth, to speak love all around
One heart, to *care for others*

I'm all here, and there -
Two eyes to see the beauty God set before me
Two ears to hear the sounds of His creation
Two hands to help those in need
Two legs to explore new pathways
Two feet to feel the shifting sands of life
Two arms to surround those I hold dear.

I'm now here in a brand NEW YEAR -
My only prayer is that I am *fully awake,*
Ready to use each part of my body,
Mind and soul, as a whole.
With one pure heart to love all of mankind.
To be *'there, or here'* for each person I meet.

Lord, let me keep living abundantly. *AMEN*

Becky Williams Buckman
January 1, 2012

I. MY POEMS...FOR ALL TIME

A MOTHER'S DAY

Today was *My Day*
To remember You, my dear.
Because of you and our love,
I am A *MOTHER*.

It was always you -
There was never another.
You crowned me with the name,
The name of *MOTHER*.

I miss celebrating *My Day*
With you and our family.
It is just not the same today
Now that you are gone.

This day will always be special
Because YOU were who you were -
The Father of our children,
The Husband of their *MOTHER*

They didn't forget
To show their love -
They called me *MOTHER*
On this, my special day.

You taught them well
To love and respect me
Every day - not just on *this* day
Set aside for *MOTHERS*.

DOWN THE LINE

What a wonderful gift
You gave me many years ago.
No other prize could have
Been given or blessed me so.

Today and every day, I miss you so -
I have shed my tears, more than I can bare.
But when I look all around me I know
Both you and God are always there!

Each time I look into the faces
Of our precious children, on *their special day*
I can still see the gleam in your eyes
When I told you they were *on the way!*

Mother - Mother - Mother
A person like no other.
A Mother's 'world' is all its very own!
Into eternity, every Mother will be known.

                                        Becky Williams Buckman
                                        Mother's Day
                                        May 11, 2008

I. MY POEMS...FOR ALL TIME

A BROKEN HEART

She has lived with a broken heart
From *bad seeds* that were sown,
Waiting to be healed with a touch
Which only GOD can bestow

When will she find relief from
Those who *hurt her* and caused this grief?
She has lived in hell - with so many fears,
With anguish and tears flowing for years

But there will come a time, one day
When pain will leave and tears will cease
Those hurts will no longer bring decay
Her *joy and peace* will then increase!

Then all darkness will fade,
She will walk in *new light*.
Mind, body and soul will all be healed
When God is fully revealed!

Becky Williams Buckman
March 23, 2013

DOWN THE LINE

SOW YOUR OATS

You sowed your wild oats.
Now slow down, young man
It's time to settle down.

You've cast your oats
All over the world
Far and wide.

The wind blew hard and pushed
Those seeds deep - so deep
They cut into your soul.

You sowed your oats
Young man - was the price fair?
Fair over here? Or over there?

It's time to settle down, young man.
Settle down. . . do it now.
Go ahead - It's time to be a Man!

The price is very high
But the price *is* fair.
Go on and be a Man…It's worth the try.

You can be a *new* Man
Start with 'new oats' and sow.
Stand back - just watch them grow!

I. MY POEMS. . .FOR ALL TIME

You will reap *true rewards* -
They too will run very deep
But they will be yours forever - to keep!

Becky Williams Buckman
May 8, 2011

DOWN THE LINE

THE HEART THAT CRIES

I never knew so much
I didn't want to know.
I never knew how much it hurt
To sit back and watch him *grow!*

I never knew the pain that came
With every step he took -
I never knew the raw places
Crammed in his every nook.

I never knew the horror of his world
Until he opened up my eyes
To see the *wicked ways of life...*
Now, all I want to do is cry!

I've cried all day, and all night -
I prayed it wasn't true – I wanted to think
'There must be some other way'
I prayed *'GOD...Don't let him sink!'*

The pain and agony he knew was passed around
To all who came close, or just nearby.
It broke so many hearts - more than just two!
For years, it made all of us cry!

I had no clue, no clue at all
That any life could be this harsh.
I had not known such *'wars'* of hell and hurt -
Nor lost in that kind of deep marsh!

I. MY POEMS. . .FOR ALL TIME

I never knew what some people would dare -
I lived in a world of people who cared.
I had been so loved, my whole life through -
If only *my love* could somehow be shared.

My eyes, my heart, my soul,
All of me aches for this life of his,
A life that is not nailed down.
I long to see him strive for a 'crown.'

Until he finds his way and settles down
The crown he *wants* is out of sight.
The crown he *needs* is not of this world -
It will only come when he sees the *Light*.

Lord, show me a way to reach him and
When I can't reach him, *I know YOU will*.
You alone can melt hearts made of stone
Now I pray: *'Make his heart your very own.'*

Becky Williams Buckman
February, 2013

DOWN THE LINE

WHAT'S A MOTHER TO DO?

What's a Mother to do
When the *babies* are all born,
And the bottles all done?
What's a mother to do?

What's a Mother to do
When the *carpools* are done,
And the *games* are all won?
What's a mother to do?

What's a Mother to do
When the *degrees* are all finished?
The *wedding* has been planned –
Now, what should she do?

What's a Mother to do
When kids rarely come home and
'Everything else' comes first. . .
What will a Mother do?

What's a Mother to do
When the *pho*ne rarely rings. . .
And *junk mail*? Give it a fling!
What's a mother to do?

This Mother is *not needed* –
She is no longer a wife.
Her house is empty yet full of strife!
How does she start over?

I. MY POEMS...FOR ALL TIME

Go shopping to buy a new dress?
Try on pretty new shoes?
Get some new jewelry?
That's what a Mother can do!

Pick up a new book?
Make some *new friends*?
Find an old garment to mend?
What will *this Mother* do?

She can find some new goals
She can quit feeling useless, and old.
She can keep on dancing - just being bold!
That's what *this Mother* will do!

Becky Williams Buckman
August 11, 2010

WHEN I LOOK DOWN

When I look *down*
What I often see
Makes a *wreck* of me.
From upside down
Or on my side -
The *'negative'* refuses to hide.

It is only when I
Stand up tall
I am no longer facing
That blank wall.
I take my ball
And throw it high. . .

It takes its course
And finds its goal.
Now, my life is on the right path -
I am going straight
To the finish line where
I am looking into *heaven's gate!*

Becky Williams Buckman
November 22, 2009

I. MY POEMS...FOR ALL TIME

DON'T TAKE ME THERE

Don't take me there,
unless you are going too.

Plan to stay with me and
Walk with me - each step of the way.

It is *not my home*, it's dark in there.
I can't go there all alone.

They will strip me of my clothes
Without a second thought.

They will force me against my will
To go against my very own choice.

They will put me in a sterile room
With cold walls and cracks in the ceiling.

Those dingy gray walls just make me sick
When I was already ill - so void of *life!*

They'll treat me like a child, spoon feed me
Spank my hand, then tie me down!

They'll take away my things
And hide them, thinking I can't see.

They'll give me *a calendar* of things to do and see
Hoping I will not want to flee!

There might be a cup of warm coffee but
Even with the sugar, it still won't be like *'mine'*

DOWN THE LINE

There will be a dozen pills for me to take
Too big to swallow - how can I fake it?

I am too old to live with you in your home -
Your life is full and frisky, just as it should be.

You think I won't notice where you take me;
You try to make me think I'll *be better cared for!*

You think I'll be happier with others like me -
That my days will be filled with so much glee!

Before you take me there, perhaps I'll just go
By my very own choice - Maybe so?

Or maybe God will *call me on home*
Before that day comes. . . Who is to know?

Becky Williams Buckman
August, 2013

I. MY POEMS...FOR ALL TIME

PUT IT ALL TO BED

Now the day is over;
What ever is on your mind
It is too much in your head -
It is time to put it all to bed.

It began with the morning sun
But what you did today is done
Put it all behind you.
Just look - just see *what you have won!*

Put it all to bed - all those worrisome
Troubles that you saw.
The *unfinished work* sits there and
If you let it, it will surely gnaw.

You may not see the banner
Flying high above your head
But when you *turn things loose,*
You can put it all to bed.

Put it all behind you - down in its' own bed
When you get up you will *face the Son!*
Face the morning with joy and laughter -
Once more *you have won!*

Becky Williams Buckman
June 30, 2008

*** written on the first anniversary of the Memorial Service for my husband, Jim.

DOWN THE LINE

I AM WHERE I AM

One day I sat there alone
In my own little world, with nothing to say.
Stripped so bare - I was *'down to the bone.'*
My song? A dull monotone.

I am where I am
because *You* came along.
I am where I am and
Now I have a new song.

The smile on your face,
The look in your eye
Gave me a reason to
Look up toward the sky

Your *new light* would take me
Out of my tunnel so dark.
You gave me *a new song*
'Twas much like a lark.

I was now singing, so full of glee.
Something *new* was inside of me!
Let me say to you, and the world
'I am where I am. . .

Because *YOU* came along!'

Becky Williams Buckman
Feb. 13, 2010

*** Dedicated to my friend, Ellen, who invited me to join the Summerville Writer's Guild in South Carolina, Fall, 2007.

I. MY POEMS...FOR ALL TIME

TOO MANY FRIENDS

Some people say
I have 'too many friends.'
Having too many friends
Is fine with me,
So - I disagree!
Read my thoughts -
Perhaps you will see.

You ask: How do you keep up with so many friends -
             Where do you find time?

I say: I find them - they're all over town -
            I try to help everyone I see
            Why can't I run from them?
            Just flee from their messes.. forget and move on?
            Why should I ignore them? Can't you see?

            They are crying for help - needing some love
            They have no one to run to,
            Never finding what they need.
            What's so wrong if I do a good deed?

            Some might be down in a deep hole,
            Alone and cold, will anyone care?
            It is black and dark down there.
            Listen, my friend: *Someone must dare!*

            Yes, I know, some can be just like a leech...
            Wanting so much more than they can reach.
            Are they looking to *me* to pull them through?
            Will I? Can I be the one to cross that breach?

DOWN THE LINE

Can we teach them to stand on their own?
To quit giving up and begging for help?
Teach them to work out their messes, one at a time. . .
With God's help and ours, their life could be fine!

I'll take a chance on *walking with them* for a while.
I'll take a chance on being their friend.
I'll take a chance on watching them smile
I'll take a chance on watching them mend!

Will you?

Becky Williams Buckman
August 1, 2011

I. MY POEMS...FOR ALL TIME

DON'T SLOW ME DOWN...

You said to me: "Don't slow me down
I have places to go,
And things to do!

Don't get in my way
I have so little time -
And it's all *mine*.

Don't tell me your feelings;
I'm already behind;
I hope you won't think that I'm unkind!"

I thought: "Oh No, sir, that is just fine,
Go on ahead - *do your thing*,
And I'll do mine - I won't whine!

I'm just saying...and *praying* that
No one will ever tell you
What you've just told me.

If they do, I'm sure it will be very unkind!"

Becky Williams Buckman
March 4, 2011

DOWN THE LINE

LIFE AFTER DEATH

I know there is life -
I know there is death.
A lot goes on *in between*
Those two cosmic rays.

I've had life, and I've had death.
There has been some heaven
And there's been some hell
In between those two worlds.

Now I know for sure
There is *new life after death!*
There is now a heaven
And a new earth for us!

How would I *know* there is life
After death....if I had not died?
Resurrection morning has now come -
'There's a new awakening' I cried.

I am now *resurrected* from the dead -
From the dark lonely days,
And cold sullen nights.
The rising sun shines along my way.

I have *new eyes* to see more colors,
Now more *awake* to the tunes of the songbirds,
More alive to all the joys of creation,
I am quickened to the smiles I see!

A new prance in my step
A new dance in my shoes.

I. MY POEMS...FOR ALL TIME

Another chance to feel love -
The kind of love I lost in death.

Life after death, Yes, it is there,
So full of beauty
You might ask: *'from out of where?'*
In the arms of others who care!

It is God and God alone
Who puts *life* back into *death*
And warmth back into a broken heart
He has given us strength for a new start!

THANKS BE TO GOD, who giveth us the victory over death.

Becky Williams Buckman
February 4, 2013

DOWN THE LINE

TRUE LOVE NEVER ENDS....

The 'never ending story' of *my true love:*
It came to me from GOD above.
He knew just where I was back then
And loved me with his *own special* love.

Because it was me, and only me?
Was that all he really needed to see?
When I looked, I saw the same
Wrapped in such *a beautiful frame!*

Our true love came at first sight and
We loved with all our might.
Yet we felt the storms come through
Some days, lasting into the night.

We walked on, holding on, hand in hand -
I was his and he was *'my man.'*
This true love could only grow more each day
Since we were *one* even when skies were gray.

Our *true love would* not bend
With any storm or strife -
Nothing on earth, or from above,
Could separate us in this life.

Never ending was our divine love -
Nothing on this earth or from above,
Could make us part our ways
Until 'the day' death stole him away.

I. MY POEMS...FOR ALL TIME

We are now apart on earth,
But not in heaven above -
Forever then, and now
Is our eternal love.

I long for that day in heaven
When once again
We will walk hand in hand
To prove *our true love* had no end!

                              Becky Williams Buckman
                              July 9, 2011

MY CALL

I don't want to live so very long.
I don't want to cry, or feel I don't *belong*.
I don't ever want to be a *burden*,
Just left to *'hang on . . .and on!'*

It's not *my way* though.
It's not *my call* to make today,
How long I will live,
Where, or in what way?

The deck is full,
The cards are now dealt
They are all on the table,
I'll keep *living* as long as I'm able!

Each day I'll do the best that I can -
There is nothing more I can do
I will be happy, and free
I will just be ME!

When *God* calls my name
I plan to be *ready and raring* to go
Knowing I've lived my best. . .and
In Heaven I will find *peace and rest!*

Becky Williams Buckman
Nov. 11, 2009

Martha's Poems...
In her time

These words were penned by me.
Martha Johnson

Martha Mae Johnson
(1919-1998)

"Poetry is the universal language which the heart holds with nature and itself."

William Hazlitt

TABLE OF CONTENTS

My Task 66
The Lonely Galilean. 67
A Little Word 69
Opportunity 70
Attainments. 71
Life 72
God's Near 73
Friendship. 74
A Young Man's Quest. 75
Reminiscent 76
Living. 77
Life's Highway. 78
The Savior of Men 79
Too Many Parties and Too Many Pals 80
To My Friend 82
A Memoir 83
Today. 84
The Vast Unknown. 85
Someone's Last Day 86
The Old Year. 87
Indifference* 89
Memoriam to Martha Johnson** 90

* G. A. Studdert Kennedy, a British Poet and War Veteran. This poem was found on the first page of Martha's little black book of poetry.

**LoDean Chapman Gresham, Martha's cousin

II. MARTHA'S POEMS...IN HER TIME

EDITOR'S NOTES

We were going through the *'worldly possession'* of our first cousin, Martha Mae Johnson, soon after she died in 1998. She had few things that were of great value in the monetary sense. She didn't buy stock in *'that part of the world.'*

Hidden in the dark corner of her closet was a little black leather notebook aged with color and time. With the greatest of curiosity, we opened it and discovered the inner being of a woman who *'against all odds'* attained high esteem in the eyes of many. As far as we know, no one in our family knew she wrote poetry, much less that one of her poems had been published: *The Lonely Galilean, in 1942*. She was twenty-three at the time.

Martha had penned her deepest thoughts that were never spoken, and perhaps uttered only to God, as she climbed every mountain in her life. Therein was her 'heart and soul' - what a significant treasure beyond all treasures! She had kept this little journal hidden many years in her meager little home, on Main Street, in Woodstock, Georgia.

She was a quiet but strong woman of faith. These thoughts opened up to us some things we never knew about her life, love, friendship, faith and her soul.

These poems written by Martha Mae Johnson are included for your journey in life. They have inspired our family since the first day we found them. May they now be a part of your inspiration, on whatever path you may choose to walk. We trust they will speak to your heart as they have spoken to ours.

Becky Williams Buckman

MY TASK

To stand above the fret of petty strife;
To stand undaunted against the storms of life;
To do to others as I would have them do to me;
To strive each day to serve humanity;
To give freely of that which is mine,
Never stopping to count the cost or the time.
Ever let me laugh and love and lift,
Until one day the clouds will drift,
And Heaven and Earth shall meet,
As one great Brotherhood around the Savior's feet.

Martha Mae Johnson

II. MARTHA'S POEMS...IN HER TIME

THE LONELY GALILEAN

That lonely Galilean
Indeed was the Master of men;
He tread the lowly paths of earth
And conquered every sin.

He went a little farther
Than man must ever go;
He knew the path of sorrow
He suffered pangs of woe.

He went a little farther
For paths of service free;
In agony he sweated blood
As he prayed in Gethsemane.

He went a little farther
In poverty, hope and love;
He gave his life as a sacrifice
So that man might live above.

He went a little farther
In every road of life
We, too, must follow in His lead
If we hope to win the strife.

Martha Mae Johnson
July 1, 1941

EDITOR'S NOTE: To my knowledge this was the only one of Martha's poems that was published prior to the printing of this book. It was published in *TESTAMENT OF FAITH: An Anthology of Current Spiritual Poetry* by Harbinger House, N. Y. (1942)

<u>**Harbinger's note about Martha:**</u> *Miss Johnson, a welfare worker, enjoys working for people. A resident of North Georgia, she is active in church affairs. This is her first published work.*

II. MARTHA'S POEMS...IN HER TIME

A LITTLE WORD

Isn't it such a funny thing?
That everything we say,
Is here, it is there,
And the first thing we know, it's everywhere.

Always think twice before you speak;
Greet each coming day with a smile;
Just remember that everything you say and do
Will always come back to you.

Martha Mae Johnson

'OTHER WORDS' we found in her little black book:

"Never leave undone what you would do on the morrow,
For Tomorrow never comes.
Our tomorrow is always 'TODAY.'"

"A good deed is never lost."

OPPORTUNITY

It matters not how rich or poor,
In worldly goods you may be;
Whether you are rich in houses or lands
Or how famous you have grown to be.
Or whether your whole life's earnings
Amount to great or small;
We're all a part in the game of life
The race must be run by all.

What kind of race we run
Only we ourselves can tell;
Each word that is spoken, each deed that is done,
Determines whether in life we fail.
The door of opportunity is open to all
It beacons men who pass its way
To rise above the vaulted past,
And to make their lives count for something each day.

Martha Mae Johnson

II. MARTHA'S POEMS...IN HER TIME

ATTAINMENTS

You can never hope to succeed
By simply saying "I can't,"
To every little obstacle in life, (or)
By just giving up
If the going gets tough
As you wade through the heat of the strife.

Each pinnacle reached
In the realm of the great
Was reached by obtaining the best -
Just not being satisfied
With just having tried,
But by putting your "all' in the test.

It may seem awfully hard
To say "I can"
Or still harder for one to say "I will"
But don't give up
For there is still a place
For you to fill.

Don't say "I can't"
Or "it can't be done"
But simply say "I'll do my best,
I'll fight to win,
Though (my) chances are slim,
Until I have won the quest."

Martha Mae Johnson
June 23, 1941

LIFE

Ah, sweet mystery of life
If it would but unfold.
And reveal the hidden secrets
That only life itself doth hold,
That little bit of trouble
Which crossed our path today
Has only made us stronger
To meet another day.

That little bit of suffering
Which came your way today
Will be dispelled tomorrow
By the flowers along the way.
And then those very little things
That are a part of each today
Help us to meet the bitter things
Which are strewn along the way.

Just give me patience to meet each day
As a valiant man would do
Not to shrink from my simple duty
But to show my colors true.
To take each joy or sorrow
And make it count for gain,
In building a better tomorrow
Toward which man must attain.

Martha Mae Johnson
March 15, 1942

II. MARTHA'S POEMS...IN HER TIME

GOD'S NEAR

A little bud bloomed forth today
Its glory is so rare,
And yet I knew not whence it came,
But somehow I saw God there.

A little bird flew cross my path
And chirped its little song of cheer.
Its music sweet went to my heart -
I thought (felt) God must be near.

I stood beside a bubbling brook
Whose rippling waters were so slow -
I pictured Christ beside Galilee
And felt that God was near.

I saw a little child at play
Its babyish prattle reached my ear.
Somehow I saw in it *implicit faith*
(And) God was very near.

I look today upon a world
Where greed and hate seem not to cease.
I pray this God who is so near
To come and give us lasting Peace.

Martha Mae Johnson
July 5, 1942

DOWN THE LINE

FRIENDSHIP

There are beautiful flowers that bloom each day
As we tread along life's way
But 'ere the heat of the day has past
They often wither and decay.

But the blossoms that are wrought
From a friendship like ours
Must be kissed by Heaven's dew,
And each tiny bud blooms anew each day
To bring happiness to me and you.

A friendship like ours can never die,
For it has been bought with a price;
Its very foundation is faith, hope and love,
That is born of sacrifice.

It is good to know that someone cares
To know that they will ever be true;
That they will always lend a helping hand,
To help you (all) life's journey through.

Martha Mae Johnson
April 10, 1941

II. MARTHA'S POEMS...IN HER TIME

A YOUNG MAN'S QUEST

A young man came to the Master one day
An entrance into the kingdom to gain;
"Good Master," said he, "What shall I do
That I, within Thy Kingdom may reign?"

"I have kept Thy commandments from childhood days;
I have lived above sin and shame.
My fortunes in this life they profit me none,
Unless I walk in the Master's name."

The Master looked at the brave, young man,
Who was rich in possessions, and fame.
"Young man," said He "Go sell what thou hast
And give to the poor, then come and walk in my name."

The young man stopped and thought on his way
These words had reached to his heart;
For he was rich in worldly goods,
With them he would never part.

He sadly turned and walked away,
He heeded not the Master's advice.
His life he chose to live for self,
Rather than give his all as a sacrifice.

Martha Mae Johnson
February 16, 1941

REMINISCENT

At evening when the lamps are burning low,
When the last of the chores for the day are o'er
My mind goes back to days long ago
To those grand old days which can be no more.

Once again to the old country home I go,
To the old slide hill and the spring below,
To the little old school house way upon the hill,
Then down the creek to the old grist mill.

There's the old swimming hole, and the fishing nook,
And the meadow lane and the winding brook,
Where I've sat and dreamed of what I would be
If and when I should have reached maturity.

My old dog Spot and my old pal Bill,
Though years have flown, they're a part of me still.
Tonight in my dreams, I feel them near,
For they're a part of all that I hold dear.

One of the greatest joys in life we will ever know
Are those dear old childhood days of long ago.
The sweetest dreams we can ever dream
Are those dreams of the old home and childhood scenes.

Martha Mae Johnson

II. MARTHA'S POEMS...IN HER TIME

LIVING

Many times we are often discouraged,
And we think that in life we have failed
When if only we would keep on trying
Right over wrong would surely prevail.

For with every bit of gladness
There must be some shadows too;
But remember it is always the darkest
Just before the sun shines through.

For after all, Life is just a picture
We're painting each day that we live;
Each cloud with some sunshine is blended,
A beautiful setting to give.

It isn't how much we receive that counts,
But it's really what we give;
The thing that counts in the game of life,
Is simply, "How did you live?"

Martha Mae Johnson

LIFE'S HIGHWAY

The road of life is an uphill climb,
From the cradle to the grave.
If we hope to reach to the heights sublime,
We must be courageous and brave.

We can't give up at each little rut,
That we pass on this highway of life;
With an ardor of hope we must keep our head up
As we pass through the mire and the strife.

There are besetting sins at every turn,
And rugged and steep is the way.
There are many precious lessons we must learn
If we are to pass a milestone each day.

What does it matter sometime, if the road is long,
And narrow and beset with woe...
If we can journey through life with a song
We will *'hope and encouragement'* to others show.

Some day we shall come to the end of the way
And we will face life's setting sun.
What a sweet relief when our Master shall say
"Welcome home, fellow pilgrim, Well done!"

Martha Mae Johnson

II. MARTHA'S POEMS…IN HER TIME

THE SAVIOR OF MEN

It wasn't so many years ago
That a lonely stranger walked here below.
His shoulders were bent with a load of care,
Yet He never faltered, for He knew not fear.

He had no place for to lay His head,
This hard, cold earth was His lowly bed;
The tree, the birds, all in nature's realm,
Knew His voice and were kind to Him.

To a darkened world as a Light He came,
To vanquish forever sin and shame.
He raised the fallen, the sick and the lame
New life He gave to all who came.

He never sought power and praise and fame.
Love and simplicity marked His name;
He walked among men, unheeded, unknown.
The agony of Gethsemane He bore alone.

He died on the cross that we might live,
His life as a ransom for all He did give;
His life is a summons to us each day
To walk in the straight and narrow way.

Martha Mae Johnson
January 9, 1940

DOWN THE LINE

TOO MANY PARTIES AND TOO MANY PALS

Too many parties and too many pals
Will break your heart someday.
Too many boyfriends and sociable pals
Will drive your sweetheart away.

Too many kisses bring too many tears…
Angles have fallen for too many years.
Those Broadway Roses and frivolous gals
Have too many parties and too many pals.

"Gentleman of the Jury", the Judge's speech began.
The scene was a crowded courtroom - the Judge a stern old man.
"The prisoner before you is a social enemy.
A lady of the evening, and you know the penalty.
Her eyes reflect the night life, her lips are red with paint
But I knew her mother - gentleman, *Ah, She was a saint!*"

"This is not like her, and yet she might have been
If it hadn't been for petting, parties, cigarettes, and gin.
We take the night life off the street, we bring it in our homes
While girls beat time with lipstick to the tune of the saxophone.
We open up the underworld to those we love so well.
Think of it gentlemen, shall we send her to her cell?"

"Remember, there's some man to blame,
That may be your Son!
If she drinks, twas you who taught her
If she smokes, you showed her how.
She is just what you have made her!
Is it right to knock her now?"

II. MARTHA'S POEMS...IN HER TIME

"And when you're in that jury room,
Remember now and then,
That for every fallen woman,
There's a hundred fallen men.
I plead with you for mercy, the testimony stands.
This girl is MY OWN DAUGHTER, the case is in your hands!"

Martha Mae Johnson

DOWN THE LINE

TO MY FRIEND

I wish it were possible for me to be
Just the kind of friend you have been to me
To be able to speak the words of cheer
That you have spoken from year to year.
To bestow upon you the happiness
That will turn every sorrow into bliss;
Just to let you know in some little way
What you've meant to me from day to day.

I know that I can never hope to repay
The many things you've done for me each day
For you have turned darkness into light,
To my weary eyes you have given sight.
The smile on your face, the touch of your hand
Makes me know somehow that you understand.
To you, my friend, may I try to be
Just the dear, kind friend you have been to me.

                                      Martha Mae Johnson
                                      May 3, 1941

II. MARTHA'S POEMS...IN HER TIME

A MEMOIR

His name was never written,
On the pages of history;
He never made a public speech,
But yet he served humanity
He only lived as best he could,
Each day he was a friend;
He always gave the best he had,
And the best came back to him.

And when his task on this earth was o'er,
No fine memorials marked his fame;
But this world was made a better place,
Because he lived in the Master's Name.
Lord, let me, like him, do the best I can.
Teach me ever to lend a helping hand.
The greatest tribute this world could pay
Is for those who walked with me to say:
"He was my Friend."

Martha Mae Johnson

TODAY

Each day as I look at the setting sun
It dawns upon me that another day is done
A day with many precious seconds was mine
Now it has faded into Time.

Today have I done my very best,
To some weary soul have I given rest?
Just a little smile or the touch of the hand
Might have helped someone to be a better man.

There are weary souls who have passed my way
Whose night I could have turned into day,
Had I stopped long enough to lend a hand.
For *my greatest service is to live for man.*

"Well done" at night is all I ask
The consolation that I have completed my task.
What we do in this life must today be done
For, my friend, tomorrow may never come.

Martha Mae Johnson

II. MARTHA'S POEMS...IN HER TIME

THE VAST UNKNOWN

Somewhere in the vastness of the sky,
There looms a Haven of Rest;
And we dream of the joy and peace we'll know
When we enter this Home of the Blessed.

There the Savior stands with outstretched arms
He bids you welcome there;
And those who enter this celestial place
Are forever free from (worldly) care.

The clouds are forever drifted,
The sun there never goes down;
And the occupants of this Holy City
Have exchanged a cross for a crown.

Someday - I cannot say how soon it will be -
I'll silently wing my flight to this vast unknown,
Once more I'll clasp hands with those gone before.
As I enter the portals of Heaven, my Home.

Martha Mae Johnson
March 15, 1941

DOWN THE LINE

SOMEONE'S LAST DAY

What if today were the very last day
That on earth you were permitted to live;
That before the break of another dawn,
An account of your life you would have to give.

Would you live today as you did yesterday,
Never giving your very best?
Just doing those things you were forced to do
Leaving undone all of the rest.

The weary, the faint, the lowly, oppressed,
Would you leave (them) to do the best that they can?
While you are so engrossed with love of self
Too busy to lend a helping hand?

Leave nothing undone at the close of the day
To your purpose in life hold steadfast;
But remember that though the dawn comes tomorrow,
That today is somebody's last.

II. MARTHA'S POEMS...IN HER TIME

THE OLD YEAR

The shadows of night were falling slow
The lights in the windows were burning low;
People were hurrying left and right -
Everywhere it was New Year's Eve Night.

There stood aloof from the rest of the throng,
A silent figure all alone.
His face was worn and his step was slow,
His shoulders were bent with care and woe.

"Good stranger," said I, "What brings you here?
Why are you sad while others cheer?"
Wearily and slowly he raised his head
Looking me straight in the eye, he said:

"Good friend, one year ago,
I was ushered into this world of woe;
People everywhere welcomed me,
And I was treated as royalty."

"To countless millions good cheer I have brought,
Many wonderful miracles in my time have been wrought.
I have seen this world mad with war,
While envy and malice others' happiness mar."

"I have served pauper and prince the same,
I have been no respecter of race and name;
And tonight when the midnight hour doth chime,
I will take my place beside Father Time."

"For one whole year I have been your friend,
This farewell message I simply send;
I am the old year - I will soon be done;
But remember soon a new year will dawn."

New hope, New courage, it offers all,
Rise up and answer its challenge, its call.
Every second wasted is a second gone,
But each minute gained will ever live on.

Martha Mae Johnson

II. MARTHA'S POEMS...IN HER TIME

INDIFFERENCE*

When Jesus came to Golgotha
They hanged Him on a tree,
They drove great nails through hands and feet
And made a Calvary
They crowned Him with a crown of thorns,
Red were His wounds and deep;
For those were crude and cruel days
And human flesh was cheap.

When Jesus came to Birmingham
They simply passed Him by,
They simply let him die
They never hurt a hair of Him,
For men had tender grown
And they would not give Him pain,
They only just passed down the street,
And left him in the rain.

Still Jesus cried, "Forgive them,
For they know not what they do,"
And still it rained the wintry rain,
That drenched Him through and through.
The crowds went home and left the streets
Without a soul to see,
And Jesus crouched against the wall,
And cried for Calvary.

* Written by G. A. Studdert Kennedy
(a British poet and war veteran)

DOWN THE LINE

MEMORIAM TO MARTHA JOHNSON**

"I watched the smoke as it curled lazily upward, drifting toward the last red ray of the setting sun. For almost an hour I had stood feeding a bonfire that was composed of clippings, cards, letters, and papers. These represented the life of a 79 yr. old lady which had just flickered out shortly after her birthday. They gave evidence of a life well-spent for God...and Man. It was *'throw away trash'* that had been sorted through by three of her cousins (Ruth Williams Pyle and Becky Williams Buckman, and myself); with her passing these things could no longer be kept.

She had been born Martha Mae Johnson on Feb. 19, 1919. The only child born to Glen and Lizzie Mae Belle Smith Johnson. Her mother had died as the result of childbirth nine days later.

Glen's parents, Robert Ithamar and Amanda May Hawkins Johnson had taken the infant child and 'til their deaths (in 1934 and 1951, respectively), had reared and loved her as their own. Her grandfather was a Methodist minister on the Blairsville charge when they took her in; pastoral changes found them moving often around the North Georgia area. She gave her heart to Jesus at an early age and spent many years deeply immersed in Christian youth work. Lecturing and striving to lead them to fields of deeper service for God. She held many high ranking positions in this field.

As I turned the trash, in its glow, I saw graduation, wedding and baby shower invitations and announcements...and as time had progressed, the same kind of invitations had come from the children of these same friends!

Get well, Christmas and Birthday cards by the hundreds; old speech notes given at different functions, old school papers from

II. MARTHA'S POEMS...IN HER TIME

Marsh Business College, in Atlanta, paycheck stubs and income tax items from J. H. Johnston Co., Dawson's Department Store in Woodstock, Ga. And ledger sheets from her venture as a partner in Williams Food Store (her Uncle Gordon's grocery store in Woodstock, where she was the bookkeeper in the 1950's and early 60's)...all of this crumbled in the heat of the fire.

It had been a full, busy life for this little orphan. Crippled by polio at an early age, surgery on her legs had shackled her to braces, a crutch or a cane for a large part of her life. But the handicap had never broken her determination to lead a full, useful life.

Stirring the embers, up drifted the remains of a love letter from the one serious suitor of her life. His name was Melvin Haynes and he had been a Chaplain in World War II during the 1940's. When the war was ended and he had asked for her hand in marriage, she 'swore to her hurt' and refused, feeling her strong obligation was to the welfare of the Grandmother who raised her, as well as to her Aunt Cliffie (with whom she had lived since 1919).

And there were tears and prayers in the smoke that spiraled heavenward. Tears and sorrow of a mother for a wayward son, and of a daughter for her dad, were in the ashes of the letters that had been exchanged between Martha and her Dad, between Granny Johnson and her son, Glen. Glen had been working in the Navy Yard in Portsmouth, Va. During 1941-42. A broken man, subject to meeting his troubles with drink, he had been unable to find true love in two other marriages, and had died Aug. 6, 1942 of bronchial pneumonia.

I snatched a part of a letter, lifting in the breeze, from the fire...it was part of a letter of consolation from a very dear friend, upon the death of Martha's beloved Granny, in January, 1951. Carl Barrett was in military service at the time and was expressing words of love and concern and his own frustration at not being able to be there for her *(Martha)* in her time of need.

The shifting smoke seemed to have an image of Martha. The 60's had showed her buying shares in the Woodstock Hospital and becoming Administrator to Dr. Evan Boddy at the Boddy Medical Center. Her aging Aunt *(Cliffie)* made her the sole bread winner of their little family of two. It was here at the Clinic she reached her full potential of usefulness as a true servant to mankind. HELP – to anyone – in any way – at any time, seemed to be the creed of her life.

Bank statements turning to ashes spoke of her thrift. She had begun work in the $350.00 range, and she retired in the $675.00 range. In my mind's eye, I could see her frail figure limping tiredly from the Clinic (just 4-5 doors up the street) toward home at 207 North Main Street. She never learned to drive, and she walked, even with braces and crutches, most every where she went until her Aunt Cliffie learned to drive very late in life! Woodstock was so small back then you could walk any place you needed to go.

Uprooting the ashes once more, I turned up frayed edges of medical bills, drug and Medicare, Insurance, and funeral bills. Her life…and her Aunt Clliffie's…glowed in the hot dust! With Cliffie's passing in 1995, a *different* Martha emerged. One who still strove to go on but it seemed her living had but one purpose in mind. To get all things fixed to the point that her passing would put as little hardship as possible on anyone. Through the very difficult pain of her last days, suffering from COPD, she lay on her 'couch of do nothing' (as she called it) and if you asked (how she was today) she would say '*I believe I am a little better today.*"

*Written by:
LoDean Gresham Chapman,
Fall, 1998.

II. MARTHA'S POEMS...IN HER TIME

Martha Mae Johnson
1919-1998

EDITOR'S NOTE: The Memoriam* was written by Martha's first cousin, LoDean.

Martha was my mentor as a young child, teenager, and young adult - she was 21 yrs. older than me - a very wise person in all walks of life. With the multiple physical handicaps in life, she could have been angry and bitter. But nothing got in her way of becoming a strong Christian witness in her own quiet and simple way, to whomever she met. Martha always had a smile for those she met daily.

I doubt that there were many people in Cherokee County, Ga. who did not either know Martha, or her family, or knew someone who knew her. She served in many leadership capacities in Woodstock Methodist Church, its Women's ministry, across other counties in North Georgia. She taught Sunday School and was a Youth Counselor for many years.

I looked up to her all of my life. She would have given the shirt off her back to me, or anyone she knew, never thinking of herself first. After every visit I had with her, there was never a time I left her home, when she didn't have a 'sack full' of groceries for me and my family to take home with us. It usually was sugar, flour, sodas or some money for the children, and a 'ticket' to fill up my gas tank on her credit card before I left town! She would never let me repay her - she simply said *'pass it on!'*

Her motto was JOY: *__J__esus first, __O__thers second, and __Y__ourself last!* She lived that JOY 24/7 and upon her death, thousands of people in Cherokee County, Ga. mourned her passing because she was such a *'beacon'* in a world that needed light.

Becky Williams Buckman

'Circuit Rider' Sermons in my time

The Rev. Robert Ithamar Johnson
(1870...1934)

"My concern is not whether God is on our side; my greatest concern is to be on God's side."
Abraham Lincoln
(1809-1865)

"If I had only one sermon to preach it would be against pride."
Gilbert Chesterton
(1874-1936)

III. 'CIRCUIT RIDER' SERMONS IN MY TIME

On horseback or in a buggy, Rev. Johnson's Saddle Bag rode along with him all over North Georgia in the early 1900's.

EDITOR'S NOTE

In 1965 I was given a wonderful gift, one that had 'lived through' sunshine and rain, sleet and snow, day and night, in early 1900's up until 1934. My cousin Martha, and my Aunt Cliffie, gave me my Grandfather's Saddle Bag. It held his typed sermons, his Bible, tracts and other special books. . .treasures untold!

I could not wait to get into its contents, and 'into' those sermons, found in a 3-ring black binder. The papers were yellowed with the age of time, the wear and tear of his soul being poured out to his parishioners.

His improper spelling and the lack of good grammar did not impede my progress as I devoured the messages he had preached. My, how I wish I could have known and walked a while with him, and heard him preach.

From things I've read or heard about him, he was a true man of God who went into the ministry after he had a family. He had married a woman who had grown up in Methodist Parsonages in Georgia. They had farmed property on Rope Mill Road, in Woodstock, Georgia until he answered the call to preach. He also was a 'PK' (a preacher's kid) and had grown up in a strong Christian home in Cherokee County. He became an itinerant preacher, following in his father's footsteps. He was *a circuit rider* serving sixty-four Methodist Congregations in North Georgia during a twenty-six year period, touching lives, homes, and communities.

As I thumbed through his little black binder, I selected four sermons that I feel are still quite appropriate for us, a hundred years later. Their message still rings true which is indicative of his theory about mankind: *the sinful nature of man is still very much alive (today), with the same factors that brought nakedness upon Adam and Eve: lying, cheating, greed, selfishness, addiction to sex, gambling, alcohol and drugs. . .all bring men and women to their lowest level of existence.* None of the above bestow *'abundant life!'* They did not in his day, nor do they bring it to us in the twenty-first century.

In these sermons, in their original form, there was broken English, improper spelling and little or no punctuation, yet the depth and eloquence of the message was as clear as a bell to me. With little formal education or seminary training his faith came through, like the Big Dipper on a clear night! His faith and witness were stellar!

When our son was the Minister at Sixes United Methodist Church in Canton, Ga. (2001-2012) I met an older gentleman (there) who recalled a story that his father had told him about 'Brother Johnson,' when he had served the Sixes Congregation from 1909-1912. The older gentleman 'recalled the story' to my son:

III. 'CIRCUIT RIDER' SERMONS IN MY TIME

There was a severe drought one year; people and their crops were hurting for rain. Brother Johnson got to the church that Sunday morning, and he threw his saddle bag under the wooden steps. Members of his congregation saw him do that and asked him 'why did you do that? His answer: 'Well, we're going to stay here and pray until it rains.'

And they prayed, and prayed some more, until the rains came - God had answered their prayers!

I can just imagine the rejoicing, and maybe even some 'shoutin' going on! Oh, to have been sitting under the power and influence of the voice of this gentle giant as he gave his heart and soul to his GOD, and to the sheep in his fold!

Day or night Grandfather Johnson could be found pecking away, pouring out his heart and soul in the sermons that he would share with his parishioners in North Georgia in the early 1900's.

HONOR THY FATHER AND MOTHER
Rev. Robert Ithamar Johnson

* Scriptures for the day:

"Honor your Father and your Mother so that you may live long in the land the Lord your God is giving you."   *Exodus 20:12*

"He must manage his own family well and see that his children obey him with proper respect."   *I Timothy 3:4*

"Children obey your parents in the Lord, for this is right. 'Honor your father and your mother - which is the first commandment with a promise - that it may go well with you and that you may enjoy long life on the earth.'"   *Ephesians 6:1-3*

To secure the divine end purpose there must be government in the family. The family is a community inclusive and exclusive, and must be governed. It is not a mere nursery nor is it a provisioning agency. It is founded upon essential relation(s) but it must be under divine law; authority maintains law by a binding and loving power over the moral nature of the child. Parental authority is born of parental relation but the power to rule well is from God. Parents need power from on high as much as did the apostles at Jerusalem, (just) as does the church now.

Not only all authority but all power is from above. *"Every good gift and every perfect gift is from above and cometh down from the Father of light......."*   *James I:17*

Physical, mental and spiritual power is from God but we must place ourselves in proper relation to receive and exert that power. Mother love is deep, rich and sweet but that alone can never

III. 'CIRCUIT RIDER' SERMONS IN MY TIME

reach the depths of the soul. Lying dormant in that little body so tender, pure and sweet is an immortal spirit that must be evoked into consciousness and by that same mother love, baptized with the Holy Ghost, it must be lifted gently and surely to a personal consciousness of the divine, and trained for eternal destinies.

The true nature of parental authority is God. It is set up by God and the ruling is in his place. Then your family government should have the same purpose and end in view that God has in the government of the race. That is your model. Turn to it. Learn your duty and how to perform it.

There are two extreme into which we are prone to fall. The one is undue severity, the other false tenderness. By the first we miss the true idea of government by a brutish despotic violence which makes no appeal to the moral nature, but drives by force, appealing to that sense of terror which destroys principle and makes cowards of our children. There is a difference between terror and filial fear. One of the greatest sins of many parents is that old idea that the will of the child must be broken. It would be almost as well to break the child's neck …NO! Do not try to break your child's will but seek to direct it. Evoke it into power to bless the world and brighten heaven forever.

Children obey your parents. Their right to govern is of divine origin in the Lord and your obligation to obey is born of personal relation. You can no more escape it that you can change your son-ship. Your mother has the command to control you - to submit and to obey is to receive blessings from God. To resist, and to rebel is to dare the curse of the Almighty. *"For Moses said, Honor thy father and thy mother; Whoso curseth father or mother, let him die the death."*   Mark 7:1

This may be done by your manner toward them as well as by your lips. How may I honor Father and Mother? *First,* by an inward esteem and love for them which is genuine and outwardly expressed on all occasions, by tenderness and sympathy toward them.

Second, by obedience to their lawful command without asking for a reason (but) by absolute perfect obedience to their authority. Come when they call. Go where they send. Do what they bid cheerfully, gladly from a principle of love. What they forbid, do not do - without asking the reason why. They honor God most who obey his will by faith and faith alone. *Obligation to honor Father and Mother does not cease at twenty one years of age, but is binding as long as they live in the world.* Boys and girls who have lived upon the bounty, feasted and fattened upon the sacrifices and suffering of their parents are sometimes ashamed of them. . . and treat them with indifference, if not with cruel neglect.

They (parents) are old, feeble, and ignorant of the ways of the modern world. They have no desire nor power to keep up with modern social life, but they know the LORD, are at home in the society of saints. They can talk the speech of heaven and point the radiant way to God, and by example, as well as by precept, make luminous the pathway to glory. That voice that once charmed and thrilled listening multitudes, is broken now, but the music in the old soul is fresh like the minstrelsy of the skies.

Are you ashamed of those withered hands, that bent form, that wrinkled face, that body that was bent, withered and wrinkled by labor and watching for you. Do you ignore or neglect your parents?

Shame on you. Love them for what they are. Love them for what they have done for you, and show them your love. Make them see and feel that you do love them. When you go home caress

III. 'CIRCUIT RIDER' SERMONS IN MY TIME

them like you did when you prattled about their knees in early childhood.

Sit down close by your old mother and take that withered hand in yours and tell her the news. She may not care much for the news but her old heart will. . . with a new life, a new joy because her son loves her enough to tell her what he heard, and what he saw. Honor Father and Mother with your care and confidence as long as they live. Now and then carry them tenderly to visit their old neighbors and friends. Let them talk over the scenes of the past. It will do them good. They will rest and sleep better.

I want my mother to have the best chair in the home, the best bed, for if she has lived for GOD, it won't be long until she will live in a mansion where all her sorrow will be joy, and happiness. My dear young people, you don't know how much your Mother means until she is gone.

EDITOR'S NOTE: This sermon was delivered to all congregations in Rev. Johnson's circuit, in the North Georgia Conference of The Methodist Church.

*I have chosen to use the *New International Version* of the scriptures he used in his sermons, thinking that perhaps they speak more clearly to us, *in our generation;* the scriptures he read in the original sermons were from the King James version of the Bible.

PREPARE YOUR HEARTS
Rev. Robert Ithamar Johnson

TEXT: *Prepare your hearts unto the Lord and serve him only.*
I Samuel 7:3

Samuel appears upon the scene as a boy – a child of promise, of pious parents who were brought up under the aged Eli at the tabernacle. He witnessed the tragic downfall and death of Eli's corrupt sons and then of the aged priest ; he (himself) was soon recognized as a prophet and judge.

At the call of Samuel there was a national assembly of the people at Mizpeh. The form of government, while it was a theocracy, was also a pure democracy in which all the people had a part. The completest divine subjection coincides with the wildest human liberty and the Bible has always promised popular government.

The power of association and discussion is illustrated in this national convention. Not much can be done with people while they are scattered, and to bring them under the conviction and motives of common ideas and inspire them with contagious enthusiasm, they must be gotten together.

The numerous and multiplying convention that gathers in the interest of all kinds of objects show this need; power scatters the members, and the fire dies out; heap them together and it burns and glows - there in heat in a compact audience. Numbers are magnetic.

God can pour more of his spirit upon a thousand people than upon a hundred.

III. 'CIRCUIT RIDER' SERMONS IN MY TIME

Revival instantly shows itself in increased attendance and attention on the day of Pentecost. The Disciples and Christians were all with one accord, in one place. By the simple process of assembling ourselves together we can invite - and compel the presence of the spirit. The primary purpose of this assembly was for prayer. The country was in a bad state but the people did not meet simply to talk about that and pass resolution, laying the blame on the government and demanding a change of administration. They were not looking earthward but heavenward.

EDITOR'S NOTE: the remainder of the sermon is missing.

TRAIN UP A CHILD
Rev. Robert Ithamar Johnson

TEXT for the Day: Genesis 18:19

"For I know him that he will command his children and his household after him, and they shall keep the way of the Lord to do justice and judgment; that the Lord may bring upon Abraham that which he hath spoken of him."

There is nothing greater than a Christian home. There is no greater responsibility than when a new born baby comes into a home. Christian character - it substantiates the home as nothing else will; in fact there can't be a real home without Christ. Train up a child in the way he shall go and when he is old he will not depart from it. That is Solomon's interpretation of the child. Look out in the world today and watch the life of the rising generation and we have to confess that *there is something wrong !* Crime is increasing - the morals of our young womanhood are decreasing; a young girl will keep company with a young man that dissipates in whiskey. That recklessness is going to destruction...

The little one gets its first inspiration in the home as it sits on mother's lap and looks up into mother's face and catches her smile. I believe in teaching children discipline; you must do it in the right way; you must deal with a child as Christ deals with you in love and gentleness. You can't teach a child like (you do) a mule.

There was once a boy - he was the only child of the home. The father wanted to make a great man of him. The son had been expelled from two colleges. The father was sitting one night thinking of what he would do with his boy when the mother

III. 'CIRCUIT RIDER' SERMONS IN MY TIME

asked (the father) why he did not come on up to bed, and the father said "I am just thinking of our boy." She said it was "too late to think of that now. You ought to have thought of that when he was a young man." That went to his heart and he decided he would teach his son discipline, so the next morning he carried the boy in and chastised him and knelt down and prayed for him; then he prayed for himself and asked God to help him to teach (his son) right and (to be able) to live right before him. And when the prayer was ended the boy lay his arms around his father's neck and told him he would obey him from then on.

So we have to do a heap of praying in raising a child.

UNTITLED SERMON
Rev. Robert Ithamar Johnson

TEXT for the Day: *"Wine is a mocker. Strong drink is raging: and whosoever is deceived thereby is not wise."*

Proverbs 20:1

The prophet Amos was a shepherd, and dresser of sycamore trees from Tekoa, in the Kingdom of Judah who traveled north into the kingdom of Israel and there exercised his ministry though not trained in a theological school, this farmer prophet, like Elisha, was called of the spirit to preach in Israel. His sermons are pointedly practical and abound in homely phrases.

Amos was a bold and fearless prophet and uttered piercing and powerful denunciation and warning against the prevailing evils of his time. The prophet lets loose a bolt of lightening against the capitals of the two kingdoms. Woe to them that are at ease in Zion and trust in the mountains of Samaria which are named chief of the nations, to whom the house of Israel came.

Amos, the cowherd, was a bold prophet and struck down the high standing among the common people. He looked up to the mountain tops and saw the pride with which they were crowned and he bravely smote them with his burning shafts of condemnation and scorn.

High places are apt to breed a haughty spirit and a love of luxury and ease. *Pride is one of the dangers of prosperity.* Nowhere else is humility more protective, as well as more beautiful than in the places of power. The day that a man begins to relax his faithfulness and diligence and take his ease, he makes his decline. The preacher must often look up and strike sin in high places. The fact that we live in Jerusalem or Samaria will not save us from condemnation and retribution in the day of our guilt. Around the loftiest

III. 'CIRCUIT RIDER' SERMONS IN MY TIME

heights of position and privilege and power, divine judgment beats and burns with the fiercest intensity. The first may be the last.

There are many at ease in the church, and they need to take heed, lest having been exalted to heaven, they may be cast down to hell. This is an argument that applies intensified force to our nation. Look in that direction: we will see people that have been enlarged and enriched by divine favor, and yet we find that we have been still more largely blessed.

However wide their borders, ours are broader still. This is a reason why we should appreciate our privileges and use them wisely and faithfully in God's service. This glittering falsehood as to the future is the devil's bait with which he decoys multitudes to destruction. A safeguard against it is the power and habit of looking ahead and considering the end. It is the farther end of every sin that we should consider most. The first end may be sweet; the last is bitter and will burn forever.

Floating with the current will not stop Niagra Falls. Shutting our eyes will not blow out the sun, plunging into and flattering ourselves, that retribution is far off will not stop judgment or put out the fires of the bottomless pit. The whole description is a picture of luxurious sensual gratification and selfishness, and is true to similar aspects of our modern life. We have been piling up wealth in our land in glittering heaps compared with which all the wealth of these ancient cities was only a handful of dust. And of this rich soil, we have been growing all the gorgeous blossoms and rank weeds of ease and luxury and voluptuousness.

We are noted as a pleasure loving people, and are growing mad for amusement. Palaces costing millions, but sometimes mere (......) and vulgar, costly clothing and ostentatious adornment that are intended to excite envy rather than afford comfort. The search for excitement and pleasure, the disposition and effort to escape work and have an easy time, the constant craving for a crowd, and itching for a new thrill...the dance hall and theater...the desire to turn all life into a picnic and moving picture show....all these symptoms of our modern life may well excite our anxiety and alarm. Such use of wealth breeds social discontent and sows the seed of socialism and anarchy.

EDITOR'S NOTE: *It appears the remainder of this sermon has been lost.*

Upon the death of The Rev. R. I. Johnson the article below appeared in the *Wesleyan Christian Advocate*, a North Georgia Methodist publication. This tribute, on his death December, 1934, is a wonderful testimony of his life. He was a servant to everyone, a godly husband and father to his children and grandchildren.

ROLL OF OUR DEAD
Robert Ithamar Johnson

The Rev. Johnson was born May 4, 1870. He was licensed to preach July, 1907; ordained deacon by Bishop McCoy, Nov. 24, 1912; ordained elder by Bishop Candler, Nov. 26, 1916; admitted on trial by the North Georgia Conference, Nov. 1926, and into full connection Nov., 1928.

For seventeen years he served as supply as follows: Dawsonville, 1910-11; Holly Springs, 1912-14; Holbrook, 1915-16; Alphareta, 1917-18; Blairsville, 1919-22; Fairmount, 1923-24; Subligna, 1925-26. As a member of the Conference as follows: Calhoun Circuit, 1927-28;East Cartersville, 1929-30; Carrollton Circuit, 1931-32; Hoschton, 1933-34; November, 1934 he was appointed to Sugar Valley, where he died December 21, 1934. Funeral services were held at Woodstock, conducted by his Presiding Elder, Dr. A. M. Pierce, and the pastor at Woodstock, Rev. L. L. Burch.

"He that winneth souls is wise." R. I. Johnson was one of the wise men of his generation. He was not versed in the methods of the seminary, he was not learned after the fashion of the schools, but he was an efficient and fruitful winner of souls.

He heard the Master say: "Follow me and I will make you fishers of men," and he took Jesus Christ seriously. Having been denied the advantages of academic training in his youth, he would not be denied the privilege of preaching the Gospel of Grace.

He knew little of the text of psychology in the art of fishing for men; he met the test as a successful fisher through all his ministry. some of his theology may not have been up-to-date; his clearcut Gospel preaching carried conviction in the power of the Spirit. He did not glory in his lack of college training; he did glory in the Cross of Christ and in the power of Divine Grace. He may not have known grammar, but he knew God. He would doubtless have felt awkward in a class-room of scientists and philosophers; he was at home and knew what to do in a room of penitent and inquiring sinners.

His preaching scored sin, without scolding the sinner. He showed sin up in its utter ugliness; he shared the Saviour with men in his divine beauty. If he caused men to wince, it was that he might win them. His fellowship with Christ, his confidence in the power of the Gospel, his clear experience of God's saving and keeping grace, and his persuasive power in presenting Christ to others place him among the great and gifted sons of God and servants of Jesus Christ.

Tender in the home, true in his friendship, loyal to his Church, faithful in life's relationships, "fervent in spirit," he had one controlling passion and that was to be a preacher of God's Word and a pastor to the children of men.

The devoted Methodist circuit rider is at home, and it is my opinion that he feels at home in any group of saints in that celestial city.

"O city, dreamed in early youth!
O city, loved till day was late!
No braver pilgrim of the Truth
Has entered through thy shining gate."
George L. King

III. 'CIRCUIT RIDER' SERMONS IN MY TIME

THE GIFT

When I received my Certification as a Director of Christian Education, in the United Methodist Church, North Georgia Conference, at Annual Conference, 1965, I was given my Grandfather Johnson's Saddle Bag. Below is a letter that was included with the gift.

June 24, 1965

Dear Becky:

"We thought of a gift that we might give you on this special day because you know that we are all so proud of you. With you have been our prayers, our hopes, and the sincere wish that one day you would attain this goal. Now that you have attained this, all of these wishes still go with you. Enclosed is a little bit of family history that we feel may inspire you to even greater things for God and His Kingdom.

And so, Becky, we feel that you are now joining the "long, long line" of dedicated persons, and we believe that 'their mantle' has fallen on you. May you catch the spirit that was theirs, pick up the torch, and carry on the blessed privilege of ministering to your fellow man and your God, wherever you go.

We are giving you this Bible, the Manuals, and the Saddle Bag used by your late grandfather, the Rev. Robert Ithamar Johnson, just as he left them on that day in December, 1934, when he died preaching a funeral in Sugar Valley, Georgia.

May God bless and keep you and may He cause His face to shine upon you."

Lovingly,

Martha Johnson
Cliffie Johnson
Woodstock, Georgia

EDITOR'S NOTE:

I am the granddaughter of Rev. R. I. Johnson, and I served in North Georgia, as Education Director from 1962 until 1984: West Point United Methodist Church, West Point, Ga.; Calvary United Methodist Church, Atlanta; First Methodist Church Atlanta; Haygood Memorial United Methodist Church, Atlanta; First Methodist Church, Marietta; and Trinity United Methodist Church in Warner Robins, Ga.

Our son, James F. Buckman, II entered the ministry in 1983, as a Youth Director and later became an Ordained United Methodist Minister, in the North Georgia Conference. Two of his appointments were in Churches where my Grandfather Johnson had preached many years before: Calhoun and Canton, Georgia.

The Saddlebag was passed on to him upon his ordination, at North Georgia Annual Conference in 1999. Here is a letter to our son that was included in 'the gift' to him:

June, 1999

Dear Son:

What a joy it is to be here today to see you take on the mantle that has been passed 'down the line' in our family. Our hearts are overflowing

III. 'CIRCUIT RIDER' SERMONS IN MY TIME

with love for you and for the calling that you have found - to serve God through the Church.

A minister friend of ours, the Rev. Carlton Anderson, once said: "If God is calling you to preach, you cannot NOT do it!" Perhaps God has been calling you all the while, and now this new door has opened for you to share your gifts with his people from the pulpit.

This Saddle Bag 'rode' with your Great Grandfather, the Rev. R. I. Johnson, all over North Georgia - sometimes on horseback, and later in a covered wagon. It is worn with 'age and use' by a man who felt the call and answered: "Here I am, Lord, send me!"

He was not an educated man, i. e. not in schools of learning. I do not know how much education he had as a child, but he never went to college, or seminary. He was a self-taught man who entered the ministry after he was married and had a family. He had been raised in a Methodist parsonage; his father, Williams Jefferson Johnson had preached in North Georgia as had his father-in-law, William Washington Hawkins. They all had set the example: a Godly life. All of them had been 'called to ministry' in these Churches in Cherokee County, Georgia: Woodstock Methodist, Little River Campground, and Hickory Flat Methodist, respectively.

As you begin your journey in North Georgia, may your gifts be exemplified to their fullest, and your example be one of which your ancestors would be proud. They will say: 'well done, thy good and faithful servant.'

Go now, with our prayers, and our blessing to impart the Gospel of Jesus Christ to whomever you meet on this journey! It has been our joy to walk with you up to this point in your life. And we will continue walking with you.

LOVE,

Mom and Dad

Tall Tales

Becky Williams Buckman

"Just cause it's a tall tale doesn't mean it ain't true."

Jonas Hackett

TABLE OF CONTENTS

Telling Stories 119
No Fools No Fun 122
Only Heaven Knows 123
This *'Birth Order'* Business 126
Mother Always Said 134
The Band Would Have Been Playing 142
That Old Time Religion. 147
The Count Down 156
Growing In Amazing Grace 160
Granny's Front Porch. 169
Sewing and So Much More 174
Adorable Aunt Cliffie 179
We Will Never Grow *'Old'*. 184
Blind Dates 194
The Dare 200
Young Love 204
A 'Gem' of a Proposal 218
Marriage and '*More*' 222
Pay It Forward. 232
Saying 'Grace' 236
My Private Plane 239
The Purple Cow 250
The Tale Ends Here 253
Newt Wilson 256
I Would not Trade 260
The Elevator 266
Fine with Florence 271
'Note' This 276
Kids Say the Darndest Things 285
It Was a 'Shoo-In' 291
Blind Man's Bluff 299
I Live Where I Am 303

Birthdays and Such...................... 306
IF.. 308
Lost and Found 310
In The Morning 317

IV. TALL TALES

TELLING STORIES

"Can I tell you a story?"

When I ask this question, friends who know me quite well, invariably respond with a grin: *"Well, you are going to tell it anyway, so go ahead."* Once they open the door, I begin rattling my tales. I never was good with *'short stories'* - telling them, or writing them! Friends sit back and *(try to)* listen patiently, knowing the saga will not be brief. If I catch them dozing, or changing the subject, I just throw in the towel! So, feel free to doze, or stop reading, and I won't know the difference. It won't hurt my feelings: my skin is pretty tough or maybe I'm just clueless!

For years people have told me I should write a book. When life gave me an opportunity, I jumped at the chance...and what an adventure this has been for me! The stories that I will share are *'true to the inth degree.'* I promise my imagination did not come into play...but I do admit I was tempted!

I hope you will sit down with me on my front porch, and enjoy the experiences that brought these stories into being. And if you should find yourself bored, I will understand. Make yourself at home, there's always a glass of sweet tea, or lemonade in the 'fridge and when you get back, perhaps, if you are lucky, I'll be through with my 'tale!'

"Join me for a glass of sweet tea!"

Each time I share a story, most often they are *my miracles*, I relive the wondrous ways that God has worked in my life. Some are hard for me to believe, even though I know things happened that way; my heart knows it, but I simply cannot wrap my mind around God's way of doing things! Such as *why was I born* or *why was my life spared? How could Jim and I have gotten back together, after years apart? How did our youngest daughter end up working on the same Naval Base in Charleston, SC where my father had worked during World War II? How did I end up moving to South Carolina, where my ancestors lived in the late 1700's and early 1800's? How did our son end up serving two of the same Methodist Churches that my Grandfather Johnson served? How did it happen that my poems*

IV. TALL TALES

were published? Or that I began a music business without really 'trying?' Was all this chance or was it foreordained? Who knows? I have lots of questions for GOD when we chat again.

Each day that I wake up, I find a 'new story' taking place in my life. That makes waking up each day a real journey. More often than not, at the end of that day, the story goes on paper! That explains why 'sleep' is hard to come by. . .once I hit the bed it seems my brainwaves begin to kick in, so paper and pens are within inches of my reach; yes, even beside my pillow! I write anywhere, anytime, any way I can.

These *tall tales* can be read in a 'pick and choose' fashion or from beginning to end; hopefully, you will get 'the picture' of my life unfolding, one day at a time! There are some missing pieces. There was no way I could cram *my wild ride* into one book. Perhaps I'll write another one someday! However, don't hold your breath. . .I doubt that I will have the energy, or patience to do another one! But who knows? I am as *unpredictable as a snowstorm* on a July day in the Low Country of Charleston, S. C.

Keep reading, get another glass of sweet tea if you will, and I will share the *'miracles on my street.'* Enjoy the journey!

Becky Williams Buckman
January, 2013

DOWN THE LINE

NO FOOLS NO FUN

The apple doesn't fall far from the tree when it comes to some things. I am definitely my mother's child when it comes to many things. She was such a hoot, all the way through her ninety-five years. Her philosophy of life was "no fools, no fun," and did she ever have fun! I'm having a ball following in her footsteps. . .

I may do a lot of "fool" things, but you'd better believe, as long as I'm alive I am going to live my life having fun. . . or I'll die trying. I have fun doing everything, i. e. except cleaning out the refrigerator!

When I began this book in 2006, I knew people were literally 'laughing at me,' behind my back. (*They didn't think I noticed. . . Wrong!*) They thought I was 'off my rocker' because I was literally writing day and night/non-stop. I might be foolish enough to think that I can write a book that people will read, but I just cannot NOT write, regardless of what others think. I might try to take a nap, and before the covers are over my body, my old mind is running way past the speed limit.

My mind would get a ticket if it were heading north on I-26 or any other interstate; and it would probably be "in jail, with *"NO bail"*, to boot! It's like there's no key to turn the switch off. The motor is running wild; the gas is being guzzled, and I'm in a gear that hasn't even been put into our modern cars yet! I don't even look back to see if anyone is chasing me. If someone does try to slow me down, well. . .I'll probably say, *'let me write this down first!'*

So, leave it at that. As mother said: 'no fools, no fun!' *I'm having fun. I'm writing. Who needs a nap anyway?*

Becky Buckman
June, 2008

IV. TALL TALES

ONLY HEAVEN KNOWS

As the story is told, I was not supposed to 'happen.' But I was born... *Only heaven knows why!*

My parents had fallen in love, and were married at Holbrook Campground, in Cherokee County, Georgia. That was August 19, 1919. Not long afterward, they moved to Atlanta and my father began his grocery store business.

Growing up on a farm in Freehome and learning the tricks of the trade, my Daddy spent his adolescent years with his *'rolling store.'* He stocked his wagon with vegetables, and produce and went door-to-door selling groceries to the entire community. The dirt roads could make his business difficult if it had rained and washed out pot-holes! But that didn't stop him.

Soon after they moved to Atlanta their first child, Miriam Lucile, was born but died at eight months of age with whooping cough. Grief surrounded them like a shroud, but in March 1922, their second daughter, Ruth Inez, was born. Life began to be rich and full again! In the latter part of the twenties, their third daughter was stillborn, and Mother was on the edge of life and death! Even with their strong faith in God, they were drowning with sadness a second time.

Mother had hemorrhaged from childbirth and was fighting for her life. She was rushed to the hospital for blood transfusions. Her younger sister had the same blood type and came to the rescue. Miraculously, Mother recovered but was warned that they should not even try to have more children.

When Mother was in her early forties, and my Daddy was in his late forties, she began to put on some weight. Thinking it was menopause, she didn't worry - i. e. until I kicked one night. *'Oh no! I can't be pregnant.'* It happened another time. She could not ignore the warning sign any longer. Two and Two equaled four, so a Doctor appointment confirmed the news! What a shock! Was it *Good news? Bad news?* What would the outcome be this time? Wow! This was going to change their lives in a big way. Ruth was a senior at Canton High School, and the nest was about to be empty - or so they thought! Surprised? You bet. Scared? Of course!

My Granny Johnson's son, Glen and his wife, Mae, had given birth to a daughter in 1919; Mae died eight days later and my Grandparents had raised Glen's baby. Granny was horrified to think that now her own daughter might die in childbirth like Mae had done three years before. I've been told that it literally 'put Granny to bed' for the duration of Mother's pregnancy.

The Doctor wasn't about to take any chances, after nearly losing his patient during her last pregnancy so I was lucky enough to be born in a hospital; the other three daughters had been born at home - 389 10th Street, Atlanta.

The time came for Mother to deliver her fourth baby; my Daddy could not get home in time so family friends, Grady and Leola Pruitt, rushed Mother to St. Joseph's hospital, getting there just in the nick of time! Funny. . . it seems men are often NOT where they need to be when their wives go into labor! What would we do without friends?

Nineteen years from the day Miriam Lucille had died, Mother and Daddy were handed a very healthy nine pound baby girl. That was April 29, 1940 and I've been *kicking high* since that day. I was given the name of Carolyn Rebecca but I have been *Becky* since 'day one!' The greatest part of the story is that Mother

IV. TALL TALES

delivered me as easily as picking a rose from the garden. She was healthy and the most wonderful Mother anyone could have. I feel so blessed that somehow I showed up in their garden. They didn't pick me, nor did I pick them but I know I was blessed to have them as parents. I trust I added a little sunshine to their garden.

Was I supposed to be born? Was I 'the accident waiting to happen?' Or was there some reason I came along without 'planned parenthood' in motion. Only heaven knows! *"I'm just so proud to be here"* as Minnie Pearl always said.

Becky Williams Buckman
April 29, 2010

THIS '*BIRTH ORDER*' BUSINESS

Have you ever given any serious thought about *why* you were born, or why you were born *when* you were, or *where*?

I had rocked along in my own little cradle for many years and it was not until I stumbled on the *'Birth Order Book'* many years ago that the rocks in my head began to rattle! I began to understand who I was. Actually, I'm still working on that but I know God isn't finished with me, so not to worry!

I had psychology in school which perhaps helped me understand a little about who I was, and what made me the person I am, but after I read that book a lot of 'lights came on.' I am who I am not only because of inherited genes, but because of 'circumstantial evidence!'

My daughter once said to me: *"No wonder I'm crazy, Mom. I'm half you and half Dad."* My thought was: 'well, guess what. . .the same thing happened to me. That's life.' Apples don't fall far from the tree!

The next question that stirs up my brain cells is: *IF this is the way I was born, being affected by my birth order, is there anything I can do about it? Can I 'change' my behavior?* Some of what I read made me a bit uncomfortable but it also gave me some consolation that I would be OK. I also read the book 'I'm OK, You are OK." Thank God, in all reverence, we are all 'winners' at that point. Actually, I didn't have to read that book to guarantee self-confidence - that I was 'ok' - *I was born knowing I was God's child*, thanks to my heritage. I've never questioned that truth.

However, it is much easier to know that in your mind and heart than it is to *'live it out'* through the childhood or adolescent years - when you don't seem to fit in, when you are not the

IV. TALL TALES

sharpest knife in the drawer. Or when you are the wallflower at the Prom - or still not married at thirty! I admit I did shed my share of tears over those issues but the older I got and the more I 'fit into my own skin' the less I cried. And the happier I became, just knowing *I am who I am; it is what it is.*

I was blessed to have a wonderful mother-in-law; she taught me a lot, and was 'another mother' to me! She had to be strong. She had seven children in eight calendar years, living on a farm in Kentucky. After I got into the Buckman family, I knew I had met a 'saint,' for sure. If I had had a baby about every fourteen months I'm sure I would have qualified to be 'Headmaster of the Funny Farm.' Not so with Grandmother Buckman; she had the patience of Job! I'm a witness to the fact that my husband, Jim, inherited that wonderful trait; if not, perhaps I would have been *'in time out'* a lot of the time. *Just saying:* I know 'me' - and if I have difficulty *living with 'me'* I know it must have been hard on him all those years. (I'm smiling because I had to employ patience with him too!)

The wife of a share-cropper, Grandmother Buckman lived without many of the luxuries that could have made raising a family (back then) a bit easier. I've heard her say she could cook seven or eight pies a day, and before bedtime, there might only be one or two pieces left. Over a hot stove, in a small kitchen, she cooked for the 'army' of workers that farmed the land. My husband said 'meat and taters' were the staple on the table every day, so he expected me to cook that at least once a day. Well. . . that's another story!

Grandmother often said that every one of her children wanted to be the *'only child.'* I could understand that, knowing that each one really didn't have much time on her clock - before one was weaned, another one was on the way! Perhaps for over ten years dirty diapers were always around. . .and they were *cloth,* at that!

I used cloth diapers too, and I only had one child in diapers at a time. That was enough for me! I cannot fathom years on end with the obvious aroma that persists regardless of deodorizers! Perhaps that is why all of her children loved the outdoors. . .who knows? I did too, but for different reasons!

My father was the last born of eleven children, born about two years apart, so if I figure things right, my Grandmother Williams might have had children in diapers about twenty-two years, with the same farm-life circumstances in Georgia. Hanging out diapers daily for that long would put me 'six foot under, ' but neither woman caved in! It was just what a mother did!

> ***I'm sure I have strayed from the 'birth order' business - but by now, you have learned that's just 'who I am.' If not, just read on.

My sister Ruth grew up as a *'first born'* and the *'only child'* until I arrived as a 'whoopsie!' I also grew up basically as a 'first born' and as an 'only child,' plus I was the 'baby!' These three factors placed me on a very unique step on the ladder! Somehow, I always knew I was a *'rare bird. . .*

'Sisters' - Becky and Ruth at home, in Woodstock, Georgia 1948

IV. TALL TALES

First borns are usually very organized, in control, and they step up to bat and take charge, leading the crowd to follow. An *only child* is doted on, gets his way more often that not, (*spoiled rotten* is more like it!) and is the star of the show. Well, in my case Ruth and I both qualified for *both* positions. So that 'mix' made matters messy sometimes! I guess my parents lived through the trauma I put into their lives, primarily because they were old enough to be my grandparents, and their patience was miraculously marvelous. Yet, I'm sure I deserved a lot more discipline and punishment than I got.

My husband told me many stories of his childhood and teen years. I'm sure he was far more mischievous than me. He got away with it simply because there was so much going on in their big family, with seven children being born in eight calendar years, it would be hard for any parent to keep their eyes on them all. He said many times a neighbor saw him in places where he perhaps should not have been, or at times when he should have been home. He would be asked: "Does your Mother know where you are?" He said, 'no' only to be asked another question: "Does your Daddy know where you are?" He had the same answer, with a bit more detail added: 'She thinks I'm with him, and he thinks I'm with her. . .' Thereby, he had a lot of loopholes on that big sprawling farmland in Kentucky.

Luckily, back then, neighbors looked out for each other's children. Telephone lines were available when we all grew up, but there were 'party-lines' so valuable information could often be picked up rather inconspicuously if a parent picked up the phone when someone else was talking to another neighbor or family member! Now, that could really (and did, I'm sure) cause a real 'stir' in the community. Children could never figure out how 'Mom or Dad' knew where they had been or what they'd been up to! Today's cell phone technology has simply re-invented the wheel of the early nineteen hundreds. . .and parents now also have a way of tracking their children! In our 'wild and wooly' society that is a good safety net.

Jim was the second born in a family of seven children. He lived under the wings of his older brother, John who was only fourteen months older. Sometimes a 'second born' child doesn't feel he measures up. *That is not necessarily the case:* if one child is born in particularly unusual circumstances, or has physical issues, either at birth, or later in life, the other children might feel slighted. The middle child and the baby can feel just as slighted as a second born. So I say: *'get over it,'* you got here when you did, and it wasn't your choice then, nor is it now! Whining over the pecking order only makes for more problems. For sure, your parents were not being 'partial!' Simply put: *'it is what it is.'* Just be happy you are in line!

Being an only child has its disadvantages, believe me. I longed for a playmate. I remember asking why we didn't get another baby! I'm sure my parents laughed under their breath while searching for the best way to tell me the bottom line: *'ain't no way, honey!'* It was quite a few years before I really knew the truth about my 'birth order!' When I got older, however, they assured me that Mother was the 'talk of the town' for months and years. . .and when I arrived, I got in on it too! Neighbors have to *gossip* about something, don't they? Duh. . .

I was always bringing friends home with me for dinner, to spend the night or the weekend; or in the summer, having cousins spend the week. I had to have playmates! *The more the merrier* was my theory, then, and still is today! And my parents never seemed to care. They both loved children and adored every friend I ever made. Often I was allowed to take a friend

IV. TALL TALES

on vacation with us, and I went on many vacations with other friends who were also an 'only child.'

The rivalry that I did experience in my own family was unlike any other. As a young child, if my 'grown up' sister did something I didn't like, I would 'never' deal with it. She seemed more like another parent to me, and I was taught to respect my parents and all adults. I *buried my issues* then, but I had to deal with them when I became an adult!

I was always 'the baby' but when I was grown, and had a family of my own, it was different. I didn't want to be treated like the baby! I wanted to be on 'equal footing' with my sister. I was a wife, and a mother just like she was. Maybe it was just my 'leftover' feelings (from childhood) but I have to admit I resented things that happened or things that were said (or unsaid); things that reminded me that "I was the *'baby'* - still under the wings of a mother hen." It took me some years to get beyond those feelings. Once I learned that "*feelings are just feelings - they are neither right nor wrong*" I was freed up from unnecessary baggage!

My sister and I were not 'close' in age, and most of the time we were at different stages of life the majority of our lives. By the time I married she already had children; by the time I had children, her children were out of the nest. After the death of her husband, it seemed we began to 'ride on the same road' more often than not, and when I lost my husband, *we were definitely in the same car!* Then we could walk in each other's shoes - our age-difference was non-existent; each of us knew what the other was feeling, what we were going through, so the thread of emotional support for each other was like super glue.

In the last few years we've grown very close. . .we talk almost daily. I have 'opened up my can of worms' so often that she's positive I am a fisherman without a pole! She's been the 'rock' on the side of my mountains; I've been able to hang on to the cliff because of her. I just wish it had not taken so many years for us to 'bond' - I guess super glue was just not 'on the market' back then! We both missed out on a lot of opportunities - each for our own ridiculous or 'silly' reasons, so *now*, we try to make up for lost time!

We are as different as daylight and dark; *personality tests* prove it big time! She was Valedictorian of her High School Class. She was on the debate team. NOT ME! I didn't have time to *debate* anything, unless it was whether or not I could go Square Dancing every week and go to every party in the county! If so, I was as happy as a dead pig in the sunshine! Still am. . .(not dead yet, *just happy!*)

I got out of high school with A's and B's, and was able to 'slide' into Reinhardt Junior College in North Georgia. Ruth could have gotten big scholarships I'm sure; instead she began working in Atlanta during the Depression and was a very successful woman, an excellent pianist, teacher, mother and wife. And. . .*the best sister I could ever have!* She's still 'rocking high' in her 90's, and sharper than a tack; she always will be sharper than me. Just recently she began quilting; her work is immaculate. She's made beautiful pieces for many of her family members. I treasure the one she made for me!

Differences of opinion, likes and dislikes are part and parcel of siblings, people and families. There is room in the circumference for it all, without the sharp edges cutting us to the bone. Bottom line: *Devotion, love and support of one another is key* to keeping us all afloat in turbulent waters. Just because we are

IV. TALL TALES

all coming from the same factory doesn't mean all of our nuts and bolts are alike. . .it does mean that our bond/*the mold, i. e. is deeper than our 'mindset!'*

When I became a wife and 'instant parent' all in one day, I realized I was grossly lacking in knowing how to deal with sibling rivalry. These are things you don't 'experience' through a college textbook! I made my share (and more) of mistakes and except for the 'forgiveness' of the children, (and my new husband), along with the grace of God, I'm sure I would have been abandoned the first week of marriage. I was as 'green as a gourd' and they might have hung me out to dry!

It's too bad that our 'birth order' has inflicted many of us with unnecessary baggage; we are charged an enormous fee to carry it around with us. It wears and tears on our tender soul to the point of being inhuman, if we are not careful.

Just remember, *you are who you are*; remember to whom you were born, and why you were born when you were, regardless of the 'birth order.' *You were born for a purpose!* As long as you are 'on time' and in sync with your destination, you are OK!

I know why I was born and I thank God daily for the journey and for those who have ridden along with me. Every day is *'thanksgiving'* for me!

Becky Williams Buckman
November 2012

MOTHER ALWAYS SAID. . .

Every mother has 'sayings' that roll off her tongue like *'water rolling off the back off a duck.'* Most children can quote them easily; perhaps they will even pass them on to their children. These were some of the ones that have stuck with me through the years!

1. *"It always good to have a little something hidden back for a rainy day."* (money, i. e.)

She had money hidden in various places around the house...like in the sugar jar! Or in the Bible! When Mom visited me, I could always expect to find that she'd hidden money in my sugar bowl, or some other place she knew I'd look - maybe between the dinner plates. I took that advice! My husband was always "amazed" to find we had a little money somewhere, when he 'thought' we were broke!

2. *"You make your bed, and you 'will' lie in it!"*

I never was good at 'making up beds' - particularly after my husband got sick; he was in and out of bed a dozen times a day. But Mother was not talking about spreading up the covers! She was talking about 'choices'. . . and there was a certain tone in my Mother's voice that said more than any words implied!

That's just the way *'advice'* is...it has a ring to it that can be heard a mile away. I guess that's why I listened to things my parents said. I respected them enough to know they *'knew some things'* that I didn't know. Yes, I was a typical and curious child, but never one to go against their advice. . .my 'people pleasing' character trait was strong.

IV. TALL TALES

3. *"You gotta' get up - you gotta' get up in the morning!'*

I'm not lazy. I'm sure of that, but some mornings, my Mother was not too sure about that! When I was growing up, I just didn't want to get up, especially if I'd been out very late partying the night before. If it was Saturday morning I knew I had to clean house. We usually had company on Sunday and *'that'* prompted me for sure! I still have to have *a talk* with myself some mornings. . .just to 'get up' and get going! Now, as a 'senior,' coffee is the thing that moves me; as a teenager, it was Coke!

4. *"Always say THANK YOU."*

Mother's dear friend, Florine, said "thank you, thank you, thank you," so many times I almost wanted to scream. Sometimes I now find myself saying thank you more than once…but I would rather be caught saying it twice rather than be ungrateful or rude. The common courtesy of *'being thankful and expressing it'* is one that all too often has gotten lost in our vocabulary, as well as in our manners, such as writing 'thank you' notes. Will stationery and stamps go by the wayside? Will we no longer have mailboxes at the street? I pray not - in my lifetime, at least!

5. *"Be sure you have on clean underwear."*

Wash day was on Monday - that was it! So you either had to have at least 7 pair of undies or turn them wrong side out, to make sure they were 'clean.' I never did have have seven pairs of panties or bras - nor figure out how to turn them wrong-side out. . .and still be comfortable!

6. *"Be on your best behavior. Someone is always watching."*

And that is true. You may not ever know who sees you, or what you do, but when you *'live above the line'* there will never be anything to regret.

7. *"Beauty is as beauty does…"*

With that in mind, I often ask myself: *how beautiful am I?* When I look in the mirror, I know the answer, in the physical realm, i. e. I just hope and pray that my actions do a better job than my skin cream does! Mother was always beautiful in my eyes - in so many ways. She did beautiful things - like set a wonderful example for me to follow. I learned so much from her and my dad. All I can hope for is that I have done the same for my children and grandchildren.

8. *Beauty is only skin deep.*

Mother was a beautiful young woman. *A smile* always topped off her pretty wardrobe. She was a beautiful teenager; and a beautiful bride, at age 21. She was *the life of the party!* I think perhaps I got my 'partying spirit' from her. . .and my sense of humor from both parents! She was still a beautiful woman when she died at age 95.

I pray I can be as content with myself, as she was, and have as much fun as she did! I regard it as my highest compliment when someone tells me *"you are just like your mother!"* That is worth more to me than anything else they could say. I've heard people tell me that my daughter is just like me. . . if that is the case, we owe it all to "Nanny" and even farther back, to my Granny Johnson.

IV. TALL TALES

9. Men are like streetcars: if you miss this one, just wait, there will always be another one right behind."

When I was born in 1940, *street cars* were the mode of transportation unless you owned a car. Mom didn't drive so she and I rode the street cars to go shopping at Rich's and Davison's in downtown Atlanta. I seemed to have missed a lot of the kind of 'street cars Mother was talking about'. . . guys, i. e. I found it very depressing to have to sit on the corner and wait for the next "streetcar"! But in 1970, *the right one* came along, (my Jim) and just at the right time!

I was fortunate that my Mom lived long enough to see me catch the right street car, and that she was able to 'enjoy the ride" with us for twenty-two of our thirty-six years of marriage.

10. *Say your prayers.*

The first one I learned was *"now I lay me down to sleep, I pray the Lord, my soul to keep. IF I should die before I wake, I pray the Lord, my soul to take."* As a young child, I did what mother said but as I grew older, I began to wonder why a parent starts teaching a young child about death when they are so young and 'so full of life!'

When Jim and I had children we tried to instill in them a different way to pray: *conversational prayers*...to talk to God as if they were just talking to us - just sharing their heart and soul! We believed that our God wanted to hear us talking to him, like we talked to each other at home. We knew that he would not 'memorize' His answer to us! He would answer each one of us, personally. For me, prayer is just the deepest or simplest thoughts I have. I know they are 'heard' and understood.

11. *I'll see you in the Funny Papers.*

As a kid, about all I wanted out of the Atlanta Journal-Constitution Sunday Paper was *the comics.* That was not too unusual for a child to be oblivious about the happenings of the world out there. That was for the grown-ups. As soon as breakfast was over, I dashed to the living room, grabbed the paper, pulled out the "funnies," and piled up on the sofa. I found my favorites: *Dagwood and Blondie,* or *Nancy and Sluggo and Peanuts!*

Mom had already dismissed me from "kitchen duty" knowing the next time she saw me that *"she'd be seeing me in the funny papers!"*

12. "Honey...a man only wants one thing!"

My Mother was born in 1898; back then it was not 'proper' for her to tell me what that *one thing* was! I soon figured it out. I was no dummy. I also figured out that was her way of being sure I was *'pure and clean'* and ready to give myself to the man she knew I was to marry! I never heard her say sex, pregnant, virgin (except during the reading of the Christmas story from the Bible) or any of the words that, *in today's lingo* are as common as candy.

It is sad that our society has gone to such an extreme corner of life when it comes to sexuality! So much so that the sacredness and beauty of becoming one with each other, and the 'creation' of a child between man and woman often has been degraded to a level that is sickening! The very essence of our sexual being is grossly exploited in every arena. . .and all for money, money, money! From advertisements about cars, toothpaste, lawnmowers, to hair products, pencils, hats, our wardrobes, you name it. The world's *economy* seems to revolve around sex. . .just say

IV. TALL TALES

the word and the product will sell! Just pick up a magazine, or watch a TV commercial. . .see how many are 'flavored' that way!

13. *"Be careful in the dark, the 'boogey man' might get you!"*

Then she proceeded to tell me, "honey, don't worry, when he gets you in the daylight, he'll turn you loose!" Then she LAUGHED 'til she wet her pants! *I knew she was joking* so I suggested to her, with a twinkle in my eye, that my sweetheart would be the only one to catch me in the dark! That's when she said, "don't turn him loose - he's a good old country boy, and just what you need!"

My sweetheart got me, in broad daylight - for thirty-six *wonderful years*. He never turned me loose!

14. *"A boy will only go as far as you let him."*

She was right on target there! I'll admit, I always had my "yellow caution light" turned on, long before we got to the STOP sign. I knew better than to play in that ballpark. As I look back on those years, I have never regretted my decision!

15. *"When you lose your health you have lost it all."*

My mother was extremely healthy for the majority of her life but she 'nursed' my Daddy during twenty-two years of declining health. Soon after I married she said to me, rather casually: *'I hope you never have a sick husband.'* At the time, that did not impact me like it did when my husband's health began to fade, after his heart attack in 1985. That began a downhill ride for us, lasting twenty-two years.

Looking back I have seen so many similarities between her life and mine: we both had dreamed of being a nurse; as life played out for each of us, we became 'full-time nurses' caring for our soul mates. My Daddy's heart attack started his slide down-ward, just as it happened with my husband.

Both men were strong willed, and *defied death* many times before they breathed their last breath. They loved life, and fought to live! They refused to give in to their physical weaknesses. Neither of them complained, or recited their medical history when they were asked 'how are you feeling.' My, what a *character trait* that is, and one that has been passed *down the line* to their descendents!

My Mother lived to be ninety-five, living in her own home, taking care of herself alone, until she was ninety. After a broken hip her wheelchair took the place of her 'old rocking chair!' Yet, it didn't slow her down too much - she put a lot of miles on her 'wheels.' Her eyesight faded significantly but her sense of humor was never dull!

She never met a stranger. When she moved into the Nursing Home, she was the 'clown of the cloister!' She roamed the halls sharing her wisdom, wit and smile with everyone - she could not see them, but they could *'see'* her zest for life.

Even after she had moved to her 'eternal' home, her beacon was still shining. Several years after her death, I ran into some employees who had been her nurses. The first thing they said to me: "We still miss your Mother so much - she made the world and everyone in it the happiest place!"

IV. TALL TALES

When Mother lost her health, *she did 'not' lose it all*. She was having as much fun as she possibly could, with whomever she shared her time. What a tribute that is!

Becky Williams Buckman
April 13, 2013

THE BAND WOULD HAVE BEEN PLAYING

When something very special happened in our life, my mother would say: *"the band would have been playing: 'Who would have thought it?'"*

That was the exact sentiment I felt the night it was announced that I was the winner of a very special prize. In fact, I'm still reeling from excitement, thinking to myself, *'I can't believe that my name was pulled out of the hat to receive such an expensive prize!'*

It was June 16, 2012. The anniversary of my husband's death had been exactly five years ago. Since his death, I had made a practice of buying some special piece of jewelry for myself around the time of Mother's Day, my birthday, and/or our anniversary all of which occurred within 6 weeks of each other. That year, the economy was still not doing well, so I decided not to spend any money on myself, knowing I really did not *need* anything. I had two pieces of 'expensive' jewelry during our marriage: my engagement ring and my 25th anniversary band. They were very special to me and I treasured the love they represented.

The week prior to June 16th, I had battled a heavy dose of depression, perhaps more than normal. The weather had been pregnant with flooding rains, and dark clouds loomed incessantly over my head, literally, as well as emotionally. I succumbed to the bed to sleep the long, fitful days and nights away. I had closed in on myself, choosing to have little or no contact with people. I didn't cry tears but I was definitely dying inside from my grief. I was void of energy the majority of the week. It had been five years since Jim died. Should I not be 'over' this kind of depression?

IV. TALL TALES

I knew God had had a hand in our move from Kentucky to South Carolina but I had no idea the extent to which it would play out! We got to South Carolina in March, 2007 and within a week, I met a wonderful friend who became my all-time *favorite cheerleader*. When she found out my maiden name was Williams, she said, "Well, we are sisters now since I am a Williams too." We bonded instantly. Her journey in life had taken her to places that I soon would be going. . .but at the time we met, I had no idea what I was facing.

This particular Saturday, she had invited me to go to a gospel concert. For some reason, I got a 'second wind' and accepted her invitation to go, without a second thought! It was a free concert at a local church, like many of the concerts she and I attend. When we arrived we were asked to register for prizes that would be given away at the reception following the concert, but the stipulation was that you had to be present to win.

We registered, and we agreed we'd stay for the reception since we had not had time for dinner. "What could it hurt?" we said, knowing we would be *chomping at the bit* to eat after the concert.

During the concert, the lead singer shared his testimony of his anger with God, how he pulled away from people after he and his wife lost their 'expected child' due to a stillbirth. He had been preaching for fifteen years; he didn't understand *why was this happening to him/ to his family?*

Two weeks after the funeral, he was asked by a friend to sing at First Baptist Church in Woodstock, Ga., my hometown. He said *'no'* more than once, but finally agreed to do it, at the urging of his friend who was the Pastor there. He went, arriving late, on purpose, of course. He sang, unwillingly, and was not very motivated, but he did it simply to get the friend off his back!

He wanted to leave the service just after he sang but that would have been very rude and awkward. So he stayed. He halfheartedly listened to his friend preach.

Somehow, in some way, he heard a voice inside of his head saying: *'be still and know that I am GOD.'* Oh yes, I know that, he thought. "But if you are GOD, WHY did you not raise my little girl from the dead, like you did Lazarus? It just isn't fair…"

Then, moments later, a peace came over him, surrounding him with the warmth of a woolen blanket, and he totally surrendered his anger. He walked out of the large congregation, knowing he was a new man in Christ. He'd been preaching 'religion' for fifteen years, but now he had a 'relationship' – one that was real. Everything looked different when he walked out that night!

This particular night at the concert, he shared that he now knew that he had been at that church *in Woodstock, Georgia, for 'a reason'* – he really didn't know what it was when he went there to sing. But when he came out, he knew God had placed him there to receive release from the hatred and anger he'd had in his heart, and to make him whole again: to fill the void left when their little *dream girl* had died.

He said to the congregation: *"You are here for a reason tonight.* You may not know why you came. You could have been any number of places on a summer night…the movies, golf course, the beach, or home with your TV remote in hand!" I was thinking *'yes, I could have stayed home and wallowed in my grief'* but Liz knew I needed to get up and get out that night! She had really not known how *'down'* I had been all week; I don't even recall talking to her that week…that in itself, was unusual. Perhaps that was her clue to invite me!

IV. TALL TALES

The concert ended. We went to the reception, more because we were hungry, than because we expected to win one of the prizes. Gift cards, inspirational books, and a $300.00 diamond bracelet were being given away. Even though it was not a packed house, we never expected that we would win anything!

All of the prizes but one had been given away, and we had not won. Now, they were down to the last 'ticket-stub' being called out. My ticket had fallen into the 'veggie dip' on my plate. Assuming it would not be my number, I continued munching on my food. A number was called out two times…and no one claimed the prize. Finally, the emcee called: *Is there a Becky here?* In utter amazement, I looked around, and no one claimed it. I realized that must be my number. I screamed to the top of my voice, literally, and said *'yes, I'm Becky!'* Meanwhile I was scrambling to retrieve my ticket-stub from the dip, to prove that number was mine… and Liz was simultaneously screaming for joy - *joy for me!* That's what a friend does!

The emcee brought a beautiful gift to me, wrapped in an exquisite box. Inside was the $300.00 diamond bracelet. When I saw it I was overcome with tears blinding me; I couldn't even see to put the bracelet on my arm. The lady sitting next to me offered to help while I cried.

'Why me, LORD?' I rarely ever win anything, much less this kind of gift. Was this your way of telling me that I was loved, unconditionally, by YOU, and that I could 'go on' without my Jim – as well as *to celebrate the memory* of *the wonderful marriage we had?* Was this the reason I had come to the concert? And especially on the anniversary of his death?

That night I received *a very special gift* that I had not chosen for myself but one that was chosen for me. It was far more special than anything I could have purchased.

DOWN THE LINE

Yes, I do believe the band would have been playing that night, as my Mother used to say: *"Who would have thought it?"*

I lifted my eyes to heaven, pointing to my new 'gift' and I smiled for my Jim…and for my Mom. I feel sure they were both smiling down on me as they watched me stare, in awe, at the bracelet that now adorned my wrist. *Amazing Grace!*

Becky Williams Buckman
June 16, 2012

IV. TALL TALES

Holbrook Camp Meeting

Holbrook Campground, located in Cherokee County, Georgia, belongs to the United Methodist Church in the North Georgia Conference. The first camp meeting was held there in 1838. The 175th Anniversary Celebration was held July, 2013.

The open air arbor was built with wooden beams, and held together with wooden pegs. It is listed on the Cherokee County Historical Register, in Georgia.

THAT OLD TIME RELIGION

Memories of Holbrook Campground run deep in my body and soul. Both sets of my grandparents had roots there. This heritage is like gold to me. I cherish that. It has helped shape me into who I am today.

Long before I was born, Holbrook's influence had been significant in the family of *Joseph Washington and Margaret Jefferson*

Williams. It began in the late 1800's. Their family farm on the Ball Ground Road, in Cherokee County, was not far from Holbrook Campground. They took their family of thirteen there; my dad grew up singing "gimme that old-time religion" and hearing the Gospel proclaimed from the large open-air arbor that still stands today. Its hand-hewn logs, held together with wooden pegs, beams and tin roof reach pointedly toward the sky. Heavy summer rainstorms never slowed the preacher down. He just preached louder, as people huddled toward the center to hear better and stay dry!

In 1838 Jesse Holbrook donated 40 acres of land to the Methodist Episcopal Church South for the sole purpose of camp meetings. Thousands of people have filled the arbor over these one-hundred seventy five years.

Families *set aside everything* to bring their children to this sacred place. Mothers have carried babies in arms; children and teenagers whispered or passed notes during worship, but the gospel singing and preaching went on. Aging grandparents ambled down the pathway to the arbor, through the white-washed oak trees that adorned the land, often with a hand-stitched pillow under their arm, and a *funeral home* "fan" in their hand. Sitting on the hard homemade pews in the sweltering August heat, made such things necessary, especially if the preaching and altar calls seemed to go on 'forever!" But worship, and having a closer walk with the Lord, was what camp meetings were all about. *Dinner could wait.*

Getting ready for camp meeting was quite a ritual for us! For weeks we boxed up everything but the "kitchen sink" for the ten days *of tenting.* Our "tent" was a rustic wooden building; the windows and doors were boarded up during the winter. The inside was a refuge for the critters that needed a place to live.

IV. TALL TALES

It required a lot of clean-up work to be done before we could move in. Hosing down the walls, getting rid of the varmints that had keeled over, and hauling in fresh sawdust or shavings, took several days. Then we could start setting up the place for the next ten days.

Dad's old Chevy truck bed was always stacked high with mattresses, cooking utensils, clothes and all, tied down with ropes and chains. I made sure Daddy left room for my bicycle. I often wonder how we made it from Woodstock to the Campground without the truck breaking down, or losing something on the way!

We went several days early, just to settle in. Services started on Friday night, at 8 p. m. There was no slowing down until camp meeting closed ten days later. Three worship services a day, Prayer Meetings for men, for women, a Children's service, and Youth services were held *every day*. After the evening service, we often walked across the road to Macedonia Methodist Church and had *gospel singings* until the wee hours of the morning! The threads of music were deeply woven in the Williams family. My how we loved to sing!

My parents, John Gordon and Leila Mae Johnson Williams, had courted each other while my grandfather, the Rev. R.I. Johnson, was serving the Holbrook Circuit in the 1900's. On *June 19, 1919 Mom and Dad* walked the 'sawdust trail' to the altar, and married after the 3 p. m. worship service. We know of no other marriage that has taken place during a camp meeting at Holbrook. *History was made that day!* So going to camp meeting was like *'going back home'* for my parents.

I was 4 months old when I went to my first camp meeting. My baby crib was covered with a mosquito net while I napped. Mosquito nets and homemade fly swatters protected us in the open-air buildings. Small tree limbs were shaved clean, old newspapers folded over them, and strips cut up and down to make swatters. When I grew up a bit, I had the job of waving them over the dinner table to keep bugs away from all the food Mom had cooked.

Old sheets were hung at our bedroom doors/windows, as well as our 'privy', to provide *privacy*, if you would call it that! The walls that separated the 3 rooms in the tent were not built from 'floor to ceiling' - so real privacy was not possible.

Nights often got so hot we'd soak our sheets, and jammies! There were no ceiling fans, washing machines, dishwashers, electrical appliances, hot water heaters, commodes, tubs or showers. We 'skimped by' without luxuries; we boiled water to cook, wash clothes, and for 'spit baths' taken at the kitchen sink or in a galvanized tub!

'Barefoot Becky,' just outside the Williams Family Tent,
early one August morning

IV. TALL TALES

Staying clean was hard for me and my many cousins! We loved to *play* on the old tire swing, throw horseshoes, have water balloon battles, and pillow fights; we raced our bikes around the circle of tents but we knew they had to be 'parked' during the services of worship. If we didn't go to the service, we were required to stay inside the tent, and be quiet, *and definitely no radios on!* That was hard for us, especially me!

We were not allowed to wear shorts or halter tops to the services. Girls had to wear a dress and boys had to wear slacks. Seems like I had to bathe and change clothes two or three times a day. Really don't know how Mother managed for me to have enough clean clothes to last ten days, but she did!

We pulled 'shenanigans', like trying to sneak in at night, past the curfew. As teens there was nothing better than a walk through the cemetery with your boyfriend, and hear ghost stories! Invariably I got 'caught' by *Aunt Sis;* even if my parents were asleep when I got in, she let me know she heard me come in, and just *'had'* to tell me what time it was. Better yet, she remembered to tell my parents the next morning before I got up! Kid that I was, I reminded her (in front of my parents, i. e.) that she was snoring when I came in, so I usually got away without being punished for being late.

My niece wasn't quite so lucky. She was staying with my parents at the campground one year, and like me, she was out past curfew. My Daddy was much older then, and happened to still be awake when she tried to sneak in. To her dismay, the screen doors were latched. I'm really not sure how long she had to 'beg' *(or cry?)* to get in before he finally unlocked the door to let her in. I doubt he had many words to say - just the look on his face was enough to cure her! From then on, I think she checked her watch carefully to be sure she didn't have to face Granddaddy again, that late at night.

Tents were so close together we could talk to our neighbors through the screened windows; we borrowed eggs, sugar, or whatever we needed, by just reaching over the back fence! *Purcell's* store, and the *Free home Store* weren't very far, but we didn't have much time to run to the store between services. Local farmers came by with fresh vegetables, milk, eggs, melons daily. The iceman came daily with 100 lb. blocks of ice for our old wooden icebox, now a treasured antique! When I was big enough, I was allowed to use the ice pick to chop up ice, and fill glasses of sweet tea or lemonade.

The first 'tents' that were built encircled the Arbor, but soon the circle was full, and now rows of tents shoot off in all directions, bringing the total number of tents close to seventy-five. Most tents are large enough for a family of six to ten people, or more, so the average number of people 'tenting' each year would be about six hundred.

I always begged to make *homemade ice cream,* churned by hand; it worked *wonders* to cool us all down in the August heat. 'Watermelon cuttings' were another good way to enjoy being with friends and family on a *steaming day.* Just hearing a big watermelon being 'split open' made my mouth water. Having watermelon juice running down your chin, and arms and legs called for 'another' bath. . .but it was worth it!

Each day started very early. The wood stove was fired up, and the aroma of bacon and eggs cooking always woke me. It was *my* chore to take the *'chamber pot'* to the outhouse before breakfast. I admit, getting out of bed to do that chore lessened my desire to eat!

IV. TALL TALES

'The privy...'

Some years, we had other relatives 'tenting' with us, so cooking for a big crowd three times a day required a lot of work. We often hired a colored 'cook' to stay with us and help out for ten days so my parents were free to go to all three services. If she got the meal ready before 'preaching' began she would walk down to the arbor, and sit on the back pew, with other 'cooks,' until the altar call was given; then she'd scurry back to the tent to get the food on the table.

Daddy raised chickens so we had a coop out back. Every day he picked a big plump one, would wring its neck, and ask me to pick the feathers. I could handle that, but not the sight or sound of that chicken 'leaving this world' just to land on my plate within the hour! Mother's fried chicken was *the best*. I couldn't wait to get the pulley bone or the biggest leg. The day the Preachers came for a meal we had a bigger 'spread'. Mother would outdo herself. And I did too, trying to *mind my manners,* letting guests go first!

An old 'dinner bell,' mounted on a pole outside our tent, rang 15 minutes prior to services to remind all of us to stop what we were doing: park the riding toys, put up the horseshoes, and get off the old tire swing, wash up, change clothes and head to the Arbor. When I was tall enough to reach the rope Daddy let me be the one to ring the bell. That same old bell still hangs there today, doing the same job it has done though the years.

Our Youth Group was impacted deeply by the tragic and untimely deaths of several of our cousins and peers. As a result, our *leadership team* raised money to erect a YOUTH BUILDING on the campground. My Daddy, Gordon Williams, volunteered his time and construction talents as Building Supervisor. (At the time, he was seventy-three years old!) He worked with The Rev. John Ozley, and others to see this become a reality in 1966. What began as *a tragedy* in our young lives became a blessing for hundreds of teens. It still is today. Teens can stay there for the week, as they would at other camps, with guidance counselors who provide them with Bible studies, and creative activities.

During the one hundred and seventy five years, children, teenagers and adults have found purpose and 'direction' for their lives during Holbrook camp meeting. What has gone on on those sacred grounds has not '*stayed there.*' Its arms have reached 'deep and wide' across Georgia, and the nation. Every year hundreds of people come to be a part of this *old-time religion* experience. I still go. I'm blessed to be a part of the Holbrook tradition. As the gospel song goes: *"It was good for my father, it was good for my mother and... it's good enough for me!"*

Becky Williams Buckman
January, 2010

IV. TALL TALES

My father, Gordon Williams, is third from the left. and Rev. Ozley, second from the right, at the Cornerstone of the Youth Building at Holbrook Campground.

*** Previously published in Autumn, 2011 issue of '*Georgia Backroads*' magazine, as "Memories Are Made of This"

DOWN THE LINE

THE COUNT DOWN

I think my Granny Johnson always had chickens in her yard, maybe even as a child. I don't know. I've seen many photos of her scattering feed to them, as they sauntered aimlessly loose, looking for sustenance! She grew up on a farm in Woodstock, Ga. and lived there again in her latter years. Back then people raised a lot of their own food - they killed hogs, cattle for meat, grew vegetables, and had fresh eggs daily.

When I visited her, Granny would take me to the nest, to gather the eggs for all the good dishes she made. It's no wonder she loved a certain oral folk rhyme - a counting rhyme, akin to One potato, two potato, three potato, four. This one began talking about chickens! It was *WILLIAM, WILLIAM TRIMBLE TOE*. It had many versions; the origin of it is difficult to determine.

From the time I was six, I grew up living near my Granny so I could run down the street and spend precious time with her. My parents also raised chickens, on a much broader scale than Granny. We didn't have just a few, like Granny. We had a "big" chicken house out on the back of our property. It was part of my "family duties" to help feed them the old-fashioned way, putting water in jars that were turned upside down on to a saucer type 'gizmo.' (I really don't recall the proper name of it!) We didn't have electric feeders - we had to do everything by hand in the mid-forties. Daddy did have a water spigot out there. That was helpful except when the pipes froze up in the winter! Then we had to carry buckets of water.

Granny reinforced my learning to count with an old folk rhyme that she loved. It was a game she loved to play. I can just hear her laughing now when I got *O-U-T!* She'd played this with all her children, and grandchildren through the years. I was the last born grandchild; she was in her mid sixties when I came

IV. TALL TALES

along and had more time to play with me! Playing with her was often the best part of my day, and perhaps a 'fun' part of her day. She'd snuggle me up, in her lap, on her screened-in porch, in the summer, in her glider or swing; or in the winter we'd edge up toward the fireplace where her old rocker sat nearby.

Then she had me spread my chubby little hands on her lap, over her *chicken feed sack* apron, and in her *sing-song voice* she began the counting game: **William, William, A Tremble Toe**. It uses all ten fingers or toes.

Here is the rhyme:

>*William, William, A Tremble Toe,*
>*He's a good fisherman*
>*Catches hens*
>*Puts 'em in pens*
>*Some lay eggs,*
>*Some not.*
>*Wire, briar, limber lock*
>*Three geese in a flock*
>*One flew east,*
>*One flew west,*
>*One flew over the cuckoo's nest...*
>*O - U - T spells OUT!*

With each word of the rhyme she pointed to one of my fingers until the last word was said. Then on whichever finger it landed, that finger had to be "tucked under" - into your palm, and we began all over again. When all fingers were hidden, the game was over, and it was time to feed the chickens! Then we went to the back porch, dipped the big scoop down deep into the bin where she safely stored the chicken feed, to keep the rats, mice and other varmints *'O-U-T.'* Then we went into the back yard to scatter the feed. Leaving their nests, the chickens came running, feathers flying, their beaks wide open before they even reached the food.

Yes, of course, there was the old Red Rooster, "the meanie" was my name for him! But Granny always said, "honey, you always have to have the Rooster…he's the one who crows every morning, and gets us out of bed." (She didn't bother to tell me the *'rest of the story' - i. e.,* the rooster's other job!) He was better known as the old fashioned 'alarm clock,' one that never had to be wound up, or plugged in. He never ran O-U-T of cock-a-doodle do's!

By now, it was time for me to get up and go back home. Not only had I memorized the rhyme, I had learned how to count my fingers, how to feed chickens and what the 'pecking order was' in her family of chickens! When I went to First Grade, I knew some things that some children my age didn't know back then, and some people my age now, still don't know, such as *William, William A Trimble Toe!*

Wow…*thanks to my special Granny Johnson.* I imagine she's smiling down on me now, knowing that I still 'know,' and can quote, this rhyme in a heartbeat. I'm teaching it, and other rhymes, to my grandchildren, sharing special times with them, just like she did with me!

EDITOR'S NOTE: The *William Matrimmatoe* chant has several alternatives: including the one above, William, A William Trimble Toe, William A Trimmy Toe, or William Trimble Trow Tran. It is a variant of a Mother Goose rhyme that was printed in 1814.

Becky Williams Buckman
January 25, 2011

IV. TALL TALES

*** Written in memory of my Granny Johnson, Amanda Euphemia Mae Hawkins Johnson, on the sixtieth anniversary of her death, January 25, 1951.

GROWING IN AMAZING GRACE

Late that evening Granny 'backed up' to the fireplace in her little frame house in Woodstock. She had become a widow much too soon...but she loved having her own home, after having lived in Methodist parsonages for many years. Her husband, the Rev. R. I. Johnson was an itinerant minister in North Georgia for almost thirty years in the early part of the twentieth century.

The winds of winter were blowing cold around the corners of her house, and the insulation had seen its better days. She often backed up to the fireplace in the 'sitting room' and pulled up her long skirt allowing the heat to flow onto the short chubby legs of her small frame. Standing there soaking up the warmth that radiated through her limbs, her thoughts rumbled in her mind, like rolling thunder behind black clouds.

She recalled those special years of giving birth to her four children: Bertha Mae, Leila Mae, Glen Livingston, and Loy Clifford. She had a lot to be grateful for - a wonderful husband, three daughters, and one son. But two of her children had faced tragedies in their lives during or after childbirth. Leila Mae and Gordon had lost their first child, Miriam, in 1921, at eight months of age due to whooping cough. Their third daughter had been a stillbirth, and Leila fought for her life but had survived, miraculously! The Doctor told her she should never try to have another child. (for the rest of that story, see *"Only Heaven Knows")*

Glen's wife had died within 8 days of giving birth to their first child, Martha Mae. Granny's faith was strong. She had grown up in a Methodist parsonage, (as a PK, preacher's kid) and then married a Methodist minister who was also a true man of God. They were 'there' to stand by their children during those

IV. TALL TALES

storms but each time tragedy struck their hearts were ripped apart as quickly as an old rotten garment falls apart under a tug-o-war.

Granny and her husband took Glen's baby to raise. They were just grateful they were healthy enough to do it. And, for sure, it had brought a lot of joy into their lives; in mid-life, when all their children were grown, it gave them something to keep living for, it kept them 'young at heart.'

Granny stood lost in her thoughts that night, tears welled up and soon fled their hiding place, spilling down onto her checkered apron. She reached for the lace handkerchief in her pocket. It could soak up the tears but not the heartache and grief. She had tried to move on, and she had. . . she had to be strong for her newest grandchild, Martha. *Her faith in God had been her rod and staff,* daily. As her tears subsided, she thought of the blessing that Martha had been to them. Smiles dried her damp cheeks.

The late night hours moved on. She began to weep again. This time she wept for her only son, Glen. After his wife died he had lost all of his bearings. He no longer wanted to go on living. Seeing Glen struggle like a young cat under the grip of a tiger was like being on the sidelines of a house on fire with no water to put it out! She had watched and prayed for him daily. After Mae died, Glen had married twice but both marriages failed due to his addiction to alcohol. Granny and Grandaddy Johnson grieved for their only son; they prayed for him to be released from those bonds, to become the father that Martha needed so desperately.

At one point, Glen had felt that he and his second wife could take Martha and raise her. He approached Granny and

Grandaddy, feeling they should be relieved of the responsibility. But Martha was now an elementary student, doing well in school, and quite well adjusted in the family. The uncertainty of their son's emotional stability led them to say *"No. Martha is ours now."* This perhaps was quite a blow to him, leading him into a deeper state of alcoholism.

Not only did Martha have the security of her grandparents' love, she had the added blessing of having her Aunt Cliffie's love and care. She had not married and still lived at home with her parents, so she was like another mother to Martha. Loving and caring for little children was Cliffie's best 'gift!'

The miraculous way God had been working in Granny's life surrounded her being that night, taking away some of the darkness she'd felt when she first approached the fireplace. Their home was one full of faith; there was a stronghold on God and his grace.

Back then, preachers mostly got paid with eggs, milk, and produce from his parishioners. Granny made most of their clothes from the fabric they got when they bought flour or chicken feed. Back then, flour and chicken feed was sold in large five, ten and twenty pound sacks of cloth - the variety of prints available was quite large. When I grew up there were only two grocery stores in our little town, and only one dry goods store, so getting to the grocery story early on "delivery day" would assure getting the best choices of fabric for our clothes. I loved going with Mother to pick out something for the new dress that Granny had promised to make for me. I couldn't wait to show her what I'd chosen, and as soon as my Mother emptied the flour sack, we washed and ironed it. I took it to Granny and she began sewing up a storm!

IV. TALL TALES

Now the hour was getting late, the logs on the fire began to melt into the small flaming red embers in the grate, the old mantle clock struck 10 p. m., breaking the silence of the room. The only station on the old radio had long since gone off the air. She realized she'd slipped into a bed of quicksand - allowing herself to woller in the misery of old heartaches. She pulled up the corner of her apron, and wiped her eyes, and saw the back of her legs were 'glowing red.' How long had she stood there?

This whole time, I had been lying on the sofa in her little *sitting room*. I was almost asleep, wrapped up in an afghan, trying to stay warm. I loved going to Granny's to spend the night, for lots of reasons. They had a cat, Spud, who was just a big ball of fur to cuddle with. And if anyone happened to be singing AMAZING GRACE, that was a sure invitation for him to curl up in your lap while you sang! Everyone in the family either sung or hummed that old hymn several times a day. It was a 'sign' that GOD was alive, and '*at home*' in their house! It was Granny's favorite - she knew every word for memory. We all did!

When Granny realized I was almost asleep she reached down for me, pulled me into her arms, and then sank down in her big cane-bottomed rocking chair by the fire. *Maybe going to bed now could be stalled off a bit,* I thought. Saying nothing, she hugged me close, as we rocked back and forth to the tune of Spud's purring, and the hum of Granny's voice - *'Amazing Grace, how sweet the sound.'* There was no room in Granny's lap for Spud. So he curled up on the brick hearth, feeling the warmth of the fireplace. He was getting old and made those funny "cat noises" that always made me giggle. She giggled with me! Granny's just do that. . .

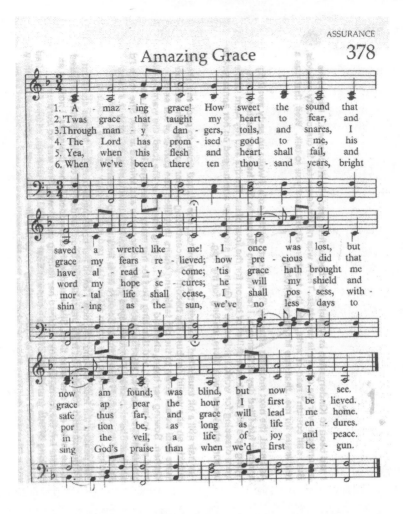

When she looked into my blue eyes, and stroked my blonde curls, she saw in me an *'extra blessing.'* I was the grandchild that was *never supposed to be*. . .but here I was! My mother had delivered me without any of the problems she had experienced with her last pregnancy. It seemed a miracle had happened right before their eyes: it had been eighteen years since her last grandchild was born.

IV. TALL TALES

Smiles etched across her face bringing dimples to her plump cheeks that characterized all the women in the family. My smiles soon matched hers, and with my biggest bear hug, I told Granny how much I loved her. Then she tucked me in bed beside Aunt Cliffie who was already snoring. Long after everyone else was asleep, I drifted off, in spite of the 'background music' of snoring, knowing that I had just had something very special: *my own special time with Granny that night.* She was the only one of my four grandparents I was privileged to know. I treasure those moments with her, but often I have wondered how many other 'other treasures' I missed by not knowing my Granddaddy Johnson, or either Grandparent on the Williams side of the family.

As usual, the next morning I woke up early awaiting another fun-filled day at Granny's. I ran into the kitchen to find her over the hot stove frying up a big black iron skillet of bacon for the four of us. Martha and my Aunt Cliffie were dressing for work. I sidled up to Granny's short legs and tugged on her apron just to be sure she knew I was there, waiting for my hug.

Her hair still a bit tousled, with a *bun* on top, she leaned down to peck my cheek quickly, so she would not burn the bacon! Concentrating on her cooking, she said no more until we sat down to the old table and chairs that sat in one corner of her small kitchen. Bowing her head, she said "grace," giving thanks for the food, the warm home we'd slept in last night, and thanking God for her many blessings, her children and grandchildren. Just as she finished she opened her eyes and winked at me. She knew I'd see her wink. She also knew I kept my eyes open most of the time during her prayer. I used Spud as my alibi so I would say to her: *"I just want to be sure he is listening too, Granny."* As grandparents often do, they let their grandchildren get away with things like that . . .

She passed the food around. My, how I loved her homemade biscuits. Martha and Aunt Cliffie excused themselves from the table and soon headed out to work. Granny lingered at the table, as if she were tired. She was deeply embedded in her thoughts. I noticed as Martha left the room, Granny watched her limping out slowly. Martha had had polio and had many surgeries, worn braces, and depended on crutches quite often during her young adult life. After my Grandaddy Johnson died, Martha was the main breadwinner for the family. She was *a real trooper* all of her life. Nothing kept her from being where God planted her, whether it was in her job, in the church or in her community. She, like Granny, always met you with a smile on her face and never a complaint of what had been put on her plate of life.

I absorbed every ounce of love I could in that atmosphere. Granny and Aunt Cliffie always had some extra treats for me when I was there - tea cakes, lemonade, or milk; and chewing gum was in their dress or coat pockets. And oh, goodness, how they did spoil me rotten, even after I was married, and had my own children! I never went to their house without leaving with a *'sack full'* of things - sack of sugar, flour, candy, popcorn, a roll of paper towels. . . or anything they had found *'on sale'* that they knew we could use. My children loved going there for the same reason I did: they knew they would get spoiled too!

Granny died when I was 11, but in those years together, she taught me to sew, embroidery, play WILLIAM WILLIAM A TREMBLE TOE, how to count, and how to relax and enjoy swinging with her, on her front porch, and to sing *Amazing Grace!* And more than that, she taught me a kind of love that I cherished then, and even more now.

She also had the most beautiful front yard - she had every kind of bush, shrub and old fashioned flower that could bloom, from

IV. TALL TALES

early spring until the late days of fall. Maybe my love of flower gardening was a gene passed *down the line.*

I began First Grade at the Woodstock Elementary School just across the street from her house. My Aunt Cliffie worked in the lunchroom there, and always managed to slip a little larger helping of my favorite food on my plate when I filed through the line. *Spoiled again?* You bet. Maybe that is why my childhood photos portrayed *a chubby child!*

Perhaps all of my Granny's life she had been burdened over this wayward son, and grandchild of hers, who had to grow up without ever recalling her own mother's face, and whose father had shifted from one woman to another seeking to resolve his anger and resentment. Glen was drinking heavily; his last two marriages had failed. He was not the father Martha needed. He was in Norfolk, Va. and didn't get back home to Georgia too often. His letters to her were sporadic.

The guilt that he felt, when he failed his responsibility as a husband and father, was killing him slowly, with each drink that he took. By the time Martha was twenty-three, her father had died. Grandaddy Johnson had been the only real father she knew but she could not have had better care! He not only 'talked the talk' - he *'walked' the Walk'* and she followed closely in his footsteps.

Martha left her footprints all over North Georgia. She too, 'walked the Walk' in her quiet unassuming way. No one ever wondered where Martha stood, she stood up for people regardless of their race, or creed. She was known in Woodstock as "Miss Martha." When she died, articles were written in local newspapers about her life, her service to her Church, her profession in the medical field, and her love for her family. She was born to love and give. She gave all she had to everyone along her pathway. The theme of her life was JOY. She told me how to spell it:

J = Jesus first
O = Others second
Y = Yourself last

She always said if you *live your life in 'that order'* all will be well with your soul. She, Aunt Cliffie, and Granny lived by that motto. What a heritage I have!

Becky Williams Buckman
January, 2010

IV. TALL TALES

GRANNY'S FRONT PORCH

When I was six our family moved from Atlanta to the small community of Woodstock, Ga. Our new home wasn't finished in time for me to begin first grade that fall, so I lived with my Granny Johnson for a while. What a treat that was! After we moved into our new home just up the street, I still *'felt at home'* at Granny's. My school was just across from her house so from her front porch my Granny could even see me during the day, on the playground of Woodstock Elementary. I have a feeling she watched me fall down many times, but also saw me get back up and keep going, non-stop...until the school bell rang to let us all go home.

When I left the classroom, all my *'schoolin''* was left behind. I was on my way to Granny's front porch, for the 'time of my life.' Once the crossing guard saw me safely across Georgia Highway 5, I ran lickety split to find *my spot* on her front porch. It was the swing. After my hug, she toddled to the kitchen to get the sugar cookies and lemonade. In her apron pocket, she usually had something else for me! It could be anything from a copper penny, to a wooden nickel, a piece of candy or chewing gum, maybe even one of her hairpins that had just fallen out of the 'bun' on the back of her head. On a few occasions she had a hen egg in her pocket!

One of my favorite pictures of her is out in the yard feeding her chickens. I can just hear her talking to them now. And if I *'dream'* of the times I spent the night there, I can still hear the old rooster crowing to wake us up! I'm sure the eggs she cooked for breakfast were 'fresh,' just brought in, perhaps, and washed off clean, then cracked for scrambled eggs and bacon along with the best homemade biscuits in town.

She was rather short and chubby, but her beauty was what counted! Her chubby cheeks were touched with 'natural rouge' - the kind you get when you just pinch up a bit of the skin and suddenly color appears! There was always a smile on her face! When I look at photos of her, I see the 'genes' were passed down for three generations - to my Mother, to me, and to my daughter. We couldn't lose each other if we tried. People tell us we are just alike! I always take that as the best compliment someone could give me.

Her hair was already growing thin, and very white; she always pulled it back, away from her face, and twisted it in a knot - *the 'bun.'* I had a lot of long golden curls, so she'd run her fingers through my hair, perhaps wishing for the days when she had thicker or prettier hair. She'd try to pin up my curls with her hairpins, but there weren't enough…so we just sat in the swing, savoring the moment. Once the lemonade was gone, and the cookies inhaled, we kept swinging. She'd begin singing 'Amazing Grace,' her favorite song.

As you have guessed by now, this song was woven into my being - even to this day, I can sing every word, of every verse, for memory. *Amazing Grace* was sung at her funeral, and at every family funeral since then. Naturally, it's on *'my list'* of music for my funeral. When the first note is played I probably will *'rise up'* and sing along. I'm just praying for a new 'angelic voice' hoping not to embarrass my children like I am often prone to do now!

Music was always a 'staple' in the Johnson family. Granny had an old pump organ in her living room, and how I loved to play it. It took a long time for my little legs to reach the pedal that 'pumped' the air to make the notes sound but I was determined to play it even if I had to stand up to reach the pedal! I don't recall Granny playing the organ but my Mother and my Aunt

IV. TALL TALES

Cliffie could play it so they taught me how to *pull out all the stops!* (I still pull out all the stops, in *'everything'* I do!)

When her living room windows were open, I could always smell the honeysuckle that crept through her lace curtains on a spring day. Nearby were fly swatters hanging on nails throughout the house. When I played in the backyard I could smell the aroma of fried chicken floating through the window screens.

On the back of her little white-framed one-bedroom house there was a porch. That's where the old wringer washing machine sat. In the back yard the clothes line was strung from pole to pole. She let me help her hang out clothes, pulling out the clothes pins from her apron pocket. Until I got the hang of using the pins, I pinched my fingers more often than not. She always had a few clothes pins in her mouth. I finally figured out why. With the heavy wet garments to hoist up on the line, you never seemed to have enough hands.

Just beyond the clothesline stood the outhouse - the 'outdoor john' or *privy*. It was a *two-seater* but I always preferred to go alone, to have my privacy, particularly if we had had beans for supper! There was always an extra supply of *'natural gas'* - you know, the kind that BEANO is supposed to curtail! That wasn't even on the market back then. At night, if we had to 'potty,' we used the old white 'chamber pot' that was kept under the bed. First thing the next morning someone had to take it out before breakfast; thankfully, it was not me!

I remember having fun out in the old garage at the back of her lot. It was filled with *'everything in the book'* except the car that it was built for! There was an old trunk out there but I was never allowed to open it. But I did see my Grandfather's old-fashioned typewriter that printed out his sermons. It was many years later when I was given his old saddlebag, and his 'book of sermons' that I got a glimpse of the spiritual giant that he was.

Behind the garage, the train tracks ran within 20-30 feet. When I heard the whistle blow a few miles back up the track, I scampered out the back door as fast as I could, to be there in time to wave at the conductor, and to count the cars on the *L & N Line!* Granny always asked *'how many this time?'* The tracks ran behind my house also, but it wasn't as easy to see them as it was from Granny's, so the 'ritual' of seeing the train was special to me!

In the midst of many of those moments, my mother often called on the phone, to say "come on home, Becky, it's supper time." Phone service then was a far cry from what it is today: we had to be on *a party line*. It was a good thing our two families were on the same line since you could often hear conversations of those on your party line! Gossip could really 'fly high' if your family was on a party line with someone who was *not* your kinfolks. And in a small town like Woodstock was back then, seems everyone knew everyone else's business!

Had I stayed there all afternoon? How the time did fly, and how I'd love to go back to those good old days when the *'simple pleasures'* in life were so very simple. No computer crashes, no 'hacking' of them, no cell phones, or 'tablets,' no mass murders committed daily - just sugar cookies, lemonade, front-porch swings, homemade quilts, honeysuckle vines, trains, and Granny games! Back to life in the slow lane where *people were 'tops'* and love flowed freely without the need for wires to connect you - a time when your batteries were charged with the 'human touch,' by getting a *'twinkle of an eye'* or the hug of a loving Granny.

Becky Williams Buckman
April 12, 2011

IV. TALL TALES

***EDITOR'S NOTE:** The last photo I have of her is very vivid in my mind. It was after Christmas - December, 1950, She had walked up the street to visit us on a very cold day. She had on her heavy long black winter coat with a white scarf around her neck. After a delightful visit, Granny gave us a big smile, said 'good-bye' and headed up our walkway toward the sidewalk. I called out to her: 'please wait a minute,' and I ran to get the new Brownie camera that I'd gotten for Christmas. I was anxious to try it out on someone special! "Granny, I want to take your picture on my new camera." She looked back at me and smiled as I snapped the photo!

She died within a few weeks, Jan. 25, 1951.

SEWING AND SO MUCH MORE

My Granny Johnson was such a great influence on my life in just eleven short years.

During that time, and until she died, I learned things I could 'use' all of my life. She was an excellent seamstress, and I think I inherited the love of sewing from her. I went on to get my State Homemaker Award when I was a Senior in high school, making everything from my own clothes, to lampshades, to reupholstering furniture, even a winter coat - wool and 'lined,' no less! That was a special project that made me proud of what Granny *(and many others)* had taught me about sewing! That passion carried over into adulthood. I made draperies for all our homes, our children's clothes, shower curtains, pillows, the trousseau for our oldest daughter's wedding, bridesmaid's dresses, their hats, my dress for the wedding. *All because* of *Granny*. . .as well as our need to be 'thrifty!'

All of her life she had to 'make do' with very little of the worldly goods. Back then, Ministers were given a parsonage (home) to live in. Their parishioners supplied them with 'vitals,' i. e. groceries, dairy products from their gardens, or their services. . .which today is called *bartering*.

The Minister's family was always treated to dinner every Sunday by some of their parishioners. Fried Chicken was always on the table, along with the home-grown vegetables from the local gardens. It was a 'feast' for sure. The only 'fast foods' in those days were sliced tomatoes, cucumbers, onions, pecans, figs, apples, peaches or watermelons!

IV. TALL TALES

Granddaddy Johnson was a 'circuit rider' minister. He rode horseback, or drove a buggy, over the dirt roads of North Georgia to preach the gospel. He was assigned, by the Bishop of the Methodist Episcopal Church South to serve five or six churches on a 'circuit' or charge. To make the rounds, he had to travel from community to community every Sunday, often preaching three times a day. This would be an all-day journey. On the Sundays when he did not preach at a particular church, Sunday School was held for the congregation. They always knew which Sunday was 'preaching Sunday' - the 'first Sunday', for example, it would be my church.

On the 'fifth' Sunday it was customary for all the denominational churches in the community to come together for the Sunday night service. Back then, and in our community of Woodstock, the three main-line denominations were Methodist, Baptist, and Presbyterian so we all were 'exposed' to varying theological beliefs and practices. The Methodists were always glad they were *'Methodists'* when it came time for baptism! We didn't have to *'go under water'* to profess our faith like our Baptist friends. We got by with just a little dab of water sprinkled on our head. I often wonder how many Baptist children wished they could be baptized like us.

'Dinner on the ground' was a highlight of the country churches - a time when everyone, for days in advance, cooked up their best dishes. And in the afternoon, they had a *'singing.'* It would be an all-day affair - one to remember! A song leader would start it off, but then call on someone in the congregation to come up and lead a special song. There was a lot of musical talent in my family - often my uncles and/or cousins would alternate leading songs. I recall having been called up to lead a song. For a teenager, that was a 'special treat!' And it was not unusual for people to *'get happy'* or shout during the sermons or at the singings. The altar was always 'open' - you could linger there and pour out your burdens while friends and family surrounded you in prayer.

* Back to my story about Granny. . Sorry, but my mind seems to ' *'wander'* around when I'm telling stories!

'Granny Johnson' - Amanda Euphemia Mae Hawkins Johnson
1872-1951

IV. TALL TALES

Granny taught me how to cross stitch. Back then, we could buy a wide variety of things at the only Dry Goods Store in town, Dawson's Department Store in Woodstock. (1940's version of K-Mart) We bought pillow cases with 'stamped cross-stitch' patterns, or a piece, when finished, that could be framed and hung on our wall. My first project was a set of pillow cases. First, she had to teach me how to thread a needle. That took a lot of patience on my part, and hers! Then I had to learn how to put the fabric into a hoop, tighten it, leaving not a wrinkle in the material. Stitch by stitch, color by color, I made something useful! Proudly, I gave those pillowcases to my parents as a homemade Christmas gift. I'm not sure it was the 'best workmanship' but at least I was proud of myself for not giving up before it was finished.

Later, as a young adult, I tackled a very large tablecloth, with matching napkins, *wondering if I would ever marry,* or have a home in which to display what Granny taught me. Years later, I did marry and used it often! After we raised the children, I began to do counted-cross-stitch while Jim inhaled the three main sports on TV: football, basketball and baseball.

If someone came to visit while I was working on a cross-stitch project I had to rush to every seat in the room, particularly where I'd been sitting. . .to be sure our guests didn't get the *'shot of their life'* with my needle! I was famous for sticking threaded needles in the arms of furniture if my pin cushion was not handy. More than once, I even got *a shock* when I sat down. . .you'd think I would have learned. Guess I've been a slow learner in more arenas than I'd like to admit!

I cross-stitched hundreds of pieces: for pillows, bookmarks, for clothing garments, 'framed art work' for craft shows. It passed many long hours, and provided the greatest satisfaction, especially when I recall who taught me how to do needlework! Today my home is decorated with special pieces of work that I have done - most of them are *'sayings'* that tell you who I am, my philosophy of life. (see 'Sign Language')

Where did time go? Now, *I'm the Grandparent* in the family. I often wonder what my grandchildren will remember about their "Memaw Buckman" when I am gone. What have I taught them? Only *time will tell.*

Becky Williams Buckman
June 19, 2013

IV. TALL TALES

ADORABLE AUNT CLIFFIE

"The Diet"

There are so many things about *'years gone by'* that stick in my memory. If only *Americans Funniest Home Videos* had been around, I think we could have won a prize!

Recalling my time with Aunt Cliffie is one set of memories I don't think I will ever forget. She was the shortest, and chubbiest of the three daughters in my Granny Johnson's family. I recall one time when she was not the 'chubbiest.' She had gone on this crash diet, and exercise plan, the likes of which I had never heard of 'back then,' nor have I heard of it since.

Cliffie's real name was Loy Clifford Johnson. I believe my Grandparents wanted their last child to be a boy! Why else would they give a beautiful baby girl a boy's name? Nevertheless, she was as feminine as could be. But still, *she was some kind of hoot!* I'll never forget going to visit her late one evening, seeing this big ball of a body in the living room floor, taking up the majority of the open space on the rug. She was *'rolling'* back and forth, from one side of her body to the other! *Yes,* that is exactly what I said.

I couldn't help but laugh, (under my breath, of course) when I saw her in such a position. With both arms joining together, hands clasped together, she rolled from one side to the other on her living room rug, one hundred times every night. You might say there was a lot of *'rocking and rolling'* going on in our little town of Woodstock. . .and a whole lot of *'shaking going on'* as well!

I had to admire her for keeping the discipline of doing it every night before bedtime. She had other tactics for losing the weight: many tossed salad meals, walking 2 miles a day. She pulled off a lot of her 'spare tires' - so much so that an entirely new wardrobe was necessary.

It wasn't an expensive diet, nor a costly exercise plan. When I was a teenager, I'll admit I did try the *'rolling'* thing, so I could lose some of the 'hippie' hiney I carried, but I could never get up the 'energy' to walk 2 miles, nor eat a head of lettuce a day! So my hips didn't fall off like my Aunt Cliffie's. I still have them, as a reminder that I am a genuine Johnson-Williams offspring! And there's not a lot I can do to cause them to disappear. . .it is all in the 'genes' that came *down the line.*

Now, I have two metal hips and when I end up on the floor - *on an accident,* as my toddlers used to say, I have to call 911 to get myself up! Cliffie would get up on her all fours. . .that too, was *a sight to behold!* Too bad I did not have my new camera with me that night. . .but the memory is as vivid as sparkles of dew on a blade of grass in the sunlight.

"The Varsity Trip"

Cliffie never married. I'm really not sure why. I guess I was too shy to ask! Well, maybe *'shy'* is not the word. . .*inquisitive,* perhaps would be a better choice. I know she dated as a young adult. She was a very attractive woman. She dressed well, her clothes always tailor-made to fit her short, stocky figure. She loved costume jewelry and had pieces to match her outfits. Her shoes and purses were always coordinated. She never owned expensive clothing or jewelry, but she 'put it all together' as perfectly as possible.

IV. TALL TALES

Her nails were well manicured. There were no nail salons in our little community, so she was an expert at doing her own. Always a file, or an emery board in her purse. . .for emergencies. (See *Newt Wilson* story)

Why some handsome man didn't snatch her up is beyond me. She loved life, had a delightful sense of humor, often dry wit, but sometimes not so subtle. Being the daughter of a Methodist Minister, and the granddaughter of another minister, I'm sure she'd had enough *'serious'* stuff in her path to cause the *'hoot'* in her to escape anywhere it could!

I remember taking her, my cousin Martha, and my Mother to *The Varsity* in Atlanta one Sunday afternoon. They were all 'senior citizens' - in their seventy and eighties. I was married and had gone back to my hometown for a visit. I knew they needed to get out of the house so I suggested we buzz downtown Atlanta for an afternoon outing. *The Varsity* is a 'famous' drive-in near Georgia Tech campus, catering to people of all walks of life. It is the forerunner of SONIC - a drive-in fast food place where the waiters (men only, i. e.) came running out to get your order at the car!

After we parked, and waited to place our order, Cliffie glanced around the parking lot, to see who she could see! Mid-afternoon, who did she see but a gang of motorcyclists pulling in beside us, in their ragged sleeveless t-shirts, long fuzzy beards, mustaches, black boots and tattered jeans. Sweaty, with bandanas tied around their heads, and tanned to the hilt! Cliffie, of course, was still dressed in her Sunday best. Now picture this:

> Our windows rolled down, on a hot August afternoon, in the midst of the 'big city' and Cliffie calls out to the

> fellow parked within 6 feet of her side of the car. . . *"hey, that is a good looking cycle you have. I bet it is fun to ride. . ."*

As I sat in the driver's seat, about to *'you know what'* I looked at her expression, and she was dead serious. . .meanwhile my mother, cousin and I wondered where this story was going. . .or if we should intervene! The not-so-bad looking man, said to Cliffie: *"Well, I could take you for a ride; how far are you willing to go?"* With a smirky grin she responded: *"Maybe I'd better take a rain check since I've got on a dress!"*

At that point, our subtle giggling soon became roaring laughter, and I felt sure we would be riding back to Woodstock on *'wet'* car seats! By this time, Cliffie was laughing with us and the entire gang of motorcyclists was joining in the laughter.

The car-hop waiter arrived with our Varsity hot dogs, topped with chili, french fries, peach pies, and a 'big orange'. . .just in time to catch the 'party' that was blowing through the parking lot. *Curiosity about killed the cat that day.* Everyone within hearing distance was wondering what all the ruckus was about - senior citizens flirting with the jet set? Why not? After all, it was a beautiful Sunday afternoon - a perfect day to take a ride in the big city, in Cliffie's old Pontiac or on a Harley! *It was FUN* for all of us and that's what counted.

Just goes to prove: life can be fun when you are single, married, young or old or when you just need a good laugh. I imagine my grandparents looked down from heaven, many times, laughing and saying: "well, that's our gal Cliffie."

IV. TALL TALES

What a hoot she was, for ninety-five years, just like her older sister, my Mother!

Becky Williams Buckman
June 17, 2001

WE'LL NEVER GROW '*OLD*'

As a youngster I recall my parents and relatives singing a song *"In a Land Where We'll Never Grow Old."* Of course at that time in my life it didn't ring any bells in my tower! I had no clue what 'old' really meant. *Now I do.* I can sing that song with the greatest of gusto, just like they did. I pray for 'landing' in that la-la land!

A dear friend sent me a wonderful Christmas gift, the book: *"Never Say Old"* whose philosophy I literally 'cling' to. What a sense of relief I had when I inhaled its advice. I think it qualifies for the best gift of the year, or maybe of all times!

People are always saying: *You're only as old as you feel.* Well, some days I feel older than dirt, and my looks, and everything else on this skeleton, confirms it. Even though I am 'heavy metal' (not referring to music either!) those four titanium joint replacements are embedded in my bones. There's no escaping the pain when it rains, or if the weather is changing. When we were kids, that was *'an old wives tale'* but it is as real as the raindrop in the middle of a downpour!

On other days (and nights) I bounce off the walls like I'm like a thirteen year old on steroids! Like when I have the opportunity to dance, every bone in my body is required to get up and move. I might 'pay for it' later but when I'm dancing I'm as near heaven as I can get! The way I see it - it's my own form of aerobics, and it doesn't cost me a dime.

I'm really glad I can shut the blinds at home when I'm in the mood to hit the floor (dancing, i. e.). I really was never embarrassed to dance in public, but late at night in my 'nighties' I'd just as soon those *'old folks'* in my neighborhood don't see me gyrating around the room, *alone*. Well, actually, if they did, all it

IV. TALL TALES

would amount to is more 'gossip' for them to chew on. I've been talked about before, so it really wouldn't cause me to lose sleep. Let's face it: *I probably dance in my sleep!*

The idea of *dancing* takes me back to my teen-age years. I grew up in Woodstock, a small town outside of Atlanta where there wasn't much to do. The movie theater had burned; there was no skating rink, not even a Youth Club. We had to do something! We would crank up our record player, the kind that used the 45 RPM records (they are antiques now) and we would jitterbug til the 'cows came home!' Anything from *'Yakety Yak' to 'Blue Suede Shoes,' or 'In the Still of the Night.'* Elvis, Fats Domino, the Drifters, the Platters were 'tops' with the best tunes! You just can't beat the tunes of our time, the 50's and 60's.

The American Legion Hall was in Canton where we went to High School. They had Youth Night every week so that was our night to dance our hearts out! A live band, no less. Before we were old enough to drive, our parents drove us, sometimes staying to watch us dance, as well as to chaperone. They never worried that we'd get into alcohol there since the water fountain and a Coke machine were our only choices!

The Band was playing the minute we walked in. . .the place was packed with *'ready to rock and roll'* teenagers. I lived all week just to get to that dance. It didn't matter if my homework was done or not - I was born to dance! My body just never knew how to stay still. It still doesn't. If there's music anywhere within a mile, I'll start *keeping time* with some part of my body - whatever is *'appropriate'* based on where I am. So far, I haven't been kicked out of any place I've been. Yes, some people do stare at me!

My Cherokee High School friends and I *'came out of the walls like termites'* when it was Youth Night. We donned our crinilans/

petticoats made with layers of net that made our full skirts stand out a 'foot' from our legs! Our skirts were made with several yards of fabric that could *fly high* when we were twirled around by our partner. Be assured, however, that we never let our undergarments show like we see now! The guys had their jeans around their waist, and not their hips, with a good looking belt and buckle. I'm not sure that most teens, and some 'old men' even know where their waist is, or that belts are still sold or that they have a purpose!

My 'steady' was in the Air Force, stationed in Bermuda, but that didn't stop me from going to dances. I could usually find someone who would take the *'wallflower'* off the wall! When we did the Virginia Reel, everyone hit the floor, and had a partner, even if it was not *your date.* Jim always knew where my 'loyalty' was - when I was dancing with someone else, my mind was always wishing it was with him! Dancing was just 'our' thing.

The Dances, the Football and Basketball games, Pep Rallies, and the High School Clubs and our Church's Youth group kept us on the go but we always had time to 'party.' During High School my friends and I always arranged to have a spend the night party, almost every Friday night. Usually, there were 8-10 of us sprawled out on the living room floor of someone's house. One of the neatest thing about those happenings was that our Mothers seemed to enjoy the party as much as we did! And for sure, they didn't get much more sleep than we did - someone had to keep an eye on *our shenanigans!* It was not our Dads; they went to bed early, and *'tried'* to sleep, amidst all the girl-y giggles.

Believe me, we weren't bad girls - we just loved to do the kinds of things you could blame on *'the devil'* - *he made me do it!* Like the night when the girls were spending the night at my house:

IV. TALL TALES

we had on our baby-doll p. j.'s, and were supposed to be getting quiet, ready to sleep. Mother had thought we'd calmed down enough that she could go on to bed. We gave her a few hours, and when we heard her snoring, we all snuck out to the barn and rigged up the pony cart. We decided we'd better not try to hitch up the pony, for obvious reasons; instead, we decided two of the stronger girls could be 'ponies' and pull the cart down Highway 5 in Woodstock. Others could ride along in the cart. Fair enough? Then, we could swap out. That was one time I was glad I wasn't strong.

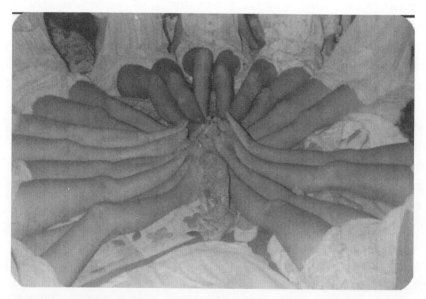

The 'baby dolls' of Cherokee High School in their *'baby doll'* p. j.'s, spending the night at Becky's in Woodstock. This was the night of the *'infamous'* pony cart ride!

Ready? Set? You bet. It was about three a. m. There were no street lights so we found a few flashlights to light the way! It was summer, and still rather warm that time of the night. The windows were open at everyone's house; we had to be as quiet as was humanly possible so no one could hear us giggling. (to accomplish 'that' it would have required us having cotton in our mouths, but we did try!) We hadn't gotten past two houses until a car met us head-on! *Panic.* Luckily, he was not going very fast and had seen an 'unsightly' bunch of silly girls in the middle of the road, at three a. m. Whoa! Was he 'seeing things?' Or were we?

Our giggles turned to screams! The 'ponies' were spooked and headed for the ditch on the side of the road. Smart move, but the girls in the cart were more than spooked. They jumped out of the cart, and began running back to my house. The driver of the car almost came to a complete stop, and yelled 'something' of a warning to us, along with a big dose of curse words. That scared us even more. We were afraid he would ask if we had stolen the cart, or where we were supposed to be; he knew we were out after curfew!

After that 'close call' we decided we had better take the pony cart back to its bed in the barn; we ran all the way, trembling like tornado winds had 'wired us;' we were hugging each other, and dripping wet not only from sweat but tears of terror! Of course, we were just glad we got home safely and had not been hauled to jail. *I do not know if my parents ever knew* what we'd done. . .if they did, they never let me know it! The gals and I will never forget it nor did we forget to say our prayers that night. Mom always said: *'God looks after fools and sinners.'* So I guess we qualified in both categories!

The mid-50's were years that impacted every inch of my life. I made friends in high school that I still have today - some 60 plus years later! I still keep in touch with my English Teacher. She liked 'our class' so much she came back to our Reunions. Hard to believe? Kids today leave high school and perhaps never see, or care to keep up with their pals or Teachers. Not

IV. TALL TALES

so, in my case. I just hope *'if and when'* my Teacher reads an autographed copy of my book, she won't correct my mistakes with a red pencil. If she does, I might not graduate! On second thought, perhaps I should have had her proof-read this before it got to the publisher. Oh well. . .

The group of gals from those days are called the *GOLDEN GIRLS*. There are over a dozen of us now - we always said things were *'cheaper by the dozen.'* Right? No, we are not on TV, but we could perhaps do *a 'Reality Show!'* You wouldn't even have to pay to see us: just find out where and when we meet. When we are together, it is 'reality check' for sure! Everyone in town knows we are around. . .they know us by our laughter! Some of us still have 'golden hair' from the bottle, but some of us just go natural with *'50 shades of gray.'*

Those kinds of surface things are not as important to us now, as they were when we were fifteen, and trying to impress the new boy in town. Some of us never surpassed the size 8-10-12 size clothes; some did. *Curves, Water Aerobics and Tops* have been real assets to those trying to slim up in their 70's. Pretty sad to think people make bug bucks off our 'spare tires' and 'sagging' wings, especially when we are on Medicare and everything 'old' folks need always costs more. It's just not fair!

These gals are 'tops' in my book. *We have not grown old.* We never will. We still have birthdays though. We don't worry about them because we are all the same age, well almost, i. e. One skipped a grade so she's the 'baby' of the bunch. On our *own special day,* we can be assured the mail carrier will know it is *'our day'* because we get a least 'one dozen' birthday cards from the Golden Girls. We are prepared to laugh all day; they send *the funniest cards.* I find myself looking at every card shop to find just the perfect card for each of them, to *top* the one they sent me last year.

When we get together *we are still teenagers* with just a bit more *senior baggage*. We always did have senior baggage with us back then; it was just of 'another world,' the kind you had when you were trying to graduate from high school, make up with your boyfriend, find the perfect outfit, or perhaps even pass a test.

Through the years some of us made the High School Reunions every 5 years, but after I married, and moved away, I missed quite a few. Through the years our friendships had remained but life had kept us from being close, or getting together as a group. Everyone had families, careers and homes to manage.

The year we all turned 55 I decided we needed to have another 'spend the night party.' I invited the gals to come to Kentucky for the weekend. Most of our 'gang' had stayed in the same area where we grew up in Georgia so they rented a van to make the five hour ride to my house. Smiles, suitcases and hugs were wrapped around the group of gals when they arrived in Kentucky. Laughter roared over the *bluegrass* the entire weekend. A few of them tried smoking 'rabbit tobacco. . .' and a few other shenanigans, just to prove we weren't too old to cut the mustard! Tears flowed when they boarded the van to go back to Georgia.

The 'lost years' had disappeared - it was as if we had never been separated by time or distance; our love for each other was the same. Our hearts had not skipped a beat. We were still marching to the sound of the same drummer, and harmonious happiness had been abiding for forty-eight hours. Our tongues had flapped, non-stop. Jim smoked a big turkey, and tried to stay out of our way. . .and to find a bed to sleep in! We celebrated everyone's birthday with one big birthday cake: with a *'A BIG 55'* greeting on top.

We had so much fun we decided that we needed to do this every year! We have gotten together for several nights, at some location of our choice, every year. For eighteen years we have found wonderful places to 'park' for a weekend, just to leave the world behind - to go back in time, to the good old days. There's nothing like it. If someone says: *'remember when'* one time, we say it a hundred times. Some of us have better 'recall' than others, so by the time the story it told, between us, we might have gotten the story close to what actually happened. It's just that at this age, 'the details' don't matter so much as *the meat of the matter!* At our age, who would know the difference?

How I wish I had had a video camera on or a tape recorder going that first weekend. Well, maybe not. However, with censorship laws so loose now we still would not get an *R rating!* We really were not that 'wild' in high school; we have just gotten *wilder with age* and some of us might even blame our children *for making us lose our sanity!* But fortunately, we grew up a bit *wiser* because of them. Our grown children might wonder about the 'getting wiser' part! That's OK, though. They too will grow 'old' someday and become much wiser with each passing year. . .we just hope we live to see that happen!

As 'seniors' we have lived long enough to earn the right to be *'free to be me,'* as Frank Sinatra sang. No guys to flirt with, no parents to please, no teachers to impress, no peers to compete with - that is *such freedom!* We all fly flags to that 'state of being!' It is so healthy, and so enriching to our souls.

These Golden Girls are my *soul-sisters.* They are prayer warriors for me. The miles/distance between us is never more than a phone call away. When Jim died, after calling our immediate family, they were the first ones to know. They came to the Memorial Service and sat as a group! They have always been 'here' or 'there' for me. The following year they rented a van and drove eight hours just to spend my birthday weekend with me...the first one since Jim died. Now, if that isn't *love*, I don't know the definition! We rented a beach house on the Isle of Palms, South Carolina and it was such a 'hit' they came back another time. It is a good thing the walls don't talk because we know things about each other that could never be 'let out to pasture!'

If you've never had a soul-mate or a soul-sister, then you have missed out on *the best bunch of miracles* God could dole out. I might have been 'behind the door' when the good brains were passed out, but I was *first in line* when good friends were out given out! I was fortunate and smart enough to pick out *the cream of the crop*. And for whatever reason, they have stuck with me for over 60 years! That says mountains about them! Of course, they are the kind of gals who would not hurt a bulldog if it were tugging on their pant leg, and I'm the kind of gal that doesn't turn loose of anything easily, much less my friends.

I have moved to a lot of places in my life, and had opportunities to make new friends in every walk of life, but I have never met a stranger; strangers are simply friends I have not met yet. When some people are asked to list five best friends, they are at a loss. I look back on my life and know that I have a 'best friend' in every place I ever lived...that adds up to more than five, so I'm very blessed! Each one is unique, a stellar star shining in their own sky, just as the Big Dipper. *'Make new friends but keep the old, one is silver and the other is gold.'* I've always carried a purse that was big enough for silver and gold, and even a little 'loose change.'

IV. TALL TALES

If I get to heaven (assuming I do!) before my friends do, I'll ask St. Peter if it is *'cheaper by the dozen'* to get inside the gate - if he says YES, then I'll run back and grab the *Golden Girls;* we'll find the best cloud to crash on, and begin the next spend the night party in my little mansion on the hilltop. Knowing God, I'm sure he'll be OK with that because he knows that, in my book, *my friends* are the next best thing to ice cream. And they don't melt! They are as solid as the rock of Gibraltar.

That's what I call *'amazing grace.'* An undeserved gift!

Becky William Buckman
June, 2008

* * *In honor of the *GOLDEN GIRLS* of Cherokee High School, Class of 1958, Canton, Georgia.

BLIND DATES

If you have ever been on a blind date, *you might get my drift* as you read on. Regardless of your age - be it 13, 25 or 'above and beyond, it is an 'adventure,' good, bad or indifferent. All of mine were *just plain BAD!* I'm just hoping that the fellows I am referring to will not recognize themselves or at least have forgotten about our date.

I've had more than one blind date. . .maybe because I wasn't the prettiest picture on the wall; sometimes, that was the only way I could get a date. I really don't know the reason, and actually don't have the time to worry over such technicalities - i. e. *at my age,* why would I even care! And beyond that, 'worrying' is the biggest waste of time, and pays a very poor salary; all you get for it is just more wrinkles. Medicare doesn't pay for 'erasers' for that condition!

I'm very grateful that I have wonderful friends - and have had all my life. When I was 'dateless' a dear friend would invariably come to my rescue. Well, I'm not so sure I was actually being *rescued.* After I went out with the guy, I knew I needed to be rescued, and taken back home!

I admit I've had my fill of blind dates. It matters not how much I need a *man around the house now,* I'm not willing, nor gullible enough to go on another blind date. *Period!* And if I had known then what I know now I would have been better off at home listening to *The Grand Ole Opry,* with my parents, on Saturday nights. Don't get me wrong, I'm sure my 'date' probably felt the same way about me. When two people *depend* on a blind date, just to get out of the house, it spells DOUBLE T-R-O-U-B-L-E! Or, in my case it did.

IV. TALL TALES

In high school a dear friend (whom I will not name, for the sake of our friendship) set me up on my first blind date. I cannot recall my date's name. . .that has been too many moons ago. *Selective memory,* I'm sure! However, I do 'recall' with the greatest of clarity, the night out. I thanked God that night that it was a double date or I'm sure I would have jumped ship, even though I couldn't swim, nor was I close enough home to walk!

A nice looking, *handsome to the hilt,* well-dressed hunk of a man came to the door to pick me up. Wow was I wooed! He didn't say much. I assumed he was as 'scared' as I was, but still I couldn't wait to be in the back seat with this guy! The 'journey' to Howell's drive-in theater in Canton, Ga. was about a 30 minute drive. It would be a great time to get acquainted on the drive up there. At least that is what I had in mind. . .but things haven't always gone *my* way!

Well, in my case, that night it was more *challenging* than fun! We were in the back seat, the summer heat sizzling through the parking lot of the drive-in theater. The windows were all rolled down. We got to the Drive-In, parked on the back row, of course. The 'sound system' was located just outside the car, on the driver's side so the couple up front controlled the speakers. By now I was wishing that I was the 'driver' and had control of something. . .

Remember, I had never met this fellow before. Nor seen a photo; my friend's date did not tell her the 'vital statistics' of the blind date he had picked out for me! She trusted his judgment, and he felt I would be pleased as punch to go out with such a 'hunk' of a guy. And I was. . . but within five minutes of our 'introduction' I knew I was in for a long hot summer night!

My date was deaf - and very little broken English rolled forward from his lips. I had good eyesight but I had been blind-sided! I was in a real tight bind. I've never had 'the seven year itch' but I'm sure I was as close to it as I ever want to get! I wanted OUT of this situation. Being young and rather inexperienced at this dating game, I did not have a prescription for curing the looming problem. To make matters worse, I was at the mercy of the couple who had set up this date.

I had looked forward to the date for a week, and more especially to see the movie that was showing. Had I been smarter, back then, or had my *thinking cap on*, suddenly I would have gotten deathly sick, choking on popcorn or something, and had them rush me back to Woodstock to the safety of my home, and my parents! I would have even offered to PAY for their tickets and the gas they spent.

But no, I was stuck in the backseat with a *hyperactive fellow* who could not hear a word I said; nor did he understand my 'sign language' and I certainly didn't know his. *Panic Plus!* They didn't teach that at Cherokee High. He was an adult, and I was a naive 'junior.' My Mother had warned me about guys and their motives, but she never gave me a hint about what to do in a case like this.

Even before the movie started all I wanted to do was scream at this fellow: *'what part of NO don't you understand?'* The sun had not even gone down all the way; I fiddled with my watch, I looked for things in my purse, I did 'anything' I could think of to occupy myself, and hopefully distract his appetite for making out!

Of course, my friend and her date were having a wonderful time, oblivious to the wrestling match I was in! I was *struggling*

IV. TALL TALES

for all I was worth, with several hours yet to endure. I went from just being 'happy to have a date' to being really ticked off; how could good friends do this to me? Sure, they were nice enough to set me up; I should have been grateful but that was the last thing on my mind.

I scanned the parking lot at the Drive-In Theater to see if I recognized any cars/couples I knew - hoping to find someone who was willing to leave early, and would take me home - I would have danced a jig, just to escape this backseat. No such luck! Every couple I saw was so wrapped up in each other, they hardly knew where they were! The thought occurred to me: if only our school had required *'wrestling' or 'karate'* in P. E. I might could have employed a few of the techniques. I'm not sure I could have passed either one, but at least it was a good thought.

My only recourse was to excuse myself and find the Concession Stand, and the closest restroom. I cried until I had used up all the tissues in my purse, and was now resorting to toilet paper to absorb the remaining tears. I don't know how long *I hid out there.* I know it was long enough that my *girlfriend* came to check on me. When I quit boo-hooing, I let her have a piece of what mind I had left! I told her if she knew what was good for her, she would never, ever, in a million years, set me up with someone she did not know. And furthermore, as soon as I had a chance I was going to tell her boyfriend that his friendship with me was 'on shaky ground.' I do forgive, but sometimes it takes a long time. Forgiveness, yes. *Forgetting,* NO!

When I got home that night, I shared *my nightmare* with my Mom. She had always said a *'half a loaf is better than no loaf at all'* but I contested her theory wholeheartedly: *No date* is always better than a blind date, particularly if it was like my first one!

THE SECOND TIME AROUND

By the time I was in my mid-twenties, memories of that first blind date experience had faded somewhat. Too bad my memory was already so poor, at such a young stage in life! And even worse, that I was still as *gullible* as ever. Somehow 'older guys' always showed up in my dating life giving them an advantage! I'm not sure why they would seek out younger gals, or why I was attracted to more mature fellows.

Be that as it may, I visited a Singles Group in a large Church in Atlanta. In a city that big, it was difficult to meet men my age but I felt sure I would meet *'a few good men'* in this group; men who had their ducks in a row, were stable financially, and whose lives were based on upstanding principles, morals, someone with whom I had something in common.

I met a man who seemed to 'fit the bill' so I accepted a date with him. But here again, I was caught in a cage without the key to get out! When I got home after that blind date, I made another vow: *'don't go there'* anymore…it is not worth the fight! If being single was my lot, then so be it. I figured when God decided I really needed a soul mate, HE would provide one, and it would be a man with whom I would not have to fight off. It would be the *'love of my life'* and someone with whom I would enjoy the wrestling match!

AND. . .God did provide! It didn't happen until 1965. Just when my time clock was ticking away, my 'first love' came floating back into my life - out of the clear blue sky! That day the rainbow was wrapped about both of us. I no longer had to depend on friends to set me up with blind dates. . .*what a relief!* God is good and I knew that He had *set me up*, again, with that *good ole' country boy*, like my Mother had said I needed! He was the best

IV. TALL TALES

date I could ever hope to have. . .neither of us were blind, or blind-sided; nor were either of us deaf! We had our own special *'sign language.'* That's the way we liked it!

Becky Williams Buckman
January, 2013

THE DARE

Have you ever dared someone to do something? Or ever taken a 'leap of faith?'

Obviously, both my husband, Jim, and I could have answered 'yes' to those questions. It was many years into our marriage when Jim admitted that he *had been dared to do something.* A dare that changed both of our lives - forever!

Jim was stationed at Dobbins Air Force Base, in Marietta, Georgia, in the mid-50's but attended my church in Woodstock. I was a teenager then and Jim knew I was already going steady with a young Navy man from a nearby town. Morris and I had met at a church function and the fact that he was five years older than me did not seem to bother me or my parents. I'm really not sure why, but who was I to question their wisdom? I felt quite good on the arm of a handsome man in uniform!

I actually thought *'I had it made in the shade.'* I had his high school ring taped with gobs of adhesive tape around it, half an inch thick just to keep it from falling off my ring finger. All of my girlfriends were dating guys in our class, but they could not *'sport a class ring'* like me, nor an older man. . .all of this boosted my ego for sure!

Things were going great for us, when out of the clear blue sky, along came my Church's Youth Counselor, Red Howell, with a different plan! Mr. Howell worked, as a civilian, on Dobbins Air Force Base, in Marietta, and had invited three other young military men from his 'shop' to come to our small church in Woodstock, and to participate in our youth activities.

IV. TALL TALES

Well, yes, these military men were 'too old' to be in our Youth group, but our small Methodist congregation was just like one big happy family - no hard and fast rules on who was in what group! These young men had to be very 'lonely' or bored to enjoy being with teenagers. . . Maybe both?

Mr. Howell arranged for our youth group to take a 'tour' of the military base. Those three airmen with whom he worked were to be our tour guides. It was June 1957. Jim Buckman was my tour guide that day. He was a tall and slender handsome guy, with sky-blue eyes, and a shyness that intrigued me. . . his good looks and smirky smile hooked me that day and *I melted in his shadow!* (not just from the summer heat. . .) I think Mr. Howell noticed my wandering eyes because after the tour was over, Mr. Howell pulled Jim aside and 'dared him' - *yes, dared him* - to ask me out! That day Jim had 'noticed me' in a different light. . . just as I had him. Jim's response to Mr. Howell's dare was: 'but I can't do it *now*, she's going steady.' Mr. Howell said 'don't let that stop you! You'll be a fool if you don't ask her out.' Jim's thought was: 'what could it hurt. . .she could always say no.'

Both men were old enough and should have known better than to 'dare' a seventeen year old to DO anything! As I think back, I can just see 'Red' and Jim going back to the shop - laughing as they recalled what had just transpired during the tour, and bragging to the other airmen! What a joke this would be.

Jim took the 'dare.' (He always was a dare devil!) He called me that night, asking for a date for Friday night. I told him that I already had plans. He asked me out for the next night. I accepted before he could finish his sentence. . .from that moment on, all I could do was think about the Saturday night date with Jim and that I would be two-timing Morris! I would not have thought that I would have done such a trick...but *'the devil made me do it'* I guess!

Somehow, I had to break up with Morris, and do it rather quickly. Friday night, I gave Morris his ring back, with some flimsy 'excuse' which perhaps made no sense at all to him. It's no wonder he took me home 'before dark' that night!

And the next night, Jim and I went to Howell's drive-in movie theater in Canton. I went into 'orbit' the moment he picked me up, and for the life of me, I'm not sure I saw any of the movie, much less recall what we saw! *THE DARE* turned into a 'lifetime of love' between us.

It was the beginning of a long, hot summer - 1957. We were both so in love! It was the best summer of my youth. I was old enough to drive, and coming up on my Senior year in high school. That makes any teenager feel grown! Yet, looking back now, I realize how very young and naive I was, but I never regretted *'daring to go on a date'* with the man who was to become my soul-mate some fourteen years later! Yes, it did take a while, but God had a hand in it all the time. His timing is perfect.

What a blessing was in store for me. We were part of each other's life for over forty-five years between 1957 and 2007. *Jim will forever remain in my heart,* thanks to 'Red' Howell, and GOD who bound us together on earth for thirty-six years, and *forever,* in eternity.

Becky Williams Buckman
June 19, 2011

IV. TALL TALES

"How about a date tonight?"

YOUNG LOVE

Sonny James sings a song about 'young love...' It was one that 'my love' and I could relate to very well. We often sang it together as we rode along on trips or just around town! If you are 'in my age bracket' you will recall the song. I still sing it often - the words could have been our very own. Maybe this is true for you as well.

> *'They say for every boy and girl there's just one love in this whole world, and I know I've found mine...young love, first love, filled with true devotion...we share with deep emotion... we will vow to one another, there will never be another, Love for you, or for me.'*

I had only *'one love'* in my life! God blessed me with a 'true love' at a very young, innocent and tender age... before I was dry behind the ears. Somehow, for some reason, boys my age just didn't flirt with me - or ask me out often. I think I was just the kind of kid who was a 'friend' to all the guys, but me being a *girlfriend* just wasn't in the mix! When it came to dances and proms, I usually had to 'ask' someone who, like me, could never get a date. And, believe me, *that* was no fun, nor did it boost my ego when some 'dud' accepted my invitation. So, now there were *two 'duds' in a row.*

I grew up in a society if a woman was seen gaining weight 'up front,' it was simply said: *she is in a family way!'* As teens, we just called it PG... behind our parents' back, of course! Today PG relates to censorship (or lack of) of movies! Parents didn't prepare us for growing up into adolescence, or young adulthood, nor talk to us about their young love, or courtship. And we certainly could not imagine our parents 'smooching...or anything

IV. TALL TALES

beyond that!' As young kids we were told the 'stork' brought us! DUH!

I don't recall any show of affection between my parents - no holding hands, hugs, pats on the butt, much less kisses! But then, too, I was born late in their life - at a time when couples tended to be less expressive, in public, i. e. In all fairness to my parents who had a superb marriage and love for each other (for almost sixty years) I think it was more a *'sign of the times.'* When I was grown, Mother told me she and Dad didn't kiss until the night of their honeymoon! (That was in 1919. . .so go figure!)

Occasionally, as I got into puberty, mother would drop subtle hints; they were never direct words of advice, and always spoken as this was all *a secret,* not to be let loose. Mother simply brought home the hygiene products I needed, handed them to me very discreetly, in the bathroom when Dad was not around. My parents owned a grocery store and it always struck me as 'funny' that Dad ordered the 'stock' for the store, so he was not clueless about the products young girls needed. He had to order those same products just like he had to order potatoes and lettuce. *'That'* was different, I suppose. It was not a 'personal' matter, as it was when his daughter had reached puberty and needed those things.

There was no 'mother-daughter' conversation about my body and emotions that would transpire as I matured. It was up to me to *'go figure. . .'* just like it was for all my other friends. Their parents didn't prepare them either. And, naturally, we had a ton of misconceptions. I'll never forget the day when I began to see life and love as they really were! It was a real *'wake-up call.'*

My boyfriend, Morris, was a gentleman and respected me but he and I both 'knew' that the moment we pulled into the driveway after our date, the front porch light would come on; it would begin to flicker on and off if we were too slow getting to the door! *We had to move fast*...getting out of the car, i. e. (you get my drift, I'm sure!)

Mother was just watching to see how long it took him to get around to the passenger side to escort me to the steps! We could always manage *a real good kiss* before she flipped the porch light switch the second time. She was a great Mom. She remained hidden behind the closed curtains, just dying to ask me about my date as soon as I got in the door. And I always told her - well, *maybe not 'everything'* that we did - but just enough to satisfy her curiosity!

Morris was my date for the Junior Senior Prom in 1957, and I was proud to show him off. . .little did I know that my romance with him was about to come to a screeching halt. (see THE DARE) Within two weeks of the Prom, I got an unexpected phone call from another 'man in uniform' and accepted a date with him before I had even broken up with Morris. So I had to do some 'tall talking' on Friday night when Morris and I went out. I told him I thought I was really 'too young (seventeen) to be going steady; *we should date other people.'* The entire time I was blubbering that explanation I had my mind on my upcoming date with Jim Buckman!

Looking back, I'm sure I made one big fool out of myself. . .and was definitely not too fair with Morris. I don't think I slowed down long enough to give him a chance to say how *he* felt! He took me home 'very early' that night, much to the amazement of my Mother who was waiting up for me.

I was just relieved to have gotten through the night without Morris stopping on the side of the county road, opening the car door, and telling me to 'get out and get home the best way you can!' (If he hadn't been such a great fellow, he might have, I'm sure). I certainly didn't know a lot about the dating game - *was I crazy?* Sure, it was a big gamble. . .was I throwing away a good apple before I had had a chance to taste the apple from the other tree? Guess that was *the daredevil in me.* . .

That one phone call from Jim resulted in him being *'the one true love'* in my life. But how it happened still amazes me. As I look back, I know it was all *a part of God's plan* for both of our lives.

From our first date, Jim and I seemed to be 'falling fast' for each other. Why was another handsome 'older man' wanting to court a teenager. . . he was nine years older than me! *Was he crazy? Or was I?* (maybe both?)

We dated as many nights as we could during that summer, and were always together all day on Sundays, at church functions. Then at the end of the summer, Jim got orders to go to Bermuda. We wrote to each other daily; each letter confirmed that *our love affair was special.* It was hard to wait until we could see each other again!

I was a Senior in high school, and wanted to be a part of all the social events, along with my peers. He understood that any dates I had were for 'convenience' only. He came home to see me that Christmas and *marriage was on the top of his Christmas list!* He was old enough to settle down and begin a family. But I was only eighteen, and certainly was not ready to marry. I knew that we needed to give this relationship more time. As great as love letters are, they are no substitute for spending time with each other.

College was on my agenda. When I was sixteen I'd felt called to serve God through a career in Christian education. Jim insisted that I could pursue my education wherever he was stationed. But I wanted to finish college first; I had a lot more 'growing up' to do. This was not what he wanted to hear! Our letters continued for more than two years, with him visiting me each Christmas. Then in early 1960, a weird scenario occurred - we had a very unusual misunderstanding that caused the *'straw to break the camel's back!'* Had phone calls or internet been available, perhaps things would have worked out differently. Maybe not. . .who is to say?

At the end of fall semester, I had broken my ankle, exams were coming up, we'd had snow, and I had not had time to write Jim daily, as I had done for years. This didn't 'fly' too well with Jim - he was clueless, of course, as to the reason. He lashed out at me in a letter, left it on his desk in the barracks and was going to mail it the following day but he didn't have a stamp. He went on to work, but kept thinking about that letter during the day. He decided *he had been too hard on me.* He planned to destroy the letter and write another one. . .but when he went back to the barracks the letter not on his desk. He looked everywhere. It was not there. *Panic! Was he losing his mind?* He knew he had written a letter; he knew he had left it on his desk! He searched high and low; no letter could be found!

Later when his roommate came in he asked him if he had seen it. "Sure, I had a stamp so I mailed it for you." He thought he'd done Jim a favor! Jim was furious. The damage was done. He couldn't afford to call me and explain what happened. I got the 'fire-y' letter. . .then I was furious!

I knew I would need to calm down before answering his letter. After I got home for the Christmas holidays, I wrote him. It

IV. TALL TALES

took a long time to say what I felt; I was hurt and very surprised he had said the things he had said to me. This was not like the man I'd dated for over two years.

In my letter to Jim, I served up the same 'soup' he had put in my bowl! I let my hurting heart pour out; I told him that if he were *'no more understanding of my circumstances at this difficult time then perhaps it was best if we broke up.'* Until he received my letter (perhaps about three weeks from the time his letter was mailed) he was in a real 'tizzy'-he stewed, paced the floor, and tried to believe I would have ignored his hasty words. But I didn't.

When he got my letter, he was devastated! And mad at himself for writing the letter, and madder at his roommate for mailing it without his permission! But the damage was done, on both sides of the fence. No more letters were exchanged. The romance was over! There was no attempt to reconcile the matter. Neither of us budged. . .We each felt the other one should have stepped up to the bat, and when that didn't happen we marked it up as 'history' or lessons learned. (there are many 'lessons' that could be learned from that scenario).

My Mother's response was: *"you'll be sorry you let him go. He's a good ole' country boy - and that is just what you need."* At the time, I never explained to her what had actually happened, and she never asked. I turned a deaf ear, trying to soothe my wounds; I told her that *'Jim will be the last man I would marry.'* I had to eat those words. . .he was *the last man I would marry!* I just didn't know it at the time.

I moved on with my life. I continued my education, got my Master's at Emory University in Atlanta; my career was as successful as I could want. I was happy and very fulfilled. I dated some, but I was never *'in love'* with anyone again. The older I got, the harder it was meet guys like the *'good ole country boy'* mother described, the kind she knew I needed! There were some dates where I simply 'prayed' to get home safely! My conclusion: *If that is all there is to choose from, I am content to be single.*

Jim had been the 'only love' I had ever known. I had lost a real treasure! To cope with this, I tried to rationalize: perhaps I was not meant to marry. . .the closer I got to thirty the more often people asked *'why isn't a nice girl like you married?'* (Duh. . .You tell me!) How was I to answer that? I just tried to laugh it off, but all the while thinking: *'well, why don't you introduce me to a great guy?'* The Custodian at my church always bugged me about being 'too picky.' Perhaps, I was picky, but I had every right to be. . .marriage, in my opinion, was for a lifetime. There would be none of this *trial and error* routine on my books!

It was five years before Jim came back into my life. With *no advance warning*. . .he just appeared! Neither of us had known anything about the 'life' of the other since the 'last letter' of January, 1960. I am always amazed at how *GOD works in mysterious ways, his wonders to perform!*

Jim was just like his Dad - always a free-spirit kind of person; one who might just get up one morning, get in his truck and take off for some destination, never bothering to call ahead, or plan things in advance. *What a way to go!* (I wasn't bent that way - I planned months ahead.)

He was 'on leave' visiting his parents in Kentucky Christmas, 1965, when he decided he would drive to Woodstock, Georgia to see if he could find me! *What was he thinking?* When he showed up on my parents' doorstep looking for me, my Mother almost dropped her teeth! He visited them a few minutes, and then inquired about me. She knew I hadn't heard from him in

IV. TALL TALES

years, and was hesitant to tell him where I was, without my permission. She called me that Sunday afternoon around 1 p.m. and told me he was there; she asked me if I wanted her to tell him how to reach me. I too, was as shocked as if Christmas showed up on the 4th of July!

I assured her it could not be Jim Buckman. I just knew she was mistaken. I had another friend, Jim Buchanan, and felt it had to be him and *not Jim Buckman*. She said: *'it is. . .I'd know him any day!'* I agreed to speak to him; he insisted on coming to Atlanta that day to see me. Meanwhile, my mind was going 'into orbit.' I had no idea what would happen when we saw each other again. His first comment was: *'I can't believe I found you, and even more that you are still single.'* All the while I *was* trying to choke down the idea that he had gone on such a wild goose chase, just to find me again.

We had a few hours to 'connect' that afternoon, just small talk - then I had to leave for work. He asked to stay in town until I got off work so we could spend more time together. We talked into the late night hours; he slowly began to unfold what had been going on in his life since we last communicated.

Soon after we had broken up in 1960, he had been assigned to Lowry Air Force Base in Denver, Co. That fall, he married and became a 'father' to the three children his wife had from her first marriage. His next assignment took them to Long Island, NY. where their two children, Jim and Robin, were born. In the spring of 1964, his wife died, after the three and half years of marriage. He was left with the five children. He had not adopted her three children so he took them back to their father in Virginia. He had questioned God: 'How could so much happen to me so fast? Why, God?' It plagued his mind day and night.

I could not believe what I was hearing. My heart was broken for him. He was so lost, so alone, so confused. He was looking for the light at the end of the dark tunnel. He felt sure I could be the one to change things in his life. When he told me that he wanted us to 'begin again' I became more overwhelmed than ever. I could not believe this was really happening. . .it felt like a dream. For days, both of our minds were in a tailspin. *Why had we 'found each other again?* What would happen next?

What were his options? At this point, he was in his 14th year as a career man in the Air Force. How could he continue his career, a single man with two small children?

His parents were in Kentucky, living on a family farm, in a small community which offered no job opportunities for an electronic technician. For financial security, he knew his 'best choice' was to continue for six more years in the Air Force and then retire. Keeping the children with him was not an option, however! His heartstrings were ripped in shreds. He'd lost his wife, had to give up the three children he had helped raise, and now to be separated from his own two children - it was *a hell of a decision,* and there wasn't much time to give it a lot of thought.

He felt God had dealt him a horrible blow. Grief was unbearable. After talking with his parents and looking at the options, they determined his parents would take his two children, both of whom were under three years old. He would continue his career. This was not going to be 'easy' on anyone involved. Jim's mother was a nurse, working night shift at the local hospital to support the family since Jim's father was no long able to farm.

It was at this point that Jim decided to find me again. *We had both changed so much* during those years apart. I was not the same person. . .no longer a 'teenager.' I had grown up and had a successful career. He had been married, a parent, and was now in his mid-thirties. I was moving up the ladder, enjoying my work, not even thinking of a serious relationship. What a blow this was to my mind!

We'd always been very different type personalities, but now there were even wider gaps. I had never been married, or been a parent! I had no idea that I should even continue seeing him, given the added circumstances of his life! It was all too overwhelming for me. Yet, we decided to continue getting to know each other, through letters. He was overseas the majority of the time, coming home on leave only once a year, always flying into Atlanta each time which gave us an opportunity to have about 2 dates a year - WOW!

Getting to know each other through letters is not the easiest way to go with a relationship; particularly since he was a very introverted personality, and I was as far from that as anyone could get! I knew opposites attract more often than not, but in my mind, I still was not sure we were compatible enough to make a marriage 'spin like a top!' It was hard for me to wrap my mind around the concept of marrying into a ready-made family. The trauma Jim had lived through was more than I could even imagine; he kept clinging to even the slightest hope that we could rekindle our 'young love.' He told me he still loved me, after all these years apart, and we could be happily married.

I had 'studied' marriage and family in college, child psychology, and other subjects that related to being married, or being a parent. . .but that *knowledge was simply that. .* .just courses I was able to pass! It was not 'real life experiences.' I was deficient in that realm. Sure, I had done my share of baby-sitting, but that too, was not enough to give me the confidence I needed to become a wife and parent all in one day!

I had always dreamed of marrying, having my own family but this kind of marriage was not what I had envisioned. Basically, I had grown up as a city-kid, and college had fostered my love of the cultural world. I loved the opportunities of the big city of Atlanta - enjoying the Opera, and big-name concerts and traveling over the USA with my job. Jim's experiences were different. His career had taken him all over the world, into many different cultures. He had grown up on a farm, in a large family, with six siblings. I grew up much like an only child, and had certainly been pampered by the many 'single adults' in my extended family. I had come along late in life when my parents were in their forties. There had not been a baby born on Mother's side of the family in eighteen years so I guess I was a novelty! *Spoiled* is another word for it, and after we married, Jim often reminded me of it! I always reminded him that *he knew that* when he married me. . .so, don't blame me!

We continued to write often and he always brought lovely gifts for me, and my family from shopping overseas. I tried to convince him that I could not be the wife or mother to his children that he *needed,* and I was sure there were many women who would jump at the chance to marry him! I felt so inadequate. If I married, there would be no way I could continue my career; it required odd hours, nights and weekends. Making a decision to give that up was a big hurdle I had to jump.

He insisted that he had '*always loved me and love conquers all. . .we can make it.*' For three years, he continued to fan the flames and deal with my indecisiveness; he never gave up on our love affair. Patience was one of his best virtues! (As I look back now, I'm sure that had a lot to do with how well our marriage did work!)

Once, I let several months go by without answering his letters; I had moved - without letting him know where I lived. Yet, he would

IV. TALL TALES

not be outdone! He called *information* to try to locate me, asking the operator for Becky Williams. She gave him the number. He called and spoke with her for about thirty minutes, the entire time, thinking he was talking to me! He asked her for a date. She said she would have to arrange a baby-sitter first, and she would call him back. He thought: *"WHAT? OMG. . .I think I have just goofed!"* He simply said, 'I think I have the wrong number!' He hung up as fast as he could. . .(poor gal, she'd just been dumped). What Jim did not know was that I never listed my phone number as 'Becky,' I always used my full name: Carolyn Rebecca! (Still today, a confusing thing for people who are trying to find me!)

His next move was to send me a Valentine, to my parents' home, telling me of his upcoming retirement in October, 1970, and asking to see me when he came through Atlanta. Mother had failed to tell me it was there for two months. When I did get it, I stalled. I was at a loss. How could I tell him that I felt we had too many obstacles; I wasn't convinced I could be what he needed in a mate.

In May, I wrote him, saying that I would agree to see him as he flew through Atlanta; we could meet for a casual dinner together. This way I felt we could have a *'farewell - let's move on' evening*, without any hurt feelings. . .What a joke that was! He had made plans to stay several days, to have more than one date with me. (All the more time for him to 'work on my emotions!') I kept insisting that he needed to go home to be with his children, and parents; After all, he'd not seen them in a long time. His argument: "I'm retired now - I've got a lot of time to spend with them! We can start over - please - I still love you and I know you love me or you wouldn't keep letting me come see you."

Was he right? I was so confused. Why had I never just closed the door for the last time? Were there still some embers burning that I had been denying all these years? What did I really know about love? My mother knew Jim was still in the picture, and I honestly believe she was praying all the time that I would wake up and smell the roses that were falling at my feet! She and God knew more than all of us put together.

When Jim retired in Oct. 1970, he came to see me. We spent a lot of time together, getting to know each other in a way that had not been possible while he was in the military. He wanted to find a job in the Atlanta area, but I knew if our relationship did not materialize into marriage, then he would be separated from his children again. Then he would be back to square one. Decisions!

As things played out, he was hired by Bendix Corporation in Marietta in January, 1971. *He had won, again!* By this time, we'd dated for three months and he had won my heart - all over again! By then, I knew our love was strong enough to withstand any obstacles we might face. (Little did we know, then, that our hurdles would almost drown us - more than a few times!) *Young love is fearless.* It overcomes any doubts. It overcomes the facts. . . it is not a *mind* thing. It is a matter of the heart which knows no logic, when true love abides.

June 19, 1971, *this young love,* which had begun in 1957, became a marital union; we were together until June, 2007 when Jim's health got the best of him. He had 'fought' poor health for twenty-two years starting with a heart attack in 1985.

We had started our family with his two children, Jim and Robin; then we had two of our own, Tim and Apryll. Those years took us down treacherous paths, more than once, and often we had no clue how we had survived the last 'crash' but never did we 'cave in.' There were times when we felt we

IV. TALL TALES

couldn't take much more, but there were always mountain peaks that remained in view. Somehow, we came out stronger than before, growing closer, and more in love than we had ever been!

Even with Jim's death, that constant and abiding love still lives in my heart. It always will. I am who I am because of him; for forty-five of my seventy-plus years, he was *my life*.

God had a plan for both of us - that plan was to be a family. It just took a bit longer than either of us expected. To GOD be the glory. . .for the miracle of love letters that kept going, *down the line* for so many years!

Jim and Becky Buckman, Alvaton, Kentucky
November 2004

DOWN THE LINE

A 'GEM' OF A PROPOSAL

It's been said that diamonds are a girl's best friend. Well, yes and no. When I was thirty I still did not have an engagement ring. Naturally, I'll never forget the day I got mine.

Every girl dreams of *'the love of her life'* falling on his knees at her feet, in some exotic paradise, with a diamond in hand, proposing to love her for better, for worse, for richer, for poorer. In my case, *'my love'* did not fulfill my dream, not in *'his proposal,'* i. e. So, here goes the story: Jim's proposal to me was a 'reality show' long before TV broadcast theirs!

It was a cold winter day in Atlanta, Georgia, February 13, 1971. We'd had snow falling all that Saturday; it the eve of Valentine's Day. Jim was coming into town to take me out to dinner to celebrate our first Valentine's Day since we had gotten 'back together.' We'd been dating 'steadily' since October and by now, our romance was in full bloom, *the second time around!*

I was hurriedly preparing for our date - the whole nine yards! I had carefully chosen just the right clothes, shoes, jewelry, purse, not to mention all the makeup I'd need to look my best for him. It was all spread out on my bed, just waiting for me to adorn myself and look good - as best I could, i. e. given what I had to work with! The ironing board and iron were ready to be put to work, when all of a sudden, the doorbell rang. Who could that be?

I had just jumped out of the shower, with my hair still wet, of course. It was four in the afternoon. I did have on a robe but was not about to answer the door looking like that! I insisted that my roommate answer the door. She was quite surprised to see Jim two hours early; he wasn't due to pick me up until six.

IV. TALL TALES

She yelled to the back bedroom, "Jim's here. He wants to come on back to see you now."

"No," I shouted, "I'm not dressed yet." I began to panic, thinking I had two full hours to be 'presentable!' My mind was about to 'blow' a gasket....how could he do this to me? He knows I had to work most of the day....and besides, he didn't call to say he'd pick me up early! (that should have been my first 'clue' about *his free spirit* - a trait he inherited from his dad!)

Walking back to my bedroom, she told me that he said *'it doesn't matter.'* He says he needs to see you now. When I grew up, a single guy did not come into a gal's bedroom, much less when she was not fully dressed! Telling my roommate to stall him for a bit, I hurried to be 'as covered up' as I could get. . .but I was a bit put out with him, to put it mildly. I always wanted to look my best - and never wanted anyone to see me less than 'dressed to the hilt!'

My roommate tried everything she could think of to stall him but Jim was not about to be stalled. . .he was very persistent! He walked down the hall to my bedroom, knocked on the door and asked to come in. I think I had a 'few words' with him before I let him come in. . .but he seemed oblivious to my 'attitude.' Some days men just don't get it, do they? He came in with a nervous, jittery look on his face. That made me even more upset.

But when I saw him give me his *smirky smile,* I melted, forgetting how I looked, or how upset I had been 30 seconds earlier. He took me in his arms, and before I could sputter out an apology for being so 'undressed,' he kissed me passionately, and then stood back, looking at me with the smirk on his face that characterized him. (By this time, I was almost *speechless*. . .that in itself is *not at all like me.*) I'd never been in this kind of predicament before. He had always respected me, never attempted to take advantage of my innocence. . .but my mind began to wonder - and *wander* as well!

Snowflakes were falling heavily and fast outside. After that kiss, he took me to the window saying: '*just look at that snow,*' a ploy to distract me, of course. While I was gazing out the window, he reached into the pocket of his heavy winter coat and, pulled out a small box. I looked down to see what he was fumbling with, and noticed he was trembling as if he were feverish! I'd never seen him so nervous.

Finally, he got hold of himself, his sky-blue eyes focused on my green eyes and he sputtered these words: "*Well, since you are going to be ironing for the rest of your life,* you might as well have this ring to make it official!" He took my left hand and placed a beautiful diamond engagement ring on my finger. At that point, I truly was a puddle of melted butter. . . trembling, soaring into orbit, tears of joy washing the 'un-made-up' face. . . and most of all speechless.

That was my '*gem of a proposal*' from my Jim! The rest is history - for better, for worse, for richer, for poorer, we shared thirty-six years with my diamond ring on my left hand - it sealed our love affair. We were now officially engaged and our souls began the journey of becoming one in the spirit, one in the Lord.

I still wear that diamond today, on the right hand. I will never take it off! In the 'jewelry' department, it is my best friend and will be with me until he and I meet again on 'the other shore.' And if he shows up early to meet me at heaven's gate, it won't bother me at all. I will run to meet him. . .and I won't be watching the clock, nor looking at the snow. I will be fully clothed

IV. TALL TALES

in my new garments. The *'dance of a lifetime'* will begin with Jim holding me close to his heart, as he always did. I just hope the ironing board is not a necessity in *our new home!*

Becky Williams Buckman
June 19, 2013*

* It would have been our 42nd anniversary.

We became Mr. and Mrs. James F. Buckman on June 19, 1971, Atlanta, Georgia

MARRIAGE AND '*MORE*'

In May, 1978 my husband and I received the most wonderful gift from some dear friends. I doubt that we ever received a gift that was so *'eternal.'* Even now, in 2014, it keeps on giving and I'm eternally grateful.

It began with a casual conversation one Sunday at our church: "Lynda and I would like to give you a special weekend - a get-a-way - to focus on your marriage." My husband, one who was usually the last one to speak up, was quick to respond, and rather defensively said: "Our marriage is fine; we don't have any problems so we don't need it; thanks anyway!"

Dee replied, lovingly: "No, we are not suggesting that you need it, but *you deserve it!*" I was anxious to know more. From my side of the fence it sounded like *'just what the Dr. ordered for us,'* so I asked what was involved. It would require that we go to Atlanta, leave our four children for forty-eight hours, in addition to the travel time. That was unheard of - just not feasible for us. We were on a tight budget; we had two teens and two children under five. I knew there was no one who would be able to care for them that long. I said, "There's no way we could do that but thanks anyway. It sounds great!"

Quick on the draw, Dee had an answer. "We will take care of the children, and your registration fee is already paid." Now *we were on the spot* again. Jim continued to deny the opportunity for this 'gift, ' but Dee and Lynda could see that I was definitely interested. I would enjoy having a weekend for just the two of us! We had begun our marriage with Jim's two elementary children, and we had two of our own, so 'time alone' was hard to come by! The whole idea sounded like a honeymoon to me.

IV. TALL TALES

We were told the motel and all our meals for the weekend were already paid for by someone whom we would never met. That didn't make much sense; how could this be 'free?' It would cost us nothing but the gas to Atlanta, and our time. Plus we would not have to pay a sitter for the children. Surely there was a catch to this offer, but I was game to go for it!

Jim stood there with a sense of wonderment but still denying his need for this. He remarked "I don't *need* this. I'm content with our marriage." Dee said to Jim: "Jim I know how much you love Becky...it is obvious! If you thought she wanted to go, would you not *do this for her*, even if you don't need it yourself?"

Jim had to admit: "Sure, I do love her with all my heart, so if you put it that way, I guess I'll have to say *yes, we can go.*" At that point, my heart began to leap like a frog on a lily pad, thinking: well, perhaps *there is hope* after all!

I knew our communication skills could use a good tune up. I had always been the more 'open' partner, Jim was the more private person, one to tuck it all away in the secret compartments of his heart and soul! That being the case, *roadblocks* were always cropping up, leaving little or no room to move ahead...often in the stalemate stage.

There was a lot of mystery about the opportunity, so we were very anxious and nervous about doing this; all we were told was the basic details, time, place, directions etc. Most of all we were told to go and just *enjoy being with each other* without any interruptions! I began counting the days; I couldn't wait; meanwhile, Jim was sweating it out, dreading the unknown.

Jim and I went on our first Marriage Encounter Weekend in May, 1978. It was a weekend like we had never known, or could have even expected! It changed our lives, individually, and as a couple. It affected our family life, and our spiritual lives. We'd found a 'new world' - a world where the two of us could emerge as lovers again!

This was truly a second-honeymoon for our romance. It sparked a renewed love - a love that was there but had just gotten put on the back burner; not intentionally, of course - just daily life - work, children, yard care, elderly parents - 'just getting through the day' was about all we could manage. We came home from our Weekend so *'on fire. . .'*

This 'new flame' led us to writing a love letter each day! On our weekend we had made a commitment to spend twenty minutes, each day, with each other, without any interruptions. The children knew this was *'our time' to focus on each other,* to deal with the deeper issues of life and love - not just 'schedules' or business matters! What a difference this made. Every day we learned something new about each other. We learned to 'love each other through any disagreement' - understanding the point of view of each other, rather than to trying to be the winner. This proved to be a win-win situation.

We accepted the leadership role in a support group of encountered couples for almost six years in our community. Soon there were several support groups that met regularly to keep the flames alive. Lives of couples were being changed one *'weekend'* at a time. Children were noticing something different in their parents. Family life was taking on a new focus! One day at a time!

The ministry of Marriage Encounter had begun many years before and had spread throughout most of the mainline denominations in the USA, but the world-wide ministry needed

IV. TALL TALES

more leadership. In 1984 we moved to Okinawa. When we left Georgia, the couples in our group gave us a wonderful 'send-off.' I recall saying to them as we left: *"If Marriage Encounter is not in Japan when we get there, it soon will be."*

Little did I know how or when that would happen. . .but within weeks of our arrival in Okinawa, the 'flame' caught fire! As I look back now, I'm sure God had a hand in the *chance meeting* of another Encountered Couple, Bob and Cheryl Ruska.

Soon after we arrived on the island, we bought a clunker of a car, got our driver's license, and I headed to the Commissary to stock our kitchen. Remember, in Japan the driver has to sit on the right side of the front seat, plus drive on the left side of the road; that took some 'brain-power' on my part! I drove very slowly, very scared but I had to do it since we were to be there at least two years.

I soon found the Commissary on Kadena Air Force Base, and as I was walking through the parking lot, a young Marine called out to me: "Hey lady, is that your blue car?" Frightened, and wondering why someone would ask such a question of a stranger, I said, "yes, is there some problem?" He gained speed on me, and my anxiety grew stronger. Here I was in a foreign country, alone, just trying to get the necessities done and get back to the security of my family! And here is a guy chasing me down. If that had been today, I would have grabbed my cell phone, but I had no recourse but to keep walking.

Before I could flinch, this very friendly gentleman was beside me, asking another question: "Did you put that Marriage Encounter sticker on the car or was it there when you bought it?" Still nervous about this 'encounter' I told him that my husband and I had put it on! Then - with the biggest of 'big smiles' he threw his arm around my shoulder and tried to hug me, saying: "Great, we have one on our car too...so we are now friends!" It was several moments before I recovered from the shock of such a happening, being hugged by a stranger! When I did, we introduced ourselves, and I realized it was safe to talk to this stranger. Then we walked up and down the aisles, shopping as we talked, sharing our experiences of being *encountered*. From then on, we were no longer strangers, just friends who had not met until now.

We exchanged phone numbers and agreed to set up a time when we could meet as couples. The Ruskas had been on the island a while. We had been there just a few weeks. Getting settled in a foreign country, a new job (for Jim), and living on the economy, was not the easiest thing for me. Jim had been in the military twenty years before we married so it was 'old hat' for him, but our two young children and I had to get the hang of this way of life...it was a real culture shock.

We were living 'on the economy' - in a concrete structured house with 800 square feet. No heat, or Air Conditioning. No phone. No shower - just a funny looking bath tub! Adjustment, after adjustment. Everyone in our neighborhood spoke Japanese - except us! The children had to ride a school bus to the military base which was at least ten miles away. The temperature there was tropical - and rarely got lower than 45 - 50 degrees, but could rise up to 100 degrees, even at Christmas time! Typhoons could happen - we could be 'boarded up' for several days at a time...with little to do inside our small matchbox sized house.

We had shipped a small TV, some toys, some clothes and a few other 'basics.' We furnished our entire abode with furniture from the military base. When we got into base housing

IV. TALL TALES

we would then be able to buy our own furniture. The less you shipped overseas, the more poundage you could ship home 'free.' What a deal that was - that just gave the 'shopper' in me free reign. The yen rate back then was great, so getting good deals were a snap.

Within weeks of our arrival, each of our children had met a new friend. Apryll had met Heidi; Tim had met Hans. Soon each child said they'd like to go home and play with their new friends. I asked where they lived, and what was their last name. They didn't really know the answer to either question. I said when you find out perhaps we can arrange something.

It was not until Jim and I found a time to meet Bob and Cheryl for dinner did we realize that Hans and Heidi were their children. Wow! Now this made it easy. We could take the children with us to have dinner together with the Ruska family. Our girls were the same age, the boys were the same age, and from there we almost became a blended family. Everyone seemed to hit it off with each other.

That night we began to dream and talk about ways of finding other *encountered couples* on the island. Would it be possible to form a support group? Within the next week, I invited some of the wives of Jim's shop' to come to our house for a brunch. One of the wives immediately noticed a Marriage Encounter plaque on our wall. With the sound of surprise in her voice, she asked if we had been on a Weekend. "YES! Have you?" Hugs were immediately exchanged...another new friend. I was beginning to feel more at home in the Orient. Could this be 'real?'

So now were had a third couple for our group. After we put out some advertisements at the Base Chapel, several more couples came forth. We were now ready to roll! Monthly meetings provided the much needed support for those of us were in a foreign land and *'out of our comfort zone.'* We knew there was a great need for the young military couples whose marriages were battling the hazards of deployment. Wives were often left at home with their children, while the husband was gone for long periods of time.

Our prayer was that somehow, someway, we would be able to make a Marriage Encounter Weekend happen on Okinawa. I began to write letter after letter to the heads of the mainline denominations to see if they could send a Team of couples to do a Weekend. We knew we could 'fill' a Weekend in a heartbeat, if some Protestant Church organization would help us.

"No - No - No - There's NO WAY," was the constant response. We became very discouraged, but we kept praying for a miracle, refusing to give up on our idea. Then, one day, when things looked the darkest, we got a letter from someone in the States, saying they knew of an organization that ministered to couples of all faiths, and creeds: United Marriage Encounter. Perhaps they could help us. We lost no time in contacting them. Once we were in touch, it seemed things snowballed so fast we could hardly see where it was going.

Within months, we had enough couples registered to fill the first Marriage Encounter Weekend, Spring, 1986! We even had a waiting list. . .this proved couples were hungry for a renewal in their marriage - in their home, and in their relationship with God. It surpassed our hopes and dreams. . .and the sparks from that weekend provided the promise of another Weekend within months. And another one after that! When we came back to the states, over 100 couples had been encountered. The ministry in Okinawa continued long after we moved back to the States.

IV. TALL TALES

The parting words I had said when we left Georgia in 1984 had now come true. We had shared the dream with Japan! We had been *blessed* to be able to plant the seed, the fertile soil had been watered, and we were able to watch God make it grow!

From there, the ministry spread to other countries in the Far East, and ultimately, to many other countries in the world. Leadership was developed. Young couples were invited to become TEAM COUPLES, to volunteer their time to help keep good marriages alive - to make them stronger - to add depth to their love relationship, in a way that no one would have dreamed possible.

Those of us who provided the initial leadership were strengthened perhaps more than anyone else; our own marriage relationships just went 'deeper' than we could have ever dreamed. Our support groups grew larger after each Weekend. The circle just kept growing. It was God's way of blessing the institution of marriage, which in turn provided a stronger society in which to live and raise a family.

This ministry is still very much alive today. Jim and I were fortunate enough to serve on the National Board of Marriage Encounter for two years, and even after Jim died, I was asked to serve on a Steering Committee to bring the ministry to South Carolina. I accepted, with some hesitation of course, because I was now a widow. I asked myself, and the National Office: *"But what can I do? I'm single."*

I was assured that my enthusiasm and passion for the ministry had not subsided, and there was a lot I could do. I realized that this was a way I could continue being of service to families. I served three years. To plow *uncharted territory* was not an easy task, but it was a big challenge. I accepted, being one to thrive on new adventures, and knowing that with God's help and wisdom, Marriage Encounter Weekends could be held in our area.

Many marriages and homes in South Carolina have been enriched since 2010. Local leadership has emerged. One local couple was invited to become a Team Couple. *What a blessing,* not only for their own family, but for the world-wide ministry.

I often wonder what would have happened *IF* Bob had not chased me down in the parking lot that day, January, 1985? Thanks, Bob and Cheryl, it was a *'great ride,'* bumps, curves and all!

Within the past six years, Cheryl and I both lost our soul-mates but she and I are still like sisters. Many miles separate us, but we still keep in touch; we have grieved together, and supported each other through that dark valley as well as our mountain top experiences. Our children are grown but we all still keep in touch. When in the military, serving overseas, especially, families bond very quickly; and when you are *'encountered'* your ties are even deeper. There is a different kind of intimacy between friends that is rarely found in other friendships.

Within Marriage Encounter, there is a 'connection' among those who have lost their spouse through a newsletter, BRIDGES. And I've been able to 'write letters' of support to others who have or are going through the grief process, and likewise, they have lifted me up with their own testimonies of their coping strategies.

To God be the glory! He works in mysterious ways, his wonders to perform.

Becky Williams Buckman
September, 2013

IV. TALL TALES

PAY IT FORWARD

When we are in school we learn a lot of lessons, but often the best lessons are learned in the day to day living. After we finish school, we launch out into the world to 'make it on our own.' We've left the comforts of our home and the security of our parents who had prepared us for the day when we would fly out of the nest.

During all of my college years, I had worked to help pay my tuition and expenses. In every part-time job I had, I learned lessons far deeper than I'd found in college textbooks. Those lessons have remained as an integral part of who I am today.

While I was at Emory's School of Theology, working on my Master's, I was living on the north side of Atlanta, but my part-time job, at Calvary United Methodist Church, was on the south side, perhaps fifty miles round trip. They had planned a 'welcome' reception for me. Everyone seemed ready to make me feel at home in their congregation.

After most everyone left the reception, this very tall, lanky, gray-haired man, with a slight grin on his face, pulled me aside, putting his arm around me, and said in a low voice: "Now listen to me. There's something I want you to do every Monday morning when you come to work." Meanwhile, my mind was wondering what he was going to ask me to do. He'd been on the Pastor-Parish Committee and had interviewed me for this job. My mind immediately went into anxiety mode: "Oh, what have I done now? What is he expecting me to do?"

He continued saying, "there's a gas station around the corner where I get gas every week. I want you to get your gas there. Fill up your tank on Monday morning before you go into the office

IV. TALL TALES

and tell the Manager to put the bill on my account." I stepped back from his gentle 'hug' just a bit, and said, "Oh Gene, I can't do that!" With a smile that would have gone from one side of the room to the other, he looked at me and said: "Yes, you can, and you had better do that – if you don't, I will always know when I get my bill!"

"But, Gene, I might not be able to repay you..." Again, he hugged me a bit tighter, and said "No, that's true, you may not, but that doesn't matter to me. I don't want you to repay me. Someday you will run into someone who needs a little boost, and you can give it to them. If they want to repay you later, tell them what I've just told you. Is that a deal?" With tears in my eyes and a lighter load on my shoulders, I said: "Yes, sir, that's a deal!"

Gene and his wife, at that time, were old enough to be my parents, and they knew the salary I was making needed to be supplemented. They stepped up to the bat that day. During the two wonderful years I spent in ministry there, I grew in the 'wisdom and statue' of those Godly people.

I've kept my part of the deal. The lesson Gene taught me that day in 1964 will never be forgotten. Now almost fifty years later, when I am more able to help someone, I can still feel the warmth of Gene's hug that day, and see the radiant smile on his face, and understand the depth of his *agape love* for a young woman who was still 'wet behind the ears.' I was just on the first rung of the ladder of life, beginning to learn what was really important in life!

'What goes around comes around' is still spinning in our world. There are still good people who live their life for others. Just yesterday it came back around to me, when I was least expecting

it. It was Thanksgiving eve, and I still had last minute shopping to be done. Even with all the advance planning and work I had done, as par, I had forgotten some ingredients.

So early that morning, I grabbed purse, keys and a heavy jacket and was 'on the run' to try to beat the traffic. I made a quick run into Dollar General (my favorite place to save money) to get some bargains; after I placed all items on the counter, I searched for my wallet. . .and searched again. *It was NOT there!* Panic - where could I have left it? Or had I left my purse unattended, and someone grabbed it? I quickly ran to the car, begging forgiveness from the six or eight people in line behind me. I was so embarrassed that I was holding them up. I just hate doing that!

No luck, my wallet was not in the car! By this time, I was truly in a flapping flutter. I asked the clerk if I could write a check. Sure, no problem. She asked for my drivers license. OH NO. . .it is in my wallet! She had already rung up the sale, put my check in the drawer, but the computer would not accept it without my license. Now what? I felt the stares of those in line shoot through my feathers like a bullet! I asked if she could take my phone number. No luck there!

I was beginning to wish I had not gotten out of bed, much less tried to shop. All I could do was ask her to void the sale. The computer would not allow her to do that either. . .dumb computers! They have no sympathy whatsoever. Don't they know I'm a 'senior citizen' and am prone to slip a bit? What happened to mercy? Grace? This kind of thing would have never happened at my Dad's grocery store, but 'that' was back in the fifties. (Too bad we're not in those kind of times now. . .a time in life where people could be trusted to be 'honest!') My dad would have let the customer bring the money back later. Someone's *word was good enough. . .but not now!*

I was still in line, I'm teary eyed, and folded over in agony, like a limp old greenback, wishing I could just disappear into thin air! The gentleman behind me had mercy. He told the cashier to put my items on his bill. "Oh no, sir, I can't let you do that." He insisted, telling the cashier to give me my purchases and he would pay for them. *I had just been shown mercy, forgiveness, and love by a total stranger.*

Wow. . .when I caught my breath, and able to speak without crying, I thanked him over and over again, and I apologized to those in line behind him. I was sorry they had to wait. As I left, I trusted they saw the *pay it forward theory* played out in the midst of their agitated souls! I wished the good Samaritan a happy thanksgiving and hoped that he would enjoy the holidays. I knew I would!

This old 'turkey' got in the car, went home and found the wallet right where I had left it! I drove back to the grocery store to get the other things I needed. I was still reeling from *the random act of kindness,* but realizing the true meaning of Thanksgiving had met me face to face, in a miraculous way.

John Bunyon once said: "You have not lived today until you have done something for someone who can never repay you."

Becky Williams Buckman
November 30, 2013

SAYING 'GRACE'

Before Jim and I married I had met a few of his relatives in Kentucky and Georgia but there were many whom I had not met. We had made the long trip from Georgia to Morganfield, Ky. where his parents lived. I would be meeting more of his family for the first time. Always the child who was eager to please, and wanted to be accepted, I offered to help Jim's mother prepare the big dinner, and help serve.

Jim's parents lived in a very old house that had belonged to his grandparents. A center hallway led straight to the small country kitchen, with a living room and bedroom just off the hall. The children were called in to wash up, while the large crowd of family members gathered around the oblong red-topped table with chairs to match, with the chrome legs, the kind that was so popular in the 40's and 50's. We were literally 'elbow to elbow.' By the time everyone was seated, with plates and glasses in front of them, there was no room for the food.

As we all bowed our heads, and tried to quieten down the house full of grandchildren, Papaw said "GRACE"; it was the standard prayer he'd been taught as a child growing up in the Catholic School: *"Bless us, O Lord, for these are thy gifts which we are about to receive from Thy bountiful hands, through Christ our Lord and Saviour. AMEN."*

There was not much room between the table and the counters; it was a tight squeeze for those of us who were serving the table. I took the Tea Pitcher and Coffee Pot around to the serve the adults; lucky for me, I was still slim! I stopped to pour coffee for the husband of Jim's sister whom I had not previously met. He wiggled to get his arm high enough to lift the cup toward me, hoping to make pouring easier for me.

IV. TALL TALES

WELL...by offering to help serve the table, *I had set myself up for being the "new kid on the block"* - usually not the favored position in any family into which you have just married. I spilled hot coffee on his arm. Of course he jumped up, nearly rumbling the table and all of the dishes on the table. As seriously as he could ever look, with his dark eyes, he stared at me eye to eyeball. Meanwhile, I was in great haste to apologize to him, and to see if he were scalded. I tried my best to use every word in the English language to excuse my *faux pas!* As usual, that just made matters worse. I just wanted to run to the barn and hide.

Shaking his wet shirt-sleeve away from his arm, he said "AND so, Mrs. Buckman, did you say your first name was GRACE?" Just as serious as he had been, I answered: *"No, Sir, my name is Becky."* Embarrassed to the hilt, I didn't crack a smile, but everyone at the table laughed until they hurt. I excused myself to the 'not-so-private' bathroom at Grandmother's house to erase the tell-tale signs of tears streaming down my face. Their bathroom walls did not connect to the ceiling, so I flushed the toilet several times, and left the water running to 'cover up' my sobs. That was one time I would have preferred having an 'outhouse' to an indoor bathroom! Then no one would have heard me crying.

I returned to the kitchen, but I let someone else do the coffee! I'm really not sure that I ever sat down to eat my meal that night - all hunger pains were gone, and I simply tried to gain my composure. When I got back to the kitchen, and heard all their laughter, I realized that it could have happened to anyone else who was working in a 'tight spot.' I saw the smirk on my husband's face, and knew he loved me in spite of my lack of waitress skills! I would be "o k" - the new kid on the block was accepted. What a relief!

By the time we had another meal together, Charlie's staunch military character had 'mellowed' and he spoke to me with a very slight smirk on his face, saying *"hello, Grace."* From then on, I could relax, knowing he had 'forgiven me'. I had never been a waitress, and that night proved that *'that was not my cup of tea.'* I would do better at the stove! For the next twenty-nine years, I never saw Uncle Charlie without thinking about the first time I met him, and the fiasco I had caused at dinner that night.

When I said my last farewell to him, I said, *"Hey Uncle Charlie it's ME, you know, Grace! I'll see you soon. Just so you'll know, you can relax now - I have given up trying to be a waitress 'down here' and I'm sure St. Peter won't let me do it up there either!"*

As I walked away that day, I could just see him smirking at me, saying: *"Good! It's about time. Being a waitress was never your cup of tea!*

Becky Williams Buckman
Dec. 30, 2009

IV. TALL TALES

MY PRIVATE PLANE

Never in my wildest imagination would I have ever dreamed I would have *my own airplane*. But I did! I don't know what I did to deserve it, but it was the 'ride' of a lifetime. Now don't get too excited, thinking that I've really gone beserk. *This is true. . .and still very 'real' in my mind.*

Late one early August afternoon, 1976, I was lying on my hospital bed; my fever was raging, nothing had seemed to stop the warring madness that was ravaging my body after a C-section, bringing to our family our second child: a beautiful baby girl. We had spent her first two weeks at Robins Air Force Base Hospital, in middle Georgia. I had only been able to cuddle and feed her several times before I was quarantined. Each day proved to be 'worse' than the day before - the darkest cloud hung over our heads.

Trying to stop the spreading infection at the incision site, every known antibiotic and procedure had been called into play. Nothing was working! Jim had walked in to see me, after work that day. The baby was healthy and was getting her share of TLC but our hearts were breaking into. I couldn't be with her!

The nurses were taking up the slack; they kept her within arm's reach almost 24/7. They played music in her room every day; they rocked her, told her stories, and kept her little bald head warm, with a stocking cap! This newborn had so many 'mamas' for so long. When I finally got her in my arms sometime later, I was given a list of *things I had to do* to keep this little one happy! Even what radio station to play for her; now if that isn't love, I don't know what is. I feel sure that is when her love of music was 'born!'

While she was being pampered by everyone in the Nursery at the Base Hospital, I was getting 'extra attention' also because of the way my body was deteriorating! Mine was not the normal reaction for a C-section! The 12" incision had become inflamed within two days of surgery, with high fevers that would not be contained! The Doctors had simply 'snipped' bits of flesh away from the wound, little by little, never giving me anything to deaden the area! Torture unlimited! A crater was beginning to form in my abdomen.

When Jim walked in from work that day, he was called to the Nurse's Station. It was 4:30. He was told I would be taken to Wilford Hall Hospital in San Antonio at 6 p. m. that day! That was only an hour and a half from now! How could he take care of things on the home front in that short time, much less be packed and ready to fly out with me? I was going to be flown to one of two military hospitals in the USA that had a hyperbaric chamber; the Doctors had concluded they could do no more for me in Georgia. I was an 'emergency case!'

The 'chamber' puts out oxygen at a higher level than atmospheric pressure, halting the death of tissue. Death results when the infection cannot be contained. I had literally been 'dying' for over two weeks - *a slow death* but it had not been said as loudly as it was said that day when the airplane arrived to pick up just one patient - me!

Jim came to tell me this news but I was so feverish I don't think I really understood. I just heard him say *'I've got to go home and get ready.'* 'I recall asking: *For what?'* Rushing out the door, he said he would explain when he got back. My sickened body and mind couldn't absorb any of this.

We had two teenagers who had been taking care of our two year old during the day while Jim was at work. Now, what was

IV. TALL TALES

he going to do? He couldn't leave the three children at home alone while he went to Texas with me. He couldn't let me go there alone, in the critical situation I was in. There were no grandparents anywhere near, only his sister. How do you make arrangements to be gone indefinitely, on such short notice?

He had not even had time to ask the Doctor any questions. He just knew he had to 'fly' like crazy to do what had to be done. He had to clean out my hospital room quickly, so he grabbed the few personal things I had in my hospital room, took them home, dropped them in the floor, then flew upstairs to pack some clothes for himself. Somewhere, somehow, along this 'flight' he called his sister and asked if she could pick up the children after she got off work. Lucky for him, she'd said yes.

After that phone call, he hurriedly called my parents. Beyond that his entire being was in orbit! It was a good twenty minute drive from our house to the Base, even without 5 p. m. traffic. He drove *'over the limit'* to get back to the Base in time to see them transporting me on a gurney out on the runway. Running for his life, with a small bag in hand, he begged them to wait on him.

The door of the large C-9 aircraft opened, the medical crew lifted the gurney up and carefully got me inside, out of the hot sun which was almost making a puddle of the tarmac. I recalled the jostling motions as they strapped the gurney on to hooks from the ceiling, with my fever hotter than the heat index in south Georgia that day. I was drifting in and out of consciousness, but I tried to get a clue about my surroundings. Where was I? What were they doing to me? This hard slab I'd been strapped to was a far cry from commercial airplane rides. I knew enough to realize I was on a military plane.

Jim and I were the only passengers! I'd been *doped up* for the trip. He sat within an arm's reach, in a jump seat; he was belted in for the trip, and I was 'strapped to the gurney' so tightly that I could hardly wiggle, much less change positions! I heard the cargo door slam shut.

As we became airborne, I felt a slight swinging motion - I was literally 'hanging from the ceiling' of the plane. I was swinging between l*ife and death* - hung in the balance, just as my gurney. I didn't know how close I was to 'taking flight into eternity,' but my family and friends knew! An unbelievable trauma.

I drifted into another world for the remainder of the flight. Jim held my hand as it lay perfectly still - clamy, feverish. He fidgeted. He wept. He prayed. He broke broke out in a cold sweat. It was near midnight now. With some sense of relief, he felt the landing gear begin to drop, but his body was numb. What was next?

Neither of us knew how many phone calls to the Surgeons at the Texas hospital had preceded our arrival; nor that hundreds of phones were ringing all over the nation on our behalf! Prayer chains were set in motion - in churches and communities we knew nothing about. Years later we met 'strangers' who told us they had prayed for us back then! How good GOD is. . .

I vaguely remember being unstrapped from the ceiling, and lowered to the transport to be taken in to the ER. Once I had been evaluated, and given something to take me 'out' completely, Jim searched for a room on base where he could catch a few hours of sleep before the scheduled surgery at 7 a. m.

He arrived early that morning, hoping to have a little time with me before I *'went under.'* But when he arrived he was told I was

IV. TALL TALES

in the recovery room! I'd been wheeled into surgery around 3 a. m.. After he had left me the night before, it was evident my surgery couldn't wait, even a few more hours! Mixed with emotions, from anger to disillusionment, he sat in the waiting room, waiting to see the Doctor and find out where I hung in the balance!

When I was moved to a room, they told him he could see me. There he found I had been placed in isolation, and was lying under a tent, with massive bandages over my abdomen. I was unresponsive. He sat for hours waiting to see even the slightest sign of life. Later in the morning, I began to wander into consciousness, but in a very confused state of mind. I was on morphine.

The first significant sign of alertness dawned much later that day when I saw my parents standing at the foot of my bed. Inwardly, I fell apart, like peas from a pod once it was split open. My mother had never flown, and had gone so far as to say she never would get on an airplane unless one of her children were dying. That remark was lodged in my mind; it stung as if I'd landed in a wasp's nest! I realized I was at death's door! Everyone else had known *that* long before that day.

Along with Jim, they stood there with masks and gloves on. . . and it was not Halloween, but just as scary - it was a haunting feeling! Gradually, I moved from subconsciousness to a very painful consciousness. Each time the nurses came in to treat my wound, I wished I had remained in 'that other world' - the one where I knew or felt nothing.

My diagnosis was *gas gangrene,* caused by a bacterial infection; toxins release gas which causes tissue to die. The amount of tissue I had lost since July 20, 1976 was greater than the size of a large soup bowl, producing a wound that could never be sewn up. That was *the entry door to hell*. . .and I walked through that vast unknown for four more weeks. The treatments to the massive wound were done every four hours. *Horrendous torture,* the likes of which I never knew were possible, nor will I try to take you there. I would not wish that on any one, ever! Burn victims will understand. When I see a burn victim now, I can identify with them, and I literally fall apart, just recalling my days of hell in Texas.

Wilford Hall was a very large military training hospital, known for its excellent staff. I usually had a team of five or six Physicians who came daily to evaluate my progress. Several of them were interns. I was 'watched over' with their careful eyes, and heard their discussions of the nature of *my rare case.* Jim and my parents sat by my bedside, almost round the clock, for three weeks. As I think back upon my 'horror' during the treatments, I cannot imagine the hell it was for them to sit by, and watch - and not be able to do anything. Being there with and for me was a comfort, but I found myself wanting to die. I didn't think I could stand much more. But I had to. I had a beautiful baby back in Georgia who needed her Mother; I had a wonderful husband, and three other wonderful children who needed me. I had to fight. I had to live. . . somehow! I knew God was in control but I couldn't pray for myself. Others had to intercede for me.

Jim was bitter and mad with God for allowing this to happen - and that 'our world together' had been slightly more than five years! One night, after he'd left the hospital, he was alone in his room crying out to God, asking *"why was this happening to us? If you are a loving God, like everyone has said, you wouldn't do this to us!"*

He had lost his first wife in death in less than four years of marriage, and left him with two toddlers, and three teenagers, and NOW, it appeared that the same thing was happening to

IV. TALL TALES

him again. *This was not fair!* How could he face this again? He prayed all night, that somehow, someway I would live, that we could raise our four children like we had planned.

The thought of our precious new baby being left alone, without us, at the Base Hospital in Georgia was another hell we both endured. We called every day to talk to the Nurses about her. They assured us they were loving her to pieces. . .spoiling her big-time! They would take her with them to the Nurses station, cuddle and talk to her, while they fed her! At every chance they would go into her room and rock her to sleep. She was the 'new kid on the block' and we heard that the staff was fussing over who would get to keep her at their desk!

We also called Jim's sister every day to check on our other three children. We were assured they were fine, but we still were burdened to know that we had been away from them for almost five weeks now. The teenagers were taking care of our youngest son, Tim, during the daytime at our home, then would go to their Aunt's for dinner and to sleep at her home.

School would be starting soon. We weren't there to do the traditional shopping for new clothes and school supplies. . .how desperately we needed to be at home! Jim's sick leave time was running out. He needed to get back to work; he and my elderly parents were worn out and needed to get back to Georgia.

I continued to be in isolation, lying buck naked under a tent, with no 'dressing' on the massive open wound. Nothing was allowed to touch it but air. All of my pride had been stripped away. Not that I was comfortable being 'seen' like this, but I had no choice! *I was on display* but who in their right mind would dare seek out this kind of display? The six Doctors, of course! I was just thankful I was in such an excellent hospital, with specialists who gave me their best. None of them had encountered a 'rare case' like mine. I was so unique that I was written up in medical history. I had never longed to be that famous, but if what they were *observing* could be used to help someone else, so be it!

Pigskin had been ordered and was used on my wound to prepare my tissue for skin graft. Another surgery? Skin from my thigh would be used to close the gaping wound; once the rectangular section of skin was adhered to my abdomen area, I no longer had pain there. But, the pain from the skin graft was another step deeper into hell. The daily treatments to heal the thigh were as unbearable as those I had endured at the C-section wound site. I began crying the moment the nurse came in; that turned into screaming fits while I was being lowered into a huge pool of hot water while the wound was scraped with a wire brush to keep the tissue alive!

I still was not allowed to wear clothing until the leg healed. I asked Jim where were my clothes? In the rush of trying to get back to the Base the day we left Georgia on our way to Texas, he had gotten his clothes, remembered to bring our Bible, and my ID card, but nothing more. . .no clothes for me! *"What? I have no clothes? How am I supposed to fly home, looking like this?"* I was sure they would not let me out of the hospital in the nude. . .much less put me on a plane!

Jim's sick leave had run out, and he was going to have to leave me there until I was healed, and able to fly home. He always had a 'fix-it' attitude, an answer for everything. He told me he would mail me a package of clothes when he got home. I had no clue what to expect. I had lost forty pounds during these five weeks; nothing in my closet at home would fit! I wouldn't have been surprised if he had mailed me a maternity dress. I figured

IV. TALL TALES

what the heck. No one would know me anyway. . .just to get home 'dressed' was all I cared about and to be able to hold my newborn baby, now almost six weeks old! For the family to be together again - that's all that mattered!

I was left there to battle the last week of treatment alone. By this time, I had been placed in a ward with sixteen other women. I was still living under 'the tent' without any adorning garments, but I could get out of bed to use the potty chair. Just so I did not step outside the four curtained walls that surrounded my bed. BIG DEAL! I now had real freedom - the kind you normally take for granted!

After being cooped up for almost six weeks, I was going stir crazy now that my family was back home. I asked the Nurse if I could use the phone. The only phone available was on a 'rolling cart' that could be taken from place to place, as needed. No, this was not the dark ages, but you couldn't prove that by me. I would never complain of course because Jim had given twenty years of his life in the military for wonderful benefits, including medical care! All that I had gone through was not costing our family anything - except the loss of a precious time in our life.

The Nurse brought the phone. I 'streaked' out of bed and dialed Jim at work. About the time he answered, I saw one of the curtains (that had been hiding my nude body) fly open. I screamed *'wait, please.'* With the redness of the 'biggest delicious red apple' on their faces, the six Doctors hastened to close the curtain, apologizing to the hilt! They gave me time to hang up the phone, explaining to Jim that I'd just been spooked by my Team of Doctors! I climbed back in bed, under my 'tent' and relaxed. . .well, that might be a stretch of imagination! I gave them the 'go ahead' to open the curtain now, and examine me. . .the faces of the young interns were still glowing with embarrassment.

Frankly, I couldn't imagine what their problem was. I was just as buck naked in bed as I was standing up beside the bed. They had seen the likes of me now for the past five weeks, but protocol doesn't condone seeing a nude body 'out of bed!' It was OK as long as I was horizontal. Go figure!

After the Doctors left my bedside, I heard 'chattering' all around the ward. Some of the ladies had noticed my feet on the floor earlier, and knew *I'd been caught off-guard!* That made me the *'joke of the day.'* By this time, I had begun to realize I would live through this hell, and to even see some humor in the situation. It was about time! We had all been in agony for so long, wondering if there would ever be any light at the end of the tunnel.

I couldn't wait to call Jim back to tell him what had just happened. Of course, he laughed with me - it was just too funny. He couldn't wait to share the story with the guys in his shop at work. . .word got around very fast, and it was all at my expense! I don't think I was ever able to look at those guys again without remembering that Jim had told them 'the naked truth.'

I will never forget having my very own private plane. . .with my very own pilot. It was *a ride of a lifetime.* I survived the trip, miraculously, flew back home to Georgia with the 'mix and match' outfit Jim had shipped, and enough money to get a coke at the airport!

He picked me up and as fast as our car would take us we drove to the Military Base to pick up our six-week old baby. We were floating in mid-air, literally, until we were told that she was not in her room. They would have to find her! *"What? Where is she? I haven't seen her in six weeks - don't tell me you don't know where she is."* Nurses tried their best to comfort us, but nothing helped: I was in tears, and Jim was shaking like a leaf on a tree in the midst of a storm.

It seemed like forever. Finally, a young airman came around the corner with a big grin on his face, an Infant Seat on his arm, with our baby! *Thank you God,* was all we could say. She was smiling too, but our smiles were bigger; our hearts were bursting with joy. I couldn't wait to hold my baby again. . .the last time I had held her she was only two days old. Many 'angels' had been holding her in their arms and hearts the six weeks I had been fighting for my life.

It was now September, and fall was beginning to appear. I was so glad to be home with our new baby and my family! I cuddled her, not ever wanting to let her out of my sight, with *tears of relief* falling like a spring shower. We were all alive, and healthy, and together again. What more could we ask for? *This was as close to heaven as I had ever been.* It was better than having my own private plane!

Since that day, never have I taken 'life' for granted. Every breath I take is a miracle. I thank God for healing me, for giving me the opportunity to raise my family with a wonderful husband and father.

Becky Williams Buckman
August, 2013

DOWN THE LINE

THE PURPLE COW

I never saw a purple cow.
I never hope to see one.
But I can tell you, anyhow,
I'd rather see than be one!
                Nursery Rhyme

My husband Jim could memorize anything. I think *'Purple Cow'* was his favorite! He loved poetry, and quoted it often! His next favorite was *'The Swing'* by Robert Louis Stevenson. We shared the love of poetry - and enjoyed quoting it to each other often. Not just the short 'simple' one like Purple Cow but poetry from the Bible, as well. He taught all four of our children 'Purple Cow' early in their lives. I had never heard it until I married him. I often joked with him, showing him it was not in my Nursery Rhyme book! He insisted it was in his, but he didn't have his book to prove it to me. We just let that volley back and forth, for years, until. . .

One day, long after all the children were grown, and gone from home, he was at The Clinic, having his blood drawn. Lying there on the table, in the room alone, he waited for the nurse to arrive. I sat in the Lobby reading a magazine. Then, I heard him call "Come here, honey, come on in here right now." Of course, the nurse went running in to see about her patient. "What is wrong, Mr. Buckman?" *"Nothing,* he replied..." *I want my wife to come in here now. . . I want to show her this picture on the wall."* Confused, she asked: *"What picture?"* He pointed to a Nursery Rhyme that was framed, hanging on the wall above his bed. There it was: *Purple Cow.* He had me where he wanted me now! He could PROVE something to me, in front of someone else!

IV. TALL TALES

Framed beautifully, and decorating an otherwise drab, sterile room, this rhyme was hanging among other Nursery Rhymes. I saw it in my own eyes, and soon began smiling at Jim. I told him *"WOW, you win."* The nurse, meanwhile, had never seen a grown man get so excited over a nursery rhyme, or call for his wife to come to his bedside while he had his blood drawn! The three of us stood there reading this little ditty aloud; he was smiling from ear to ear while we squeezed hands.

He was still grinning when she stuck his arm for the blood. I walked out, just shaking my head, and getting dozens of wild stares from the twenty or so people in the waiting room. They had all heard him call for "his honey," had seen me go running to him, and then they heard the *Purple Cow* rhyme being recited by 3 grown people!

"What is this hospital coming to,' was their thought, I'm sure! Who would have thought that a nursery rhyme would create such a scene, much less hear it recited with the 'joy juice' that Jim used when he taught our children this rhyme!

This was just the beginning of the things I learned from him! I always knew he had the memory of an elephant, and was reminded again that he would always be *a kid at heart.*

Our daughter Apryll made her dad a ceramic PURPLE COW as a gift. I shared that rhyme in the eulogy I gave for him at his Memorial Service. It was *'so him.'* Along with other special momentos of my husband, the *Purple Cow* sat on a table, that day, for our friends and family to see. It was a tribute to his significant ability to memorize poetry as well as his deep and abiding love for children.

The *Purple Cow* is in a Curio Cabinet near my front door now. I teach each of my piano students this rhyme as I tell them about my husband. If he were still living, he would have met them at the door, and began teaching them *Purple Cow*; he would have loved every one of them just as I do! He would be listening to them take piano lessons from his wife: the kid who didn't know all of her nursery rhymes!

I imagine when we meet again, we'll join hands, smile at each other, and '*in a wink*' we will start looking for *Purple Cows* as we are led through the green pastures of heaven!

Becky Williams Buckman
August 19, 2010

IV. TALL TALES

THE TALE ENDS HERE

I'll never forget the day. . .

Our family had just moved to Okinawa, Japan. My husband had taken a civil service job there and this was going to be a wonderful opportunity and education for all of us. The children and I had never been, so we were eager to explore our new world in the Orient.

I had had a college roommate from Japan with whom I had kept in touch through the years. Jim had always wanted to take me to visit her family in Yokahama. Instead of that being a dream, it would now be a reality! I was elated beyond belief.

Jim had served in Japan during his military career and had been exposed to the unique customs of the country but he had not shared any of the surprises that the children and I were *'in'* for! I had no clue of the culture shock that lurked ahead. I'm really not sure I could have understood, even if he had tried to prepare us. The *'adventure of a lifetime'* was in our reach.

We had bought a cheap old clunker of a car. Since cars rust out quickly on the island there was no need to spend much on one. As long as the doors would close, the windows not broken out, and it would run without a 'knock' it served its purpose. The island was only about 60 miles long and about eight miles wide, at its widest point, so there wasn't a lot of driving to be done. The weather was great most of the time. Temperatures rarely got below 45 or 50 degrees, and it would be cold only if it was raining.

We had gotten to Okinawa Dec. 29, 1984, and were anxious to see our new world. One Sunday, early in January, 1985 we had been to worship at Chapel Three on Kadena Air Force Base. After a quick lunch at the TIKI the four of us piled in our old blue Nissan. With a simple map in my lap we headed up toward the north end of the island, chugging along at 40-50 kilometers.

Remember, we did not know Japanese, and if Jim did, he didn't admit it! I always carried my little Japanese dictionary in my pocket, but it didn't always do me much good, especially on this particular day, just when I needed it the most.

Whatever I had eaten for lunch decided to 'talk to me' in a very loud rumble. . .if you get my drift. I needed to find the 'ladies room' - like 30 minutes ago! But we were out in the middle of nowhere, on narrow roads, with little or no civilization.

The longer we drove, the sicker I got. This was going to be *some more disaster* if we did not find a restroom. I think I even threatened Jim that if he didn't drive faster and find a facility I would just have to have him stop by the side of the road, and let me run to the woods! By this time, our elementary aged children were perhaps hiding in the floorboard of the back seat, hoping no one would see these crazy Americans who were literally lost in the boonies. I was using every known muscle in my body to stay in control. I was even praying to find something like the 'outhouse' I had used as a child!

Finally, Jim spotted a Japanese facility. He parked the car and before he shut the engine off, I ran for all I was worth to get in, only to discover there was *no American toilet*. When I saw there was nothing to sit on - just several open holes on the concrete floor, I shouted out loudly: *"Oh my Lord - I can't do that."* I'm sure Jim heard me, and laughed until he hurt. I was hurting too, not only my stomach, but *my pride*. At that point I really didn't care

IV. TALL TALES

who heard me - I was desperate! I had on a nice 'Sunday' dress but I had no clue *how* I was going to protect it while I took care of business. But at that point, only one thing mattered! Need I say more? You understand.

No one ever taught me to squat, low to the ground, with my best dress on, wadded up around my waist, much less aim for the 'goal!' That day our *'sightseeing was cut short!'* I cried all the way home, wondering what kind of life had we gotten ourselves into. This was just the beginning of my education in the Orient!

We lived in Okinawa almost three years, and I never accomplished 'the Japanese way' of life in that arena. . .but I did learn enough Japanese to read the signs that said they had the kind of 'facilities' I was used to.

Once that was accomplished, I loved sightseeing in the Orient!

Becky William Buckman
June, 2012

DOWN THE LINE

NEWT WILSON

I never knew Newt Wilson, but for years I've wished that I had had the privilege. He came along in my Mother's life before she married my Daddy.

My Mother was a beautiful and charming young woman in the early 1900's. Photos of her as a teenager assure me she had no problems in the dating arena. I even think she might have been a flirt! She was always dressed to the hilt, often with stylish boots, and a hat to accent the natural beauty she had inherited from her Mother, my Granny Johnson.

Mother had a younger sister, my Aunt Cliffie; they often double dated. I imagine young men would flock to the Johnson home to set up their dates before any other fellows could get out of bed that morning! Through the years I heard Mother mention the names of her many suitors, one of whom was Newt Wilson, as well as those of my Aunt.

These two Johnson gals grew up in a Methodist parsonage, under the roof of an evangelical minister and his wife. They moved around, from one rural community to another in North Georgia for over twenty-six years. I'm sure these teenagers were well known, and perhaps even 'checked out' as soon as word hit that there was a new preacher in town! You know how 'word' gets around about *PK's* (preacher's kids) They were always up to something - fun or otherwise. Mother and Aunt Cliffie were no different - they were just 'happy kids' and probably didn't get too many spankings: maybe a *'good talking to'* from time to time from their Father.

My family had been living in Japan for three years, and had just come back state-side in 1987. We were all excited about seeing

IV. TALL TALES

Mom, after so long! She was going to be 89 on August 23rd that year, and was still able to live in her own home in Woodstock, Ga. My sister's husband shared the same birthday so that was all the more reason to plan a big party.

I have the reputation of being a 'party gal' and special occasions like this were always putting my brain in high gear! I got busy, getting things organized, and delegating tasks for other family members to do. There's nothing I enjoy better than 'playing games.' I can stay up all night making up my own *crazy games*. And most of the time, they go over well, but not always from 'my doings;' after all, it is the 'people' who make the party. At this party, Mom was the 'celebrity' in more ways than one.

There were hats, horns, streamers, banners, and even a special T-shirt for Mom to wear - the whole nine yards. We had worked diligently to keep this celebration a secret. All Mom knew was that we were coming home for the weekend. She had always said: *"I'm just living 'til you get back home from Japan."* My husband had an answer that always 'topped' her own sense of humor, so his response was: *"Well, we'll just stay in Japan - that way you will keep living longer!"* They were like two peas in a pod - how they loved each other. I often wondered if he married me just to have her for a mother-in-law!

By this time Mom was still in pretty good shape for her age. Her 'funny bone' was never found to be out of place, and I really think laughter kept her young and as happy as anyone could be. Every now and then, you might catch one of her gears 'slipping' just a bit, but what would you expect for someone almost 90?

All of her children and grandchildren arrived; one by one we poured into her living room singing "Happy Birthday." I'm surprised she didn't drop her teeth or wet her pants! She was speechless. We dressed her in the special MAXINE T-Shirt. It said: *"I've still got it but nobody wants to see it."* She took it in stride, of course, laughing all the while.

After we settled in, she caught her breath and the fun began. I began to ask her questions about her youth. . .things like how old were you when you had your first date, what did you do on that date, or who gave you your first kiss. She would ponder the question a bit, and then proceed to tell us, always with some response that cracked us up.

This went on for several minutes. Meanwhile Mother's baby sister, my Aunt Cliffie, was sitting beside her taking all of this in, but not saying anything. She always was well dressed, 'made up' like a doll, with matching costume jewelry; her nails were perfect and polished to the finest of fine. Now remember, back then, even in the late 1970's Woodstock did not have a Nail Salon. We didn't even have a traffic light until I was grown.

Seems Aunt Cliffie had nicked one of her nails, so she pulled out the emery board from her stylish purse. She began to take care of the problem at hand, but still with her ears perked up to what her 'big sis' was saying. She never missed a trick, and had a delightful dry sense of humor which made her all the more fun.

When I asked Mother about what boyfriend do you remember the most, other than Daddy, she was stumped. She paused, looked real serious, obviously was trying get her mind in gear - his name just wouldn't roll off her tongue. We all sat in anxious anticipation of her answer. Finally, she turned to her sister, and in all seriousness, said: *"Cliffie, what was Newt Wilson's name?"*

Cliffie never looked up, nor cracked a grin; she continued to file her nails, and simply said: *"Newt Wilson."* The laughter

IV. TALL TALES

bounced off our rib cages like basketballs dribbling down the court! I'm really not sure Mother realized that she had answered her own question, but she looked at me and grinned, saying: *"Well, what else do you want to know?"* We asked a few more questions, like who kissed you first? *"Your Grandaddy was the first man I ever kissed, and he didn't kiss me until after we were married."* My nephew asked her how she knew that she wanted to marry him if they had never kissed.

Today, the walls of Mom's sixty-eight year old house are still standing in Woodstock, but I'm sure there are some big cracks among the bricks and mortar! It was just the laughter that shook everything loose that day.

That story will live on - through eternity. When someone new becomes a part of our family, this is the *'signature story'* that welcomes them in. It gives them a little clue of what they got into when they married into the Johnson-Williams families. The good thing tho,' it hasn't stopped any of them from becoming one of us!

To crack us up, day or night, just say *Newt Wilson*. Nuf' said?

Becky Williams Buckman
January, 2011

I WOULD NOT TRADE

It was April 13, 1993. Spring was bursting forth in all of its *'glory'* in Bowling Green, Kentucky. I stood looking from the hospital window, into the parking lot; the Bradford pear trees were beginning to burst into their heavenly white blooms - soon to be a 'ball of white fire' to the beholder.

The hospital had called me *very early* that morning, telling me my Mother had taken a turn for the worse. I had to get there immediately. I felt as if lightening was striking all around me with no way to escape its effect.

My aging mother had been a patient there for several days, fighting the congestive heart failure that had been eating away at her body, now for several years. She had moved, from her home in Georgia, to be with us in Kentucky. That move was perhaps not a choice of hers as much as it was a necessity for me to assume *the care giving role*.

Mom's mind was really quite good for her 95 years; she knew she was with me and my family, but she did not realize she was living somewhere other than Georgia. We think she was OK with that; at least she never mentioned that she'd moved north! She always seemed happy wherever she was! We were just happy to have her with us. Most of our life we had not lived too close to her so it gave our young children a chance to know their Nanny in a way they could not have otherwise.

Mother was a 'fun' person. Her *sense of humor never left her.* That was a trait that always marked her life - she was a happy loving soul! Life had been very good to her, until recently. She had been blessed many times over. She had had a great marriage - fifty-nine years. She and my Daddy had married on August 19, 1919

IV. TALL TALES

at Holbrook Campground where my grandfather Johnson had served the Holbrook Circuit several years before. As far as anyone knows it was the only wedding ever performed there. They had walked the 'sawdust' trail down to the altar after the three o'clock worship service. How I wish we had photos of that day!

Before Mother came to live with us she had broken her hip several years before. After that she had moved a bit slower, graduating from her own pace of walking to a walker, then finally to a wheelchair. Her eyesight was fading. She never complained but she often commented that *'someone should turn on some lights in here.'* She did not let those 'inconveniences' hinder her from enjoying people. . .her ability to carry on an intelligent, *and often quite funny,* conversation was phenomenal. I never knew her to meet a stranger! She had a dry wit about her, so she had met her match when my husband came into the family. They literally gave each other a 'run for the money.' There was never a dull moment when the two of them were together! They kept us all in stitches, with their 'digs' at each other. I don't know how each of them could think up such things to say, so fast that the other one often had no chance for rebuttal!

Given the crisis of this particular morning, I made arrangements to be off work all day, knowing this was an urgent call! When I walked into her room, Mother knew me, and as par for her, greeted me with a smile, glad to see me. It was not the smile that I was accustomed to seeing. . .it was obviously tagged with pain. I rushed to her bedside, hugged her and pulled my chair as close to her bed as I could. She reached for my hand, as best as she could, considering all the tubes that were tied to her frail body.

Our hands stayed clasped for the longest time. The warmth of our bodies touching brought moisture to our hands but we never turned loose! We could almost feel each others heart beat. There were no words between us - just the flow of mother-daughter love that had bound us for fifty-three years. I was born the last of her four daughters when she was forty-two - the *whoopsie!* Be that as it may, *I never felt I was an accident. . .*we both felt God had had a hand in it! I'm just glad it happened that way; I wouldn't have traded it for any another plan. What a blessing she was for my life!

The nurse came in to brief me on what was transpiring at the time. The monitors were beeping loudly. Mother was go*ing in and out* of consciousness, perhaps not hearing the 'real story.' I was trying to piece it all together from the Nurse. I tried to be calm, and take all of this in, one heart-beat at a time; meanwhile the heart monitor was showing significant signs of erratic beating. My eyes were glued to the machine, but my ears had to stay open for the news I knew I was not ready to hear.

I was given the options that were ahead. I pondered them. Mother already had a pacemaker but it was no longer keeping her heart in rhythm. They could replace it but that would be risky at her age. That did not seem a wise choice or a chance to take. Run more tests? Put her through more pain and suffering to borrow nothing more than a few hours or days? NO!

Her life had been 'over the top' with joy and fullness of living. She had enjoyed every moment of the ride. Sure there had been the typical hard knocks along the way, but her faith had steadied her grip. *She came from strong stock!* Taking every setback in stride, she looked at them as 'lessons,' preparing her for the next big step, knowing she was on solid ground with God as her guide.

Here I was alone, in the room, with the *'giver of my own life'*-Mother's beautiful body and soul was struggling to hang on. She had always

IV. TALL TALES

been my *best friend*. She knew me backwards and forward. She had always given me good advice, but not the 'bossy' kind. She never pried into the corners of my being. But I always knew 'she knew best' - from experience. True, she had grown up in a totally different era, with different rules to play by, but I trusted her implicitly!

My husband and children were in their own worlds that day - at work and at school. My only sister, was three-hundred miles away, in Georgia, having multiple physical issues of her own. She had had to release the care giving role of our mother to me a year earlier. That had been very difficult for her since they had always lived close to each other and had a close relationship.

Cell phones were not 'in' back in the early 1990's. Well, maybe they were, but they were not common necessities as they are now. I found the nearest pay phone in the lobby. I was scared, like never before. . .scared for Mother. I dreaded making the phone call to tell my sister the 'news.' I shook with grief and fear as I attempted to dial Ruth's number. I did not know how to tell her that the end was rapidly approaching. . . The phone rang several times before she picked up. I told her everything that I had been told. There was a long silence; we both simply tried to get a grip!

There was little or nothing we could do but stand by and wait for the time; I would not leave Mother's side. It looked like Mother would be slipping away within hours. Granted, when you are in that situation, watching your loved one move over into eternity, your mind is so frazzled, just as the winds would be if they trying to blow leaves in opposite directions at the same time. I was being volleyed from one side of the world to the other - all in one moment!

After I had spoken with my sister, I stood in the hallway sobbing until my body shook as though I were having the worst chill of my life. I could not control anything: the tears, the sadness that was engulfing my soul, and the thoughts of *'what should I do next?'*

I did not leave Mother's bedside except to go to the restroom. I do not recall leaving the room for food. . .the nurses brought me drinks when I needed them. If I ate at all that day, it was to 'pick at' the food on the tray that was brought for Mother. Every moment could be Mother's last breath. . .I let my husband know that I would be at the hospital indefinitely. I needed him to be with me, to hold my hand, to listen and wait with me. I was so alone but I knew Jim needed to be at the house to take care of the 'home front' when our teens got home from school, to prepare them for Nanny's impending death and our trip to Georgia for her funeral.

I stayed at her bedside, in my chair. . .the kind of chair that is not welcoming to a tired and stressed out family member! Mother seemed to be coming back into consciousness. Her eyes met mine, she reached for my hand again, squeezed it for all it was worth and said: *'will you stay here and hold my hand while I go? You won't leave me, will you?'*

'NO, Mother, I will never leave you. . .I am here with YOU!' Leaning in to her, I laid my throbbing head on the bed, as close to her head as I could. She closed her eyes, and seemed to relax, knowing *it was OK for her to 'go' now*. She slipped into unconsciousness and toward the end of the day, she met her *Master* face to face.

I was there, watching and waiting, as she crossed the bar. Yet, even so, I was *face to face with my dear Mother*. I saw her walk

IV. TALL TALES

through the door of her new home; she was with all her loved ones, especially my Daddy. I could just see him - he was smiling for all he was worth. He wrapped her in his arms just as he had when they married seventy-four years ago. I was at peace knowing they were *'in high heaven!'* I could just hear everyone singing *Amazing Grace*. And if cats go to heaven, Granny's cat, SPUD, was right there, alongside the angels, purring til his hair stood on end!

I slowly slipped toward the door, hesitating for quite some time. I just stood there, letting the tears roll; my face, and soul were being bathed in saltwater! I could do no more. I waved to her: *"I'll see you soon, Mom."*

I would not trade April 13, 1993 for anything!

Becky Williams Buckman
April, 2009

DOWN THE LINE

THE ELEVATOR

It was October, 1995. The elevator stopped on the fourth floor at a Nashville, Tennessee hospital. The door opened. "Going down?" someone said. Looking very down trodden, my Orthopedic Doctor stepped on. A fellow surgeon looked at him rather quizzically. He'd never seen his friend look so forlorn. "What is going on, Joe?"

My Doctor shook his head, then put his hands in his face, and let his burden flow free. "I wish I knew! I have a patient who had a hip replacement a few weeks ago; now infection has set in and we cannot seem to get it under control. I've tried every antibiotic possible. The incision area opens wider every day!"

"I've been doing surgery over twenty years; I have never had this happen. I just don't understand what went wrong. My only option is to take the prosthesis out, to see if that is the problem, but I don't know what other complications I'll find. It appears to be staph infection. I've just left her room; she's being prepared for surgery now. I'm going now to scrub."

The other surgeon said "Please tell me more about this case before you go any farther. This sounds very serious! I know a Physician at St. Thomas who has a patient who would not respond to antibiotics either. If you are willing to go to my office now, I will get in touch with him." Immediately my surgeon felt a slight ray of hope. His mind was raging like wildfire with questions: 'maybe there was a way out... should I pursue this? What could it hurt?'

Upon arriving in his friend's office, the Doctor had his nurse page the well-known Dermatologist at St. Thomas. Within minutes he was on the phone with him describing my case in great detail. In less than an hour my surgeon and the Dermatologist were in my hospital room, ready to examine the 'rare bird' who was lying there crying, with a high fever, in great distress, waiting to be wheeled down to surgery!

Jim was there, pacing the floor, as nervous as a cat in a room full of rocking chairs. He'd been through so much with me through the years; he didn't know how much more of this he could take. He took a deep breath when the *two* Physicians walked in. Now, what did this mean?

After being briefed by my Orthopedic Doctor, the Dermatologist examined the gaping red wound from my hip replacement surgery. It was now grossly infected; I had a 12" incision which dug into my thigh at least 3" deep; it presented itself as raw meat. Jim and I were so afraid; I had always had trouble healing after surgery. Would I dance around death's door again, as I had when our last child was born, nineteen years earlier? It seemed like a repeat performance. God forbid!

After a brief moment, the dermatologist looked at my surgeon and said that to go back in to remove the prosthesis would only cause 'the fire' to rage more. It would cause the infection to spread into other parts of my body, perhaps never to be contained. Antibiotics were definitely not the answer. *Then what was?*

My surgeon looked at me and Jim, wondering the same thing. The Doctor from St. Thomas told us that it appeared that I had a *very rare condition,* which was not curable, only treatable with steroids. *Pyoderma gangrenosum.* He suggested that the upcoming surgery be canceled; that a regimen of steroids be given to me for the next 24 hours. My body's response would determine if I actually had that condition. If my fever dropped, and the infection seemed to be held at bay, then he would treat me with steroids until such time as the wound would be ready for plastic surgery!

With tears in my eyes, and a trembling hand clinched to Jim's, I laid there in an ocean of emotions. . .fear, anxiety, yet with a slight feeling of relief that there might be something that could be done to save my leg and my life! This meant that a longer hospitalization was ahead, but it would be worth it if I could just be healed.

After a long sleepless night, I saw the dawning of a new day. I wondered when I would know something for sure. Would I really be one of the *'one in a million'* people who had this rare condition? The day dragged on. It seemed the Doctors would never come. Each moment I prayed asking God for the strength to live through whatever was on my plate!

Jim and I feared the worst but hoped for the best. In our minds we re-lived those six weeks after our youngest daughter had been born, when I was in a very similar situation; we wondered if *'this diagnosis'* was what I had had nineteen years ago? At that time, the Doctors at Wilford Hall Hospital in San Antonio had simply said I must have had gas gangrene, and that I was very prone to infection. They had checked me for diabetes, thinking perhaps that was why I didn't heal. But that was not the case.

When the two Doctors arrived, my fever had dropped; the open wound appeared to have come to a standstill - it had not increased in size. We all were so relieved! Maybe we were on the right track. I shared with both Doctors the scenario of 1976 with my C-section incision not healing. The facts were parallel!

IV. TALL TALES

I did not have to have more surgery. . .not that day, at least. It would take about a month for the wound to be ready for plastic surgery, but we all began to see the rainbow at the end. Prayers were being answered; just as they were in 1976!

The days rolled by, ever too slowly; each day was full of torture. The treatment of the incredible wound was the worst hell I had known since 1976! The 'crater' in my leg was so large that stitches were out of the question. The raw skin had to be 'kept alive' - the tissues had been literally dying for the two previous weeks. I cannot *(nor would I try)* describe the treatment I had to undergo, every four hours, twenty-four/seven for a month or more.

I didn't think I could stand or go through that process one more time. I had survived that same hell years ago, *when I didn't think I could!* But that time, I was too sick to know how close to death I was. And here I was going through it again. *How? Why?* I do not know. Outside of God's grace, healing power, and *the miraculous intervention* of the 'one' surgeon on that elevator, I would not be here to tell the story!

Why did I live? How did I get through it, with a desire to keep living? Why did two surgeons end up on the same elevator, at the same time? And why did they begin a conversation about me? And how was it possible that my Surgeon was able to touch base with the Dermatologist who knew the answer to our dilemma - all within a matter of 20 minutes?

The 'timing' was incredibly miraculous. Another 10-15 seconds sooner, or later - or without the 'middle man' / the friend of my surgeon, on that elevator, or without the two surgeons consulting on my case, everything would have been different. If any one thing had changed, the entire picture would have had different colors! Not only for my life, but for the life of my husband, and children. I shudder to think what might have been! *None of that was coincidence.* The way I see the picture: *for some reason, my life was spared.* I would live. Why?

Somehow, in my wildest imagination, I could not understand the *why* of all of this at the time. The next six weeks were long, tedious 'out of the ballpark' plays, but when I got to home plate the game had been won. I walked off the field that day knowing I would have this 'rare condition' the rest of my life but we knew the Doctors now knew how I had to be treated. *That was 'healing' enough for me;* my body and my soul had been restored!

That was eighteen years ago. Today I know, without any doubt, why *my life was spared, for the second time!* I give God the glory for the things he has done, in and with my life!

Becky Williams Buckman
September, 2013

IV. TALL TALES

FINE WITH FLORENCE

People have come into my life *'for a reason,'* which at the time I could not explain. Florence was one of those. From her I learned things I never knew I would *need to know*. It was like an internship, preparing me for my future. But it was worth every minute of it!

She and her husband were getting up in years, and had moved from Boston to Kentucky to be near her son. Within weeks of their move, her husband had a massive heart attack and suddenly she was a widow. She had not wanted to leave the north, she had not wanted to 'downsize' from their luxurious and prestigious home to a patio home one-fourth the size they had owned up north.

She was appalled at the *country life* she had to try to melt into! Moving to 'redneck' country, and losing her mate, all within weeks of each other was such a culture shock that it threw her into severe depression. It was at that point that I came into her life…and she into mine.

Within six months of our move to Kentucky, my husband's health began to decline at a rapid pace. He wasn't able to work the majority of the nineteen years we lived there. We had two teenagers, in seventh and ninth grades, the most expensive years of our lives were facing us! I needed to step up to bat and supplement our income, somehow. Any way I could!

I scoured the classified ads of our local paper daily. I found a job that I felt I could qualify for; I called the number, had an interview the next day and was immediately hired as a caregiver for Florence.

DOWN THE LINE

What a character she was! In her early eighties, she was *a very classy lady,* in every respect. She had extreme pride in herself, always dressed in style. They had been used to a very wealthy social life. They had a 'top of the line' car. Her home was immaculate. She had many fine things, beautiful clothes, and was used to having luxuries that I had never known, i. e. until I got so 'old' that I couldn't do my own toenails! But she had had it all . . . pedicures, manicures, massages - the works!

Now, when she looked out her living room window, all she saw was a county road and open fields across the road. Occasionally, deer would cross the fields before her very eyes! The closest grocery store and 'filling station' was just up the road. It had been there for many years, owned and operated by a family whose house was built on to the store. My, what a disaster that 'sight' must have been to Florence; she was 'in the sticks' in Plano, Kentucky. None of this added up to her dreams of retirement years.

When I was interviewed, I had been briefed on a few things that I could expect. But upon meeting Florence, I knew I had a real challenge on my hands. Her driving privileges had been taken away. . . that, in itself, knocked her down a notch or two. She felt imprisoned by the shackles of life in the south! *Culture* wasn't draped from the power lines where we lived, like it had been in Boston. Street lights were unheard of. Sidewalks were out of the question.

For the most part, I worked 'on call.' Our home in the country was just a few miles away so when she called I knew I needed to go – if not then, very soon! Often when I walked in she was in tears so we sat on the sofa and I listened, sometimes for an hour. *She was alone…so alone,* and so lost! There was little I could say – I had not *'been there, or done that'* but I tried to

IV. TALL TALES

grab hold of *the feeling* that was pulling her like the undertow. When she finally calmed down, I began trying to engage her in conversation.

She had a piano so that was a 'starting point' - a way to talk about something we had in common, the love of music. Florence was a wonderful pianist. She loved to play for me, and would talk to me about all the times she had entertained her friends in Boston. Her hands had become arthritic and were twisted, causing her some difficulty, but she became a new person when she could perform for me! She was used to being *'on a pedestal'* in the north; in the South, she felt *buried underground!*

I, too, loved to play the piano but I had let my skills slide while raising our family, so this opened a door for me. We'd go to the piano and play for each other - we could light up a dark night, like a shooting star streaming across the sky. We spent hours lost in our own little world. The therapeutic value it brought was immeasurable.

Healing comes with *the sound of music.* That was the one sure fire way I could draw her out of her misery; it helped her achieve relief from her anger, from her hatred of life in the south, from the blizzard she had found herself in.

Florence had to take medications for her illnesses; she was in psychiatric counseling the entire time I worked with her. We spent hours going to Doctor appointments, shopping and taking care of her errands. Once she found she could *'trust me,'* one step at at time, she opened up to me, pouring out her many disappointments at this stage in life – a time when she and her husband had planned to travel, and enjoy the benefits of being so wealthy! But…life had dealt her a difficult set of cards. She didn't know how to play *'that hand.'* She was bitter, sad, hurt, frustrated, angry, confused, lost, alone. . .she had been in a wreck before she had even hit the road!

All I could do was listen, and try to put myself in her shoes. There is little you can say to someone when you have not walked where they are walking. As I look back I wouldn't have known how to play that hand either. The 'books' don't prepare any of us for that kind of shell shock. Many books are written on 'living life' but very few are written to prepare people to die, or to accept the death of someone you love.

Within a few years Florence had to downsize again due to her health. This time to a retirement home. Another massive culture shock…but the salvation in *that move* was that she was around people and she could still play the piano! It would be easier to make friends there. When she'd lived in the country, she had never made friends with neighbors, nor had she had a social life. She had missed that. Her family and I were the only contacts she'd had with the 'outside world' for the two previous years. After she'd been in the Retirement Home a few months I began to see her beautiful personality emerge, once again. *What a miracle;* it was a joy to visit with her. We were just friends now. I could see she had dropped a lot of her baggage. The load was much lighter, and her visits to the Psychiatrist were not as frequent.

In the country I had been her only friend, but it had been a joy to play that role in her life. She taught me things about 'high class living' that I had never known, nor would ever experience in my own life. In time, she had learned to loosen up, and deal with the deck she'd been given. She learned to let me into her world – and allowed me to share my world with her: a world she had never conceived of. . .the world of the *'common folk'- especially southerners!* She found out that people in the South had

IV. TALL TALES

feelings just like she had: *hurt is hurt, grief is grief,* any way you cut it, regardless of where or how you grow up. In that sense, we both were the winners. Little did I know then that what I had learned from working with her would 'come into play' in my own life, almost detail by detail!

In our retirement years, Jim and I moved to South Carolina to be near our daughter; within the first week he had a stroke. And within three months, he died. Here I was in a new city, a new state, with only my daughter and her new husband here. I was miles away from my other three children, and friends. *I had to start over,* just like Florence!

It was a new journey for me, too; perhaps not as hard for me since I grew up a 'southerner' and simply moved a bit farther south! I look back and see that my time with Florence had been *God's way of helping prepare me* for what I was to face up the road - the roadblocks, the signals, the destination! No, it still did not take the 'edge' off of my grief, nor did it hasten the healing process, except to realize I was not the first woman to become a widow, nor would I be the last. Each one coped, and I could too. I just needed *Time and more Time* along with the determination to keep living and not die on the vine!

It simply proves that everything that happens to us, day by day, is for some reason. We may not know the reason at the time, but someday the picture will be perfectly clear. Things happen in *God's timing,* not ours. Our God works in wonderful, miraculous, and in mysterious ways. An awesome God, he is, for sure!

Becky Williams Buckman
February 13, 2011

'NOTE' THIS

American Author Joseph Campbell once said: *"When you follow your bliss, doors will open where you would have not have thought there would be doors, and where there wouldn't be a door for anyone else."*

In my life I have always followed my bliss, not having any idea what doors it would take me through. I walked through them, but having faith that all would be OK.

IV. TALL TALES

In the spring of 2007 my husband and I moved to Summerville, SC to be near one of our children. Our declining health had been the 'straw' that had become a burden; we were no longer able to keep the 'home place' in Kentucky. It had been our dream-come-true. . .a work of art that had been in progress almost twenty-five years, from the time we sketched out the first rough floor plan, until the last tree and flower had been planted!

We had built our home on thirty-six acres of rolling bluegrass plains, open fields with the sounds of cows, birds, horses, deer, skunks and an occasional red-tailed fox keeping us in tune with nature. The nearest home was almost a half-mile away. It was *our own little sanctuary* where we could walk the aisles of solitude or delve into cheerful conversations as we tilled the soil, spreading myriads of color on what was once bare fields.

It had been heart-breaking for us to leave our little *'mansion on the hilltop'* (not a mansion by Webster's definition!). We had spent thousands of 'happy hours' planning it, building it, and making it a 'garden for our souls.' Not being able to keep it *'blooming in all its glory,'* was literally eating us alive, physically and emotionally.

Moving to an unknown city and state, we were starting a new life in our senior years. All of this was overwhelming. Our youngest daughter and her fiance' were the only two people we knew there. Her wedding was within a month of our arrival; the other three children were coming in for that, so our agenda was already over-booked, simply trying to unpack, find the bare necessities for daily life. Three months earlier, Jim had broken his hip and was still recovering when we moved. It was a 'rough ride' in every sense of the word!

On the third day, after our 'move-in' date, Jim had a stroke; blood clots were in his heart, brains and lungs! He was hospitalized for six weeks. The stroke simply added more stress to the 'brokenness' of our lives. The next three months literally tore us to pieces; we spent more time in the hospital and rehab than we did in our new apartment. With the multiple health issues that he had accumulated over the past twenty-two years, the quality of life had left both of us devastated. Depression wrapped its strong arms around us, squeezing our energies into nothingness. Our minds were so boggled and warped with anxiety that getting through another day was almost more than either of us could tackle! We were grieving. . .daily!

His death came three months after our arrival in Summerville. For him, it signaled *a release from the prison of many health issues*, and moved him into a peaceful and eternal rest! For me, it simply drug me farther into the pits, swallowing me whole. I was farther down than I'd ever been before! Jim had been 'my life' for over forty-six of my sixty seven years! We'd met and fallen in love when I was seventeen - and except for five years, we'd been in each other's life all of that time...*what would I do now?* I was as lost as a needle in a haystack!

I'd been in the caregiver role for so long that I could hardly recall what life was like *'before illness.'* Every waking hour, twenty-four seven, *his needs were my only priority*. I had not had much time to do anything but take care of our necessities. It seemed everything we did revolved around doctors, hospitals, surgeries, medications and medical bills.

Now what? I had time on my hands, like never before in my life! For weeks I was numb, but I simply had to do more of the necessities, endless paperwork, phone calls, trying to wrap up all of the loose ends when a death occurs. I could see nothing beyond

IV. TALL TALES

the moment; I just took one step at a time, sobbing through each one! I could not think of my future, except in terms of me being 'alone' the rest of my life. That in itself was more than I could imagine. . .I had always had a family. After I left home at eighteen, I had always had roommates. *I had never lived alone.* What was I to do when I got out of bed each day? I didn't want to go on living without Jim. '*Why am I still here?*' played over and over in my mind.

The notepads on my desk and by my bed were blank - twenty-four hours a day, with no agenda except to try to make a new life for myself in Summerville, SC. I was no longer a 'couple.' I felt as I were only half a person, left with no limbs to help me function. My heart was lame; I was so restless, everything was out of rhythm. My mind was constantly stumbling over the roadblocks in my path. My soul seemed to have disappeared and my prayers bounced off the walls, often flying back in my face!

Looking at boxes, still unpacked, stacked on top of each other, simply made me cry more. Inside them was all we had 'saved' from our thirty-six years of marriage. I could not bear to open them up. When and if I did, I knew the tears would never stop flowing. So I let them sit - for several months. I simply walked around them, trying to ignore the memories they signified. But you cannot ignore *death*. It is real.

I got by, just one day at a time. The cards, and phone calls came, from friends all over the world. Each one took me back in time, to the '*heavenly history*' of the life and the love we'd always known as a married couple. After each one, I'd slide back into the darkest corners of the world, hiding my hurt, my alone-ness, my lost-ness! Repeatedly, I closed the draperies and went to bed, regardless of the time of day, a glaring sign of depression. I knew the 'sign' quite well, and what to do about it, but *I caved in* to the horrors of it that first year.

Our four-poster canopy bed had been a wedding gift from my parents. It was now my place of escape, for hours on end. Sunlight often did not reach me, nor moonlight by night. I lost myself in the world of books, reading novels, and non-fiction by the dozens, to fill the void that had engulfed me; I was Jonah, inside the whale that had swallowed me whole. I tried to keep the 'world' shut out as best as I knew how. I avoided contact with people as much as possible. I cried at the least little thing - perhaps in the grocery store when I passed the candy aisle: I'd see Jim's 'favorite' bar and would melt just as the candy bar would if left in the sun!

This was not like me - not at all! I had always been very successful in keeping my chin up through any storm we had faced, through losing both sets of parents, and Jim's younger sister. We'd kept the home fires burning for years, taking each hurdle in stride, together. We had been through it all. But when his health began to hit rock bottom, he was unable to do much more than survive on his coffee, cigarettes, and TV. Once Jim made the comment: *"I don't care about anything anymore, and the worst part of that is that I don't care that I don't care!"* That attitude began to eat away at me as well.

Now that Jim was gone, *I 'felt cold, sick, scared'* and unable to pick up the pieces to move on. I had never felt so deserted, so helpless, or angry. Even though Jim had had several 'close calls' with death, during the past eight years, I had always 'brought him home' from the hospital, but the last time, I walked in the front door *alone that night in June.* We had not been here long enough to make friends, or participate in our new community, but a wonderful Methodist Church 'found' us in the hospital

IV. TALL TALES

the week Jim had had his stroke; they began to reach out to us before we had ever visited there! They began to spread some light on the dark shadow of death. That was *the* 'miracle' that helped pull me through that first year!

Before we had gotten here I had looked forward to 'starting over' - to scaling down. We were older and needed to be close to one of our children. I felt good about our choice of moving to South Carolina, but I had not envisioned it like this. How was I to start my life over *alone?*

I was sixty-seven. Until now I had not felt that being that age was so 'old' but now I felt like my life was over too. I just wanted to 'check out' and catch the next bus for eternity! I couldn't bear to think of 'going on' with my life, *without the love of my life!* But, I had to. . .I had no choice in the matter! I simply had to focus on the fact that Jim was free of pain and the misery of his poor health. He had lost his will to live, and depression got the best of him.

I had to deal with my own depression, to get over my pity-party, realizing that he was 'free' of all of his baggage, and I had to get rid of mine! I could not put off 'unpacking' much longer. I had stumbled over boxes for months. I began unwrapping the memories. . .little by little, and began to *try* to make the apartment my 'home.' But it never was. It was still *empty!*

I'd seen an advertisement at our apartment, left by a 'cleaning lady.' I asked her to come clean for me. She brought her four-year old daughter, who was eager to check out everything in the crowded apartment; she found places to go that I didn't know existed! In an effort to 'free up' the cleaning lady to do the job I had hired her to do, I took the little tyke over to the piano, hopefully to entertain her, as well as to keep her out of trouble!

As we played the piano, the mother came over and asked me if I would teach her two older children piano lessons in exchange for weekly cleaning.

It took several moments for it to 'register.' I'd been involved in music all of my life, at church, at home, at school, in college, but I had never taught piano! Both sides of my family had musical talent. I'd studied music in college, and had private lessons in piano, voice and organ. We worked out a plan and I began teaching piano the following week to two of her three children. The youngest child was deaf (with hearing aids at the age of six) and the other child was eight. I was not at all sure I could do this, but I thrive on challenges. I will try anything once and if I fail, I'll shoot for another star!

Soon other children in the apartment complex noticed the children coming to my house, and asked where they were going. The word got around that I was teaching piano, and other children wanted to come as well. And within a few weeks I was *'in business,'* without making any effort. It never occurred to me that I could teach piano, much less open up a Music business. I'd owned several businesses previously and 'doing business' is just that. My public relations experience was an asset so I began to get organized; it filled my thoughts and consumed some of the time that had previously been just *hanging on the line.*

I had always loved and worked with children; they can say the darnedest things to crack you up. They are good at making you forget 'grown up' problems! Now I had a 'reason' to get out of bed - to prepare to teach these precious children. My business began to take off like a rocket ship, with no end in sight. . . and *Ms. B's Music Biz* was officially launched in the fall of 2007. This was fun, fulfilling my need to be back in the 'world of music,' with an added benefit: adding a little cash to the 'kitty!'

By word of mouth, more students came. The business grew from two, to four, to eight students, until I reached the maximum number that I can teach each week - fifteen! All of this was a *'miracle'* dropped in my lonely lap! I would have never dreamed up this idea on my own, much less had the confidence that I could teach piano. I still have to pinch myself to believe it has happened. This was a 'miracle!' I just wish Jim could be here; I think he too, would be as pleasantly surprised as I was.

During my courtship with Jim, I often played the piano while I was waiting for him to pick me up for a date. Before he came in the door, he could hear me playing, and would insist that I continue for a while before we left for our date. Placing his hand on my shoulder, as I played, I could feel the 'warmth' in his heart and I knew our souls were 'connecting.' Even today, each note *I play* seems to rise above the keyboard, reaching upward to heaven, *just for him* - as he watches me play my heart out. That makes it all worthwhile!

Quite often big things come in small packages…and this *gift of teaching piano* was a big thing that came 'two by two,' like the animals in the Ark! Moreover, it changed my life, from being a lost and lonely person, to resurrecting the real 'Becky.' Now I have a constant source of joy, giving me a purpose for living. It keeps me in awe of the way **GOD** worked to heal my broken heart!

God's timing is perfect. My healing began at the piano. The children teach me more than I teach them, I'm sure. They fill my life with 'joy juice' that flows through my body and soul! John A. Logan once said: *"Music is the medicine of the mind."* For me, it truly has been that, and more!

Becky Williams Buckman
May 30, 2013

IV. TALL TALES

KIDS SAY THE DARNEDST THINGS

You just *have* to love kids. Anyone who is 'lacking in love' for them has missed out on the most wonderful creation God made! They are just miraculous little minds that will blow yours off its deer stand. While you are perched up high, they are 'on the level' where things show up just as they are. And be assured, they will tell it like it is, be it great or gross!

What comes out of their little mouths is literally music to my ears. There's nothing pretentious about them. They are smart, much smarter than I ever was, thanks to today's technology. They are quicker than lightening, out of the clear blue sky, and you never know when or where they will strike. They will leave you rolling in the floor with laughter, or with a tear glistening in your eye, 'thinking' seriously about the significance of what came off the press! They have no inhibition whatsoever.

All my life I have gotten a double dose of teasing. It was just 'in the air.' My Father and Mother were 'King and Queen of Teasing,' so early on *I learned to laugh* and watch the world laugh with me. It is the healing ointment for any ailment. Having had my share of ailments, it has surely soothed my soul, and made the ride a lot smoother. I'm sure I'd have become a *'bitter old bitty'* if I had not known how to laugh. Heaven forbid!

All my life I have worked with children and we had a family of four children, so my ears have been tuned in to their 'unexpected' thoughts and expressions. I love it. Just when you think you are drowning in your own misery, they will lift you up by their affirmations – their encouragement and sunshine will squelch any cloud and stomp out the raindrops.

Like most children, I've always had a jar full of questions. As a kid, my dad always said "Becky, you can ask more questions; how can you think up so many?" Mother came to my aid quickly, responding: "well, how do you think she is ever going to learn anything if she doesn't ask?" Kids today are still 'full' of questions!

A young friend has a darling 6 year old who feels I am his own 'grandma Becky.' He was here one day when I was dressed casually, for 'home', not the public. I was wearing a tank top because the heat in South Carolina was topping off well above 100 in August. As he headed to his car, he hugged me. As I was waving good-bye, he looked back at me, yelling: 'Grandma Becky,' what is all that stuff hanging down from your arms?" After his Mother and I quit laughing, I said: *'it is just the wings on my airplane.'* That really confused him, of course. Quizzically, he looked at his Mother and asked what does she mean? I'm not sure what she told him, but I just marked that 'observation' up to the fact that I've lived long enough to have wings. However, I doubt they qualify for being angel's wings.

I was teaching Music at a private school recently, sicker than a blue-blooded horse. The last thing I felt like dealing with was children. The bed was where I really needed to be. But at the end of the day, my perspective had changed. Youngsters can do that for you!

IV. TALL TALES

I barely had a voice above a whisper. I was as raspy as the wolf in Little Red Riding Hood. I explained that my students needed to 'help' me by being extra obedient, quiet and watching for my hand signals. I struggled through 40 minutes of teaching, being a 'clock-watcher' the entire period. Finally, as I was lining them up to leave for the day, these cheerful children brightened my day with:

> "Mrs. Buckman, I hope you get better."
> "Mrs. Buckman, please take your vitamins"
> "Mrs. Buckman, I will pray for you to be well enough to be here tomorrow"
> "Mrs. Buckman, your earrings are so pretty"

The next day at School, we were honoring those who lost their lives in the 9/11 attack in 2001. We were singing *America The Beautiful*. My voice was some better; I was barely singing, but it seemed to croak like the biggest frog in the pond. I soon discovered my pathetic voice had been heard. One child was far too kind in her comment; she said: *"Mrs. Buckman, you have a beautiful voice!"* That was music to my ears! Yes, as poorly as I performed that day, this child still thought I scored 'ok'.

Then another day, I was teaching a piano lesson. I had asked my astute seven year old student to play his piece one more time: "I think we need to look at a few notes." He looked at me with the greatest of concern, and said: "Mrs. Buckman, I think you are tired." Admittedly, I was! I said: "what makes you think that?" His observation and rather honest opinion blurted out: "because you have all those bags under your eyes!" I had to laugh! I'd tried to hide those bags with layers of makeup, but you can't fool a kid. They can see right through you! I'm not rich enough to get a make-over, so *'baggy eyed Becky'* just keeps rolling along.

Recently, a student was playing the 'simple' version of "Ode to Joy," a piece that every beginning student has to learn. She played it very well; I bragged on her. Then she told me that she was planning to try out for the *Middle School for the Arts* here in Summerville next year. (It is a competitive process; children work hard for several years to be good enough to get in.) She told me her cousin had been accepted to that school playing that same very simple piece.

Here is the kicker: With a big smile on her precious face, and her eyes full of delight she said: "Miss Becky, why I bet *you* could even get into the Middle School for the Arts!" WOW - what a compliment that was for me! I had to tell her that *I'm not as smart as a 5th grader* so I probably shouldn't even try out! But it is nice to know my students have some confidence in their teacher!

And at this age I'm sure I'd really be a misfit in an elementary school. I'd love being with all the children, and I could probably handle lunch and recess, but math and science would put

IV. TALL TALES

me in the 'failure' department for sure. I struggled with those two subjects in high school and college. I even had a Math teacher suggest if we had a 'Failure Club' I could probably be the leader! That was *not an encouraging word!* I admit I did not have complimentary words for her: they never hit her ears, but I'm sure GOD knew my thoughts! Yes, I failed Algebra that year. Who wouldn't, with that kind of TLC? If it had been in today's world, I could have sued her for knocking me off my totem pole! In my humble opinion, she was really a bit too old to be influencing my generation. She had sliced my ego like she was slicing tomatoes, and my tears flooded my heart and soul that day. That cut to the core. There's an old saying that: *sticks and stones may break my bones but words can never harm me.* I disagree. Physical wounds heal much faster than harsh words. I guess that teacher's mother never taught her what my parents taught me: *'if you can't say anything nice, say nothing at all.'*

Recently I was visiting my youngest grandchildren. I usually take them a little something for us to 'play with.' Luckily, they are still young enough to find time for me. That in itself, is an ego-booster! They always know I will have something for them, and greet me at the door wondering what 'Memaw' has for them this time.

When I pulled out something for Caleb, his eyes glowed; he came out with this: "Memaw, is this expensive?" I usually try to answer a question with a question so I asked him what did 'expensive' mean to him. "Over a hundred dollars" he replied. My answer: "Well, no, darling, it isn't." The bottom line was it didn't really matter to either of us. We played together, and that was music to my ears.

Not long ago, the TITANIC movie came on TV. My seven yr. old grandson had been very enthralled with it; his curiosity was overwhelming enough to ask me *if I was alive when the Titanic sank!* No, I am not *that* old but I have seen the movie so we had a great *granny* discussion about that tragic event. I was in awe of his take on that scenario! I told him my father was living then and remembered when it sank. In 1912, when it sank he was 19 years old and in the Army. I'd heard him talk about The Titanic many times. It had impacted his life just as JFK's assassination impacted mine in 1963; and like 9/11 has impacted Americans today.

I had a piano student who was exceptionally shy. I had tried for three or four months to draw this student out of her shell. Conversations were nil. I was the 'monologue. . .trying to evoke some response but all to no avail. I had all but given up hope. Until one day. . .

We had worked diligently on her assignments. Time had flown by. When I looked at the clock I was amazed we were out of time. Breaking the silence, I said: *'where did time go?'* She looked at me for a moment, as stoic as always, when out of the clear blue sky, she looked around the piano, on the bench, in her book bag, and finally she lowered the music stand on the piano. . . looking intently to see what was behind it.

Nothing was there. After a few moments she looked at me and quietly said: "Well, *it didn't go there.*" Finally a grin overtook her face. I laughed and she began to let me see her true personality, her subtle sense of humor that had been kept a secret. That day, the silent spell was broken. From then on, it was no longer a monologue, thank goodness!

I hope I never lose my hearing. I would never want to miss the things that come from the mouths of babes! If I did, I would be robbed of one of the greatest joys of my life. I hope children will always be at my feet. They will forever be in my heart.

Becky Williams Buckman
September, 2013

IV. TALL TALES

IT WAS A SHOO-IN

There is a *'shoo-in'* and then there is *'shoe-in.'* Right? In our family we have known both. One was at the wedding of our youngest daughter. The scenario that day fell in both categories!

She and her fiance' had chosen the month of April for her wedding, in Charleston, SC., found a beautiful venue, and put down the required deposit early on. Now that that was done, they could move ahead with other details. Several months later, she got an unexpected phone call that the venue had lost its lease and was no longer available. It was a scramble to find another venue that close to the wedding date.

They settled on a wonderful venue in Mt. Pleasant, SC. They wanted to marry in April, but as they looked at the calendar for the weekends available, there were several major issues. The first weekend included April Fool's Day. *No way* would they choose that weekend. The following weekend was Easter. Her brother was to officiate the wedding and there was no way he could be out of town that weekend.

By this time, they were getting a bit exasperated. The remaining weekends at the venue were already booked. What was the next alternative? They began to explore the option of a week-night wedding! And so, it was: *Monday, April 16th* at six in the evening. Invitations went out in due time, but it was not long until some of the guests began inquiring if there had been a misprint. No! Nothing was amiss.. . .after all, *a wedding is a wedding,* anytime, day or night, or in any season; the couple would be united in love, 'for better for worse, for richer for poorer, in sickness and in health.'

That scenario was *a 'shoo-in'* - easy enough!

DOWN THE LINE

I am a 'browser' shopper, and had found my wedding attire before we moved to South Carolina. I was not even shopping for my dress. It just 'jumped out' at me. It was a perfect size, color, and the price was right. Shoes to match were easy enough, and the perfect purse was on a shelf, just waiting for me! When I got the dress home from the store, I realized the jewelry I'd worn at the last family wedding would be perfect for the dress!

This was the second *shoo-in*. It gets better as we move along!

Members of the wedding party had to travel from the west coast to the east coast, and everywhere in between. Each one had had their measurements taken at a local shop in their area, and told their attire could be picked up in Charleston on Sunday prior to the wedding. One less thing to have to pack.

That was easy enough! Another *shoo-in!*

For almost a year, we had been planning to move to Charleston just waiting on our Kentucky home to sell. The wedding was less than a month away, when a suitable apartment became available to us. It seemed everything was coming together, despite all the roadblocks that often crop up in times like these!

Perfect timing: another *shoo-in?*

My husband, Jim, had fallen in December (prior to the upcoming wedding) It left him with a broken hip, six weeks of therapy and a lot of frustration for all of us. He was still in 'recovery mode' when had to 'get moving' to South Carolina for the wedding.

I'm known as *the organizer* and *list maker.* I'd been packing up things for a year!

IV. TALL TALES

Some things to go in the moving van, some things to go in the car with us as we made the long trip, and some things to just 'leave' for the dumpster!

Jim had been fitted for his tuxedo, shirt, tie etc. but all the groomsmen were to get their own black patent shoes. No problem. Jim had a pair that had rarely been worn so I packed them in the 'wedding suitcase' that would travel with us in the car. I wasn't about to trust the moving van with our clothes for the wedding!

I had everything I assumed we would need, both on the road, and until our moving van arrived a week later. We headed south early one morning, late in March, leaving the beautiful land and 'home place' that we had dreamed of for years; it had been custom designed and built for the special needs of our family. It had been our *fellowship hall* for friends and family. If those walls could talk, I'm sure they would tell plenty of 'tall tales.'

We had thought we would live out our remaining years there but life had not turned out that way. As we locked the doors behind us, neither of us could utter a word; we were swallowed up in an ocean of emotions! The 'mix' was as varied as the ingredients of a dump cake simply piled one on another, How could we possibly know our own feelings, or those of our spouse - much less express it or deal with it? Both of us were *numb* from the impact of the whirlwind that surrounded this move. I wasn't sure my body had energy enough to crank the car, much less make the drive to South Carolina!

Within the first week of our arrival in our new state, Jim had a stroke and was in a rehabilitation program for the next three weeks. He had incurred blood clots in his heart, lungs, and brain. There was no guarantee that he would be able to go to the wedding. *Now what?*

A lot of juggling went on during those weeks trying to rehab Jim to the point of being able to be at the wedding. Between the hip that was still not totally healed, and the stroke he could not walk our daughter down the aisle! Our son, Jim was the Officiating Minister; our other son, Tim was to be a groomsman, but he would also need to walk his sister down the aisle. He 'wore three or four hats' that day. He wheeled his Dad down the aisle, then walked me down, and finally, he took Apryll on his arm to meet David at the altar. He was in charge of the music too! All of that took some juggling, for sure. But, it all came together beautifully, *literally, by the sheer grace of God,* and with the prayers of many, from all over the world.

All of that had to be a shoo-in, for sure!

When the minister asked: *"Who giveth this woman to be wed?"* Jim and I stood up and said: *"we do."* Tim then took his place alongside the other groomsmen. Then we began to relax and watch the wonder of it all, meanwhile being washed in the glory of love.

*To back up a bit:

Our son, Tim had flown in from Denver the day before the wedding, and had gotten his wedding attire, he had even checked to be sure it fit. Suddenly he realized there were no shoes. He asked Apryll: *'Where are my shoes?'* She reminded him that he was to provide his own shoes. *"Oh, no,"* he said, *"I don't have any dress shoes with me. I thought they came with the tux; all I have is my boots!"* It was Sunday - the Tuxedo shop was closed!

IV. TALL TALES

Early the next morning, he called to arrange to drop by and get shoes on the way to the venue. That did not seem to be a problem. We would get them after we picked Jim up at the Rehab hospital. We left several hours early so we could help Jim dress. He was still confined to his wheelchair and unable to walk.

Tim and a wonderful hospital employee got Jim 'dressed to a *t.*' He looked as handsome as he did on our own wedding day! Now, we just had to put his black patent shoes on his feet. I'd made sure they were shining like crystals. You could even see your reflection in them! But, there was a slight problem. . .even with black silk socks, his feet would not shrink enough to get his feet inside, even with the laces undone! Several of us worked for more than a few minutes, but it was to no avail! *"Oh well, no problem. . .we are on our way to the tuxedo shop anyway. We'll just get him a pair of shoes also."*

I am basically organized, the 'listmaker' in the family but it had never occurred to me to have Jim try on his shoes before the wedding day! It had not been a concern of Jim's - he depended on me to have my act together. But both of us had been running on *'overload'* for the past year. I look back now and wonder 'how' we even got this far south, with any sense left at all!

While we were discussing the issue of Tim and Jim not having shoes for the wedding, the hospital employee suggested that Jim just wear those nice white NIKE shoes - the ones he'd been wearing to the gym every day! After all, they were new, and had never been worn outside of the hospital. His theory: *'why pay to rent such expensive shoes for two hours when you have a new pair of Nike shoes?'* (It made sense, saved time and money, and who would even notice?) Jim was perfectly OK with that idea. . .and at that point, I was ready to get the show on the road! Our daughter would be just as married as if her Dad had on black patent shoes! So, the NIKE shoes were on, all laced up and Jim was ready to be rolled down the aisle.

A 'shoe-in!'

IV. TALL TALES

I looked at my watch. Time was running out, we needed to get Tim's shoes, and on to Mt. Pleasant for the 6 p. m. wedding. About that time, my brainwaves began to roll. I thought I recalled our son wearing a size 12 shoe. We had a size 12 there in the hospital room! *"Try on your dad's shoes, son; they just might fit!"* What would be the odds? Yes, you are right! He put them on, they fit well enough that he thought he could get through his sister's wedding with them.

Now there was another *'shoe-in!'*

We got to the wedding. The bride and her attendants were dressing, helping each other, with zippers, hairpins, jewelry, and finally they were ready to get on their shoes and walk down the aisle. The two attendants had matching dresses, but they too, were to choose their own shoes. Neither had discussed with each other what shoes they'd selected. When they opened their shoe boxes, their shoes were almost identical! I was astounded! I couldn't believe this.

Another shoe-in?

Now it was time for the bride to put on her shoes! Within minutes of six p. m. she slipped into her carefully chosen shoes. Having recently suffered from a broken foot, heels were not a good choice. She had to be comfortable for walking down the aisle and to dance the night away with her beloved! Let's just say: *they weren't white,* but only the 'gals' in the wedding party and her husband knew her secret!

That was the last *'shoe-in!'*

No one knew that Tim's shoes were not from the Tuxedo shop, nor are we sure if anyone noticed Jim had on his new white

DOWN THE LINE

NIKE shoes or that our daughter didn't have on heels! It really did not matter! We were all there in one 'fashion' or another!

All of God's chillen' had shoes!

Becky Williams Buckman
April 16, 2010

IV. TALL TALES

BLIND MAN'S BLUFF

I've lived in a lot of houses. We've always had blinds at our windows. But until I moved to South Carolina I had never known blinds would *'eat'* things. Well, they do!

I began wearing glasses in elementary school, and after three eye surgeries I still don't have great eyesight, but I have not been declared legally blind. I will admit to looking straight at something, and not seeing it, particularly if I'm in a tizzy to get out the door for an important date, but I'm not 'alone in that ballpark.' It even happens to the younger generation. Sometimes we think we are 'losing it!'

Once I had to be checked out by my Physician to see if I had lost my marbles. He said, "actually, NO, you are 'off the scale' when it comes to your test score. . .you knew the answers even before I finished asking the question; you scored more points than was possible." (*OK, folks, that is a true fact; I didn't make that up!*) I just wish I'd been that smart in high school and college. I might could have gotten a good scholarship, but oh well, better late than never.

    * Back to the 'blinds' now.

Last winter I got some terrible bug that laid me flat for almost 10 days. I don't remember much about the first few days, for sure. I had been to a concert and when I drove in my driveway, I recall my cell phone ringing. I stopped the car, but sat there for about thirty minutes chatting with my best friend. I had an unusually bad headache with piercing pain behind my eyeballs. So I slid my glasses to the top of my head.

Once inside, I put down my purse, and other things I'd brought in from the car. Went to the office, turned on the computer, let the blinds down. I worked in the office about an hour and then hit the bed. Except for the headache, I didn't feel sick. Just very tired.

Saturday morning, another story! I tried to dress so I could teach piano, but that was hopeless! I canceled all lessons and went back to bed, slept the majority of the day, and ate little or nothing for the next two days. By Monday, I knew I was sicker than a skunk who had inhaled his own aroma.

I needed to go to the bank but I could not find my glasses. I looked and looked in every possible place they had ever 'rested.' They were nowhere to be found. I won't drive without my glasses so I grabbed my sun-glasses. It was a cold, dark and rainy day. I crept my way to the bank 'in the dark' - maybe not the wisest thing I'd ever done, but *my strong independent will* always pushes me! Perhaps I could have called a friend, but why inconvenience someone when it is just a five minute errand?

I was getting sicker by the minute. I passed the Urgent Care facility and knew I had to get in there quickly! When I walked in with my sun-glasses on I was the center of attention, being 'looked at' rather strangely, of course. Who wears sun-glasses on a day like this?

I was checked in quickly. When all the 'vital signs' were taken everyone realized what a basket case I was! I was very dehydrated, and had multiple other issues. After four hours I was dismissed. In the downpour, I made my way to the Pharmacy, then home to guzzle down the 'horse pills.' I've never figured out why some pills are so small you can barely see them, and others are big enough to make you gain weight! Go figure.

IV. TALL TALES

I knew I had to find the missing glasses sometime. I got tired of people asking me why I had sunglasses on inside! I emptied every trash can, thinking they might have fallen into one of them. No luck. The next week I had the cleaning lady to move all the furniture, check under all the cushions, under my bed. Still, my glasses did not show up. Where in the ??? could they be? I had been not been anywhere, except to the Doctor, since Friday night. It was a mystery.

This wildness went on for days. Finally, after 3 weeks, I ordered new glasses, much to my dismay! The 'lost pair' was hardly a year old but I had no choice but to dole out the money for new ones! I gritted my teeth all the way, thinking how could anyone lose a pair of glasses when confined to the house. I'd been too sick to even need them. Was I really *'losing it'* upstairs?

Sometime later that spring, I was working in the office after sundown. I always let the blinds down in the evening. So, as normal, I pulled them down. *Clunk! Something hit the floor.* I had nothing in my hands, nor had I knocked anything off the desk which sat in front of the window. Being so near-sighted, I could not see what fell. I was clueless. . .things falling from the ceiling! Now this was getting scary!

I was not sick but I knew I was 'seeing things' - without my glasses on! I was as surprised as an elephant trying to swim in a kiddy pool. I looked down to see my 'lost glasses' on the floor, in pure and simple disbelief. Where did they come from? I had let those blinds up and down twice a day for the past two months. I looked around the area, and there was no place those glasses could have been all that time, except trapped *IN THE BLINDS!*

YES, that is what I said. *NO*, I could not believe it either; to be real honest, it was a freaky scenario. I hesitate to tell it for *'truth,'* but it is. However, I don't have any witnesses, so you will just need to trust me! I didn't know that eye-glasses could be so sneaky and hide for so long. Nor I did not know that BLINDS would *'eat'* anything that got in their way!

Hindsight is always better than foresight. In hindsight, the way I SEE this mystery is:

> That Friday night when I came in from the concert, and let the blinds down, the glasses, which had been sitting on top of my head, decided to 'rest' in between the slats! How I could have overlooked them for six weeks is still a mystery. Why had they never fallen out before now? IF the cleaning lady had dusted the blinds like she was supposed to, perhaps I wouldn't have had to buy new glasses.

Oh well! Who knows? Maybe I was playing 'Blind Man's Bluff' the whole time. I always always did love to play games, but who would have thought I would have been *blind* that long?

Becky Williams Buckman
June, 2013

IV. TALL TALES

I LIVE WHERE I AM

At a recent Reinhardt College reunion I asked a friend where he lived now. He said *"I live where I am, but my house is just up the road."* What a testimony that is. He has his feet 'on solid ground' for sure!

To live, wherever our feet take us, wherever our minds or souls fly, there we live. Home is in the heart, and can never be left behind. Sure, the house we lived in as a child, or young person is in our past and perhaps no longer standing. Our house is nothing more than a temporal dwelling. It too shall pass, just as our bodies shrivel and die.

When our son, Tim, was almost 5 years old, my father died. He didn't understand why. I tried to explain it on *his level*. I told him that *Granddaddy's house,* his body, i. e., had just gotten run down, and was in great need of repair. It had been repaired many times, but this time, it just couldn't be fixed! Tim was old enough to have some good memories of my father and I wanted him to understand that my father's death was not a bad thing: it was *a relief* from being sick; now he had been healed, he had a healthy body and was in heaven.

Meanwhile, I was struggling with my own grief. I was going to miss my Dad so much. I was his "baby". All of us would miss *Granddaddy,* but I knew his spirit would always be with me. I can think of no better role model! He had such an impact on my life, as I watched him go through life, *living where he was* at the moment!

He was a devoted husband and father; he was a fantastic business man. As a young man he began his own business by having a *'rolling grocery store'* in the Freehome community, in north

Georgia, where he grew up. His family owned a farm and had a big garden to provide food for the family of thirteen. My dad would gather vegetables from the garden, put them in a wagon and went door to door selling them to neighbors.

After he married, he bought his first grocery store in Atlanta, and through the years he owned other stores there; his last one was Williams Food Store in Woodstock, Georgia. He truly served the community. He was an honest man and was highly respected by people of all ages, race and creed. He was not a 'Sunday Christian' - *he lived his faith daily.* His leadership skills were displayed in his church and community organizations throughout his life. When he was seventy-six he went to the United Nations in Washington, DC to be a Youth Counselor for a week. What zest for life!

When I was a teenager, (and he was in his early sixties) he was always 'ready to roll' with me, even after a long hard day at work. He took me, and my friends all over the county to Youth Fellowship meetings, or school functions. He never complained or asked 'why' I thought I had to *go to every school or church function.* (I had followed in his footsteps, being involved in dozens of organizations). I often wonder where he got the energy!

He was a Veteran of W. W. I., having joined the military forces from Cherokee County, Georgia. During and after W. W. II he worked as a civilian, for several years, in Charleston, SC. My mother, sister and I stayed behind, but he came home periodically for a weekend visit. We visited him in that historic city several times. Little did I know *then* that many years later my daughter would work on the same Naval Base, as a civilian. Nor did I know that my retirement years would bring me to the Charleston, SC area.

IV. TALL TALES

During his service in Charleston he spent many lonely hours at night, and on weekends in a woodworking shop. We have many beautiful pieces of woodwork that my father crafted. In his retirement years, he loved finding old furniture that had been dropped at the dump. In his truck, he would haul it home and refinish it into a beautiful antique! His mind, nor his body, was ever idle.

He also lived his life fully through his musical talent. He sang, as did most of his family. His musical ability still "lives" in the life of his children, and grandchildren. *My Daddy lived where he was* until the day his soul came to rest in November, 1978.

It is my goal to follow in his footsteps: *to live where I am,* just as he did, and to dance through life, until my last breath is taken!

Becky Williams Buckman
August, 2009

BIRTHDAYS AND SUCH

You're getting *old* when you wake up and don't remember it is your birthday…until you get on FACEBOOK and see that your 'friends' and family remembered it! Well, you can't be 'that old' if you still know how to turn the computer on, and how to get into FB, can you? *So not to worry. . .*since every day that you get out of bed you are a day older, and it isn't even your birthday! What's the big deal anyway?

When you are my age, *special days* don't mean the same as they did when you were not quite as young or *wise*. Now you look at *each day* as very special!

After all, you made it to the floor, without falling out of bed, or dropping your false teeth – the ones you forgot to 'take out' for their nightly cleaning last night! And you remembered who you were when you saw that face in the mirror, and wondered *"how can I still look that bad, after 10 hours of sleep?"*

You get to the kitchen, without your glasses, and without stumbling over the recliner. Better still, after pushing 4 buttons on the coffee pot, you found the *right one* to turn it on, and finally heard the drips, and smelled the aroma, telling you that you really are going to be able to 'move' those old bones enough to get to the Doctor appointment today.

Coffee down, and glasses found, you wonder what else you have to do today, thinking if I forgot that it was my birthday, I must have forgotten something else! I'm usually more organized than this…

Then, after four trips to your closet you found clothes that fit, and 'almost' match; next you make several rounds in the

IV. TALL TALES

bathroom, apply a heavy dose of makeup, not only on your face, but on the bruises on your arms, knowing for sure the Doctor will wonder if you have been in a dog fight with someone. (Well, he should know you live alone, and you don't own a dog....that brown spots and bruises come with the territory)

Of course, the Doctor will 'know' you are older when he sees your chart and says *'so today is your birthday. What are you doing to celebrate?"* Your answer: *"I'm paying for your new convertible...so I assume I'm getting a ride home in it. I really don't have the money for a taxi today!"*

He looks at you, quite concerned....knowing for sure you are getting older, and might need to take the competency test before you leave the office! He pulls out a sheet of paper, and asks you to put the numbers 1-12 on the CIRCLE in the center of the page, making a clock. You do it, perfectly; then he asks you to put the hands on the clock indicating it is 10:45 a. m. You do that, only to remind him that 10:45 a. m. looks the same as 10:45 p. m.

AH HA....you've got him in a 'tight spot!'

In disgust, he throws his hands up and says, *"I give up, you got me on that one...You are in good shape, maybe better than me! You're dismissed. I'll see you next year, and by the way, we've called a taxi for you. It's on 'the house' today. Have a great birthday."* The yellow-cab was at the curb waiting, but the top wasn't down! Oh well, that's LIFE in the slow lane.

Becky Williams Buckman
April 29, 2013

IF. . .

It is human nature to say: *'if. . .'* or ask *'why. . .?'* when things happen the way they do. We beat those two words to a pulp, yet never seem to get the 'juice' out of them!

My husband was a man of strong convictions. He didn't stand on the corner to preach; if you heard him, you would have to be listening closely. Yet, he was a deep thinker and he had a lot to say. He was right about so many things.

In our fifty years of knowing each other, hundreds of things happened to us, none of which we could explain, even if we had another hundred years! We were constantly in awe of the way our lives played out - the way the die was cast. He always said: "if any *one thing* in your life or mine had changed, we would not be who we are today, or where we are today, nor would our life together be the same."

We were both convinced things happened to each of us, for a reason, but it was not up to us to question *'why.'* Or to think: "*IF I had just done this. . .or not done that, things would have been better.*"

Before I married Jim, I was prone to analyze and critique my actions, trying to convince myself I could have done better but I finally learned, from him, that it was no use trying to figure it all out. He was so right. There is no harm in learning from 'mistakes' but there is no use in crying over spilled milk either!

Probing around with 'if' and 'why' can drive anyone insane; it is merely wasting time and energy that would best be used giving God the glory for the food dished up on your plate! At the time, it might look like spinach (ugh) but once it is digested and fully integrated into your system, it provides growth.

IV. TALL TALES

As we grew older (and had time!) we 'walked down memory lane' quite often. Things like this came to mind:

> *What if Jim's military assignment had been 'correct' and he had not been stationed at Dobbins Air Force Base? (YES, his *orders* were for some other base!)
> *What if Jim had not visited my church?
> *What if he had not taken the 'dare' to ask me out when I was already going steady?
> *What if I had turned him down?
> *What if his roommate had not mailed the 'nasty' letter Jim wrote to me?
> *What if I had ignored his *one last try* to mend broken fences?
> *What if we had chosen to not have children?
> *What if we had not gone on a Marriage Encounter Weekend?
> *What if we had not gone to Okinawa and shared Marriage Encounter Ministry?

Our *what if's* could go on and on. . .but every time we 'rehearsed' those factors (in our memory walk) and saw how they played out, we knew God had a plan for both of us - *a plan for our lives to be 'one in the spirit, one in the Lord.'*

All *we* had to do was go along with the plan. . .and *every time*, we rejoiced together, knowing all the pieces of the big puzzle fit together perfectly. There was no reason to say IF, nor ask WHY? It simply was what it was! *Amazing grace!*

Becky Williams Buckman
February 13, 2013

DOWN THE LINE

LOST AND FOUND

I don't recall getting lost as a child, or as a teenager. As a young adult, a few times. And as a 'senior citizen' it has been more than a few! (but *isn't that part of life,* at this age?) I was never so 'lost and alone' as I was when we moved to Summerville, South Carolina.

We had an empty nest; our four children were living in four different states, from the east coast to the west, and we were in yet another. We had to leave our home in Kentucky, after nineteen years. We'd never lived anywhere that long. We had moved six or seven times before but the circumstances had never been so difficult or overwhelming as they were in 2007.

After Jim's heart attack in 1985, cancer struck him twice; he had had multiple broken bones, and surgeries through the years; COPD constantly plagued him, along with a rare blood disorder. His medications were up to 15-16 pills a day. Keeping 'that' straight was a tall order for sure.

He was no longer able to drive, nor work in our yard and flower beds. That had been our passion, so all of these *'no-no's* brought on severe depression for him. When he broke his hip in Dec. 2006 that seemed to be the straw that broke the camel's back. It didn't do me any favors either! Trying to scale down from the big house and yard, and getting ready for the move to South Carolina added a new dimension to my agenda.

In the *'shape we were in'* we knew we had to go south for the good climate, to a small community where I could navigate traffic easily; a place with excellent medical facilities, and preferably one where there was a military base. Charleston, SC was our choice since our daughter was there.

IV. TALL TALES

Once that decision was made we had to wait almost a year before we could move. Our home had been on the market for a year, with no nibbles, much less 'bites.' We had built the home we had designed with our unique family needs in mind. It was our dream come true. Jim loved the thirty-six acres of wide open fields. Our home sat on the crest of a knoll in a large open hay field at the back of the property. *It was our sanctuary* - wildlife was prevalent! The deer danced around us daily. The closest house was over a half-mile away, and we were near the end of a county road. It was so peaceful there - just the sounds of silence, occasionally broken by the sounds of wildlife.

I had searched the 'net' and located an apartment for us, knowing that we could no longer maintain a home. I had also located a Methodist Church which offered an excellent music ministry; I'd been in touch with several staff members through the year and had been assured we would find what we were looking for at Bethany United Methodist Church.

Until our house and property sold we could not see our way clear to move to SC. Our daughter's wedding was set for April 16, 2007. A month before her wedding our concerns about getting there in time for the wedding mounted. Jim's hip was still in the healing process, not able to walk without his walker or a cane.

I had been pitching junk, sorting, selling, and giving away things for a year since our apartment would be about one-fourth of the size of our Kentucky home. *What a task that was!* It didn't help that we were both 'pack rats' extraordinaire. We should have moved more often! I went to bed every night, bone tired, in tears, having nightmares over the next day's agenda. I had always 'juggled' many things at once, as a wife and mother, but I had always had Jim's help. We had worked together as a team. Now *it was all up to me*. . .I didn't know how I could get it all done alone!

Every box was marked, with contents labeled, and the room it was to go into when it arrived in Charleston. The movers came, and did their thing for several days. We moved into a motel during that process, 'closed the door' on those years, and began the long trip to Summerville, SC (a small bedroom community outside of Charleston.) A stop-over at our son's house in Georgia gave us a few days to catch our breath - but not nearly enough time for me to face what was coming for us! I guess it is good that we didn't know what was ahead. . .

We arrived late on Sunday evening, in mid-March, 2007. We checked into Lodging at Charleston Air Force Base. Our furniture was to arrive on Tuesday morning. It was on schedule, but I was not! On Monday evening, sometime in the night I had fallen and dislocated a hip, and woke up in the nearby hospital. *Now what?*

I had the keys to the apartment, and the car. Jim still could not drive. He was stranded at the motel on base with no way to do anything but wait! The movers were to arrive at 10 a. m. A friend from Georgia was also to arrive at that time to help us get settled in. Our daughter was supposed to be at work. How was all of this going to work out? *What else could go into this 'mix?'*

Just hang on - there's more to it! A number of phone calls, and some good timing helped me get out of the hospital in time to meet the movers. Once my hip was back in place, I was like new. Of course, I had to be careful not to move the wrong way, or lift anything! That is a hard order to follow, especially when you are in the middle of a major move and your husband is on a walker, feeling helpless. We were in some kind of 'kink' for sure!

IV. TALL TALES

There is nothing like a true friend. The kind that comes to help *two helpless friends* settle into their new apartment. Linda had been my roommate when we were at Emory, and we had remained close through those many years. She is the kind of friend who 'walks a mile in your shoes' right along side of you, smiling every step of the way, turning this disaster into a delight! There is no way I can describe *this angel* - she was *the miracle of the month!*

Our daughter's wedding was in four weeks. Our other three children were to fly in for it; two planned to stay with us at this tiny apartment. I'm really not sure how I had planned to pull that off. . .since we only had two small bedrooms, one of which was Jim's, filled with his hospital bed and handicap equipment. The apartment was filled with boxes - there was little room to walk but *where there is a will there is a way* so somehow we would manage!

On Friday of that first week in SC, I saw *signs of a stroke* in Jim, but he denied them and would not hear of going to the hospital. In our lifetime, between the six of us, we'd spent over three years of our marriage in hospitals! On Sunday morning I finally called the ambulance. They confirmed he had blood clots in his heart, his lungs and his brain. Several days later he was placed in rehab to begin a strenuous process of getting his life back! It would take at least three weeks of six-hour workouts, each day, in the gym. I went to visit him every day. I was stretched thinner than a spaghetti noodle. I simply ran from pillar to post on adrenaline, with little sleep.

The long-awaited day of the wedding was upon us. Luckily, our daughter had everything under control. The mother of the bride was not so lucky! When in the name of goodness had I had a moment to think about the wedding? I wondered how in the world we were going to get Jim there; get him checked out of rehab long enough to withstand the 'wedding festivities.' Even before Jim's stroke we knew Tim would need to walk his sister down the aisle.

Among the hundreds of questions you are asked when you arrive at the Emergency Room, you are asked if you have a religious affiliation. (*I wonder how long that question will still be allowed, with things as they are now?*) Of course, all I could say was "I've been in touch with Bethany United Methodist via *'the net'*."

I had no clue we would meet a Bethany staff member in the hospital, even before we were able to attend a service! But it happened that way. . .believe it or not. The third day in the hospital a Minister from Bethany was visiting us in Jim's room. He was retired military, from Kentucky, Jim's home state. They both were avid sports fans, so there was no lack of conversation and the bond between us began to form.

Pastor Mark continued visiting Jim daily. Two days later I got a phone call from a member of the Church who wondered if there was something she could do to help me. She had heard of our 'circumstances' - that we had just moved into our apartment, new in town, no friends, a wedding within 3 weeks . . .and Jim suffering from a stroke! Something between us *caught fire* immediately. When I told her my maiden name was Williams, her response was: *'well, we're sisters!'* Truer words were never spoken.

Those were the most welcoming words I had heard in years. I knew from the sound of her voice, and the beat of her heart, that *I was no longer lost, I had been found,* and we had been connected through a wonderful friend, Dr. Fentress. Liz arranged

IV. TALL TALES

to visit me the next day, offering to help unpack or shop for me - anything! With all I had been trying to cope with during the last year, and now all of 'this' happening, I desperately needed to just 'flop down' and talk to someone. Unpacking was the least of my concerns. . .I had the basics unpacked, the rest could wait.

When I met Liz at the door, I knew I was OK. She hugged me, with her biggest smile and embraced me as a sister, not as a stranger! From that point on, I felt I could cope with whatever came my way.

How could a Church of 3200 members have time to visit someone who had never even visited there? *Well, this one did!* That, in itself, speaks volumes about the body of Christ that dwells within that congregation.

Three months later, on the evening of Friday, June 15, 2007, our pastor, Dr. Fentress, had felt the need to go to the hospital to see Jim. I'm sure his wife was wondering why he would leave his easy chair, when it was his day off! He simply said: *"I haven't seen Jim today. I just need to go."*

He walked in Jim's hospital room within minutes after Jim's heart had stopped beating. Luckily, it had kicked back in on its own, but leaving Jim wondering what had really happened. The two Kentucky fellows chatted about what had just happened: they talked about his relationship with God, and about heaven. . .about Jim being ready to move into a new home. *God's timing is perfect. . .it always is, and always has been.*

Within a few hours Jim moved to his eternal home. God knew our every need - He provided for us then, and has continued to be here for me. I *'once was lost but now I'm found'* by a fellowship of believers. It was *'Amazing Grace'* at work in my life, once again!

Becky Williams Buckman
August, 2008

IV. TALL TALES

IN THE MORNING

I grew up singing the old gospel song: "I'll meet you in the morning," at our Methodist Camp Meeting in Cherokee County. Even as a child, I knew its meaning. But on June 16, 2007, the truth of that hymn rang loudly in my heart and soul. As I drove home from the hospital at 5 a.m. that morning, I sang it with tears flooding my face, yet somehow, I knew *it would all be o. k.*

The day had been long, the week even longer. The day had been hard, and the week even harder. The past few years had been *'hell on earth'* for both of us. Our family had been through the mill. . .there was too much on my plate and *'even more of the same'* on Jim's. I could not seem to digest any of it without reflux! There was no 'pill' that could help either of us to cope. *God had to be our rod and staff* - to comfort us! Our bodies simply went through the motion of living; all we could do was just exist moment by moment, just long enough to keep our heads above water. That was not the life we had dreamed of; instead it was *a slow form of death.* And the knife was as sharp as a two-edged sword, painful beyond imagination. No words could describe that sphere.

*** My thoughts and tears began to fall onto the pages of my love letter to Jim on June 16, 2008, the first anniversary of his death.

'My Love:'

"Darkness had fallen on us that Monday evening, June 11, 2007. You had been quiet, pensive, responding only with a *yes or no* in answer to my question about what you wanted for dinner. Lately, our communications between each other had been reduced to 'question and answer' dialogue, almost *like a test*. Not the intimate kind of communication we had enjoyed during the majority of our marriage. The joyous life had been drained from us, every move each of us made was sheer drudgery - just to get through the moment, the day, the night, the week, the month, the year. We had lived that way for longer than either of us wanted to recall. Your declining health, and mine, had plagued us for almost twenty two of our thirty-six years of marriage!

If not verbally, subconsciously, we both cried out: 'Why, GOD, why? Have we not already known enough pain? Enough trauma? Enough heartaches to top Mt. Everest?'

For many years daily dialogue, (our love letters to each other) and our face-to-face communication had been the 'best' of the best times! Now, deep sadness and severe depression overwhelmed both of us to the point of desperation. Illness now was the 'ruler and commander' of every waking moment.

While I worked through the mess of having recently moved to an apartment, in a new town, in a new state, my mind was like the shifting sands of the nearby Atlantic Ocean. The tide was in, then out, then everything became quiet; suddenly high winds approached, and roared; *'emergency after emergency,'* as 911 had become the number most often called from our phone. So often that when our phone number showed up they knew where to find us, and what treatments were necessary! That's pretty sad!

I had finished the dishes that night, unpacked a few more boxes, trying to make 'this' our new home. That in itself, was very hard. We'd begun our marriage thirty-six years ago in an apartment, and now in our 'golden years' we had been forced to

IV. TALL TALES

do that again. A hard thing to swallow. We had built our home in Kentucky and had planned to live out our last years there.

For the past *'who knows how long'* I glanced over to where you were sitting. You began to slump over. . .and couldn't manage to make a sound. Grabbing the phone it was 911. . .again!

The local hospital was literally next door. The EMT's arrived within minutes with oxygen, knowing from my call, that this was an acute pulmonary edema attack; while they stabilized you, I began my 'job' of getting all your medicines together, and to spend the night at the hospital. We had been through this seven or eight times already. Many times it turned out to be a 'close call' but being a fighter, you pulled through every time! Was this *our routine?* Well, yes, to some degree, but the *'panic button'* in my heart was always set in motion the moment I realized you could not breathe on your own.

You had been admitted to the hospital, settled in your room, and visiting hours were over. We were both very tired, so I went home to rest for the night. The phone rang. It was the realtor saying we had an offer on the house. That was the first offer in a year, but it was not an offer I felt we could consider. Giving away what we had worked so hard for was not an option for us so I began to bargain. I made an offer. The client refused.

We had been making two house payments for three months; that had to cease so we volleyed back and forth several days, and finally caved in to a price less than what we had hoped for, much less than what our investment was worth!

By Wednesday your health saw an uphill trend - you were going to be moved from Intensive Care to a private room. This was a good sign! The paperwork from the realtor arrived that morning by Fed X, and together we signed the papers, and had them notarized there in the hospital. I returned them to the Realtor in Kentucky within the hour.

Now, we could breathe easier. A load was off our shoulders. The process of 'signing' all the paperwork had literally worn you to a frazzle, physically and the emotional struggle of 'closing the door' of our life in Kentucky had taken its toll on both of us. We knew starting over at this age/stage in life would be a challenge but we had no idea our new life in South Carolina would begin like the cold winds of winter that creep up on you, leaving you without a warm coat!

I left so you could rest. I too needed to get some rest. I got to the apartment, hit the bed, and within an hour, a terrible thunderstorm came; lightening struck our apartment. I saw it dance across the bedroom, not realizing the damage it had done until I reached for the phone to call you. The phone was dead. Within seconds, my cell phone rang. It was the charge nurse, calling to tell me you had just taken a drastic turn for the worse! I needed to get there immediately.

They had had you in the hall, in your wheelchair, waiting for a private room; suddenly you bottomed out, barely breathing. By the time I arrived, perhaps five to seven minutes later, they had you in ICU again, hooked up to all the machines. These roller coaster rides always made my head wiggle like a worm, but I simply had to be calm, and do the things I had to do when life throws curve balls.

We had known these kinds of roller coaster excursions early on in our marriage. . .not only with the scenarios of each of us/ health-wise, but with our parents. I had once thought that nursing would be my career. It was not, but in reality, I now feel like

IV. TALL TALES

I have been a nurse, most of my life, without having to pay taxes on a salary! More than fifty times in our thirty-six years of marriage we had been hospitalized!

So perhaps, nursing was my 'calling' after all. For sure, I had learned the 'lingo' of the medical science. The good thing about it: I didn't have to 'pass a test' like I would have had I gotten a nursing degree. Those big medical words soon became part of my vocabulary - almost second nature to me. One day a nurse asked me if I were a nurse! When I asked why she wondered that. . .she said I knew words that *ordinary people* did not know. That was scary!

After you were settled in ICU again, quietness engulfed both of us. It was an eerie feeling, once again. Words would not come. Silence lasted, it seemed, for hours. When words did come, they were empty, and pointless; we felt a distance in our souls. Our minds had always wondered 'would this be the last time?' Every time you had an 'attack' it seemed as if our bodies and souls were already being pulled apart between earth and heaven, just knowing that the time was coming when death would part us. We were not ready for it! All of these experiences should have prepared us, but nothing could get us 'ready' to be apart. Always before, you had come out of the crisis, defying the odds!

Maintaining the status quo you made it up to Friday evening. I was at home waiting on the nurse to call me when you woke up for dinner. Somehow, the nurse failed to call me. Apryll and David were visiting you when your heart stopped beating - *'Code Blue'* and the staff rushed in. Your heart took its own course - it kicked back in and began beating on its own. *That was a close call!*

I got a phone call from Apryll telling me what happened. I was at your bedside within five minutes; you were alert, and told me something 'funny' happened to you earlier, pointing to your heart, saying it just felt different. You told me the Doctor would put in a pace-maker the next morning. You had agreed to that. I was fine with your decision but very apprehensive about surgery, in your weakened condition with COPD. But that would buy us some time.

I stayed well past visiting hours. It was eleven p. m. now. I hesitated to leave you, even for a moment but I had to go to the Waiting Room across the hall to make phone calls to all the family, alerting them of the recent emergency. When I got back you looked at the clock and reminded me I was not supposed to be there since visiting hours were over! The nurse came in, insisting that I go on home and get some rest. I resisted time and again, saying I would be fine in the ICU waiting room. I finally gave in. She knew I had been there all week, and that I was physically and emotionally exhausted. I was a roaming zombie. She promised to call me if anything changed.

I knew you needed to rest, and knowing perhaps the nurse knew best, I went to your bedside to tell you I would be back in the morning. Your mouth was so dry and I offered to get you a coke. You were very agitated and adamant saying: *"I do not want a damn coke from the Nurse's station; they are half water. You know what I want! I want a coke in a bottle - the kind I have at home!"* There were none like that in the machines downstairs, so when I left to go home I promised you: *"Darling, I will bring you one in the morning."*

As I walked in the door at home, the phone rang. It was the nurse: "He's going, Mrs. Buckman." I got there in five minutes! Apryll and David arrived but the nurses would not let us in to to see you! They were working frantically to save your life. We paced the floor, speechless and in tears! The Doctor worked

IV. TALL TALES

with you for over an hour; then he came out to tell us he had done everything he could to save you but you didn't make it!

Darling, I knew there would come a time, but I didn't know it would be then! None of us were ready to hear those words. The Nurse told us we could be 'alone with you' as long as we needed - so I sat in your room and held your hand for over an hour, pouring out my love for you, praying that you could hear me, somehow. . . amidst my flooding tears. I was so broken, so alone in the shadow of death. As I lingered, dreading to go home without you, I kept promising you: *'Darling, I will come in the morning. . .I will bring your coke then.'*

You were escorted into heaven before I got back with your coke, but I hope God assigned a special angel to care for you, one who would give you the special kind of coke you wanted. If not, I'll bring a six-pack with me when I get there; they will be chilled just like you want them. We'll sit on the front porch and share our cokes, between hugs and kisses, of course!

Looking forward to our reunion, *in the morning!*
'Your love,'
Becky

"*Significant Others...*"

A collection of writings for ALL time

By various authors, and lyricists

"Bathe in the warmth of the sunshine of these utterances, thereby cleansing the mind, the heart and the soul, finding a taste of heaven therein."

Becky Williams Buckman

TABLE OF CONTENTS

Christie	Timothy Buckman
From Dusk Til Dawn	Timothy Buckman
Giving Thanks	James F. (Jim) Buckman
Mari's Untitled poem	Mari Buckman Snell
A Love Letter To My Wife	James F. (Jim) Buckman
My Recipe for Eternal Love	Becky Williams Buckman
Promise Song	Heidi Ruska Krone/ Timothy Buckman
Smiling All The While	Becky Williams Buckman
Words To Live By	Becky Wiliams Buckman
Our Songs	Becky Williams Buckman
Things Are Hard Right Now	Claudia McCants
The Dance of a Lifetime	Various Authors
Numbers Down *'Our'* Line	Becky Williams Buckman
To My Parents	Nancy Legat
When I'm An Old Lady	Author Unknown
Beautiful Hands	Author Unknown
Footprints	Author Unknown
For Moms and Grandmas	Author Unknown
What If	Melvin T. Haynes
When You Thought I Wasn't Looking	Author Unknown
On Death and Dying	Pamela Jekel
Something Meaningful	J. Carie Sexton
We Buried Her Beneath The Willows	Author Unknown
Growing Old	Author Unknown
What Is Life About?	Face Book
Moving Forward	Becky Williams Buckman
God Saw You	Author Unknown
Relax	Becky Williams Buckman
Games People Play	Becky Williams Buckman

CHRISTIE
Lyrics and Score by Timothy Buckman

Hey Christie, where did we go wrong?
I haven't felt this feeling in so very long
But I know you'll be alright
You've got someone there to love and hold you tight
There's not much I can do or say
I'm more than a phone call, I'm a million worlds away.

Hey Christie, what is left of us today?
I hope it's more than the memories and words I couldn't say
I'm sorry that I left you so lonely
All the time I prayed to God and swore you'd be my only one
There's not much I can offer you
But you've got to know that my heart is breaking in two.

Christie, I can't help that feeling I get when we're together
It's a feeling I wish would last forever
I know it's not right
The winds of change have had a say in our lives
There's not much more I can try
I guess we weren't meant to be
My head knows that we are out of time
But the truth is, Christie,
My heart doesn't want to leave.

I never dreamed that we'd be saying goodbye
But the roads of life have all but taken us side by side
I'll wake up someday, sometime
I just hoped you'd be right there in my life

DOWN THE LINE

Christie, I can't help that feeling I get when we're together
It's a feeling I wish would last forever
I know it's not right
The winds of change have had a say in our lives
There's not much more I can try
I guess we weren't meant to be
My head knows that we are out of time
But the truth is, Christie,
My heart doesn't want to leave.

There's not much more I can try
I guess we weren't meant to be
My head knows that we're out of time
Christie, my heart doesn't want to leave.

V. "SIGNIFICANT OTHERS…"

FROM DUSK TO DAWN

We walk hand in hand in the twilight
A shimmer over broken sands of stone
Share a glance at memories of despair, but
I'm still alone.
Here we walk
Hand in hand across the sands
Woven so tight as stone
We're together in my heart
But my soul feels all alone.
I'll travel without you on the long journey I must take
To a castle built from the grains
Of the stones of time.
It's not far
I can feel it near.
I'll walk no more for I am weary
In my age of old.
And the legend tells no lies,
It tells I can fly
If so, then maybe before my time
I can make a whole new life in that
Castle in the sky.
Now sets the sun
And the whisper of mist brings the dawn.

Timothy Merriman Buckman
1991-1992

* * *Previously published in Greenwood High School Anthology, Bowling Green, kentucky 1991-92

GIVING THANKS*

Our daily dialogue question for the day was: "What Do I Have To Be Thankful For?" My husband, Jim, wrote this to me in his love letter:

"My Love,

Your most endearing quality is your desire to keep raising our relationship to a higher plane. I am thankful for God, you and our family. If not for you, I wouldn't be the person that I am.

You are the one that led me to God, gave me two wonderful talented children, and took on the job of raising the two that I already had. It does my heart good to know that you care for all of us, and want the best. Although life isn't always easy you fight through the down times and keep a positive outlook for the future. Even with my physical problems, you still desire and want my love and companionship! For this I am thankful."

Love,
Jim (your love)
May 6, 1999

V. "SIGNIFICANT OTHERS..."

James II, Robin, Tim and Apryll 1988

EDITOR'S NOTE: During our courtship of many years, 'love letters' kept us together. Military duty kept us apart, but we wrote three-four times a week. Even after we married, Jim and I wrote 'love letters,' to each other daily, for almost 25 years. Each time they were written in response to a question about a concern, a need or an emotion that either of us had: *a feeling* we were experiencing at the time. We read our letters to each other in silence, and then shared from the depths of our souls, connecting in a miraculous way through God's love for us as a couple, and a family.

Jim struggled all of his life to be able to express himself verbally, in a way that people understood. Often, he was 'misunderstood.' Yet, he had a phenomenal way of expressing himself 'on paper' and once he realized he was 'free' to open up in that way, without any threat of being judged, he found he was then more able to express his feelings verbally. He was a 'new person' from then on!

*This particular love letter stands out. *I read it daily.* I treasure it and the soul from which it came!

V. "SIGNIFICANT OTHERS..."

MARI'S UNTITLED POEM

Mother, I don't want you there
waiting in my house.
It's bad enough you wait in yours
Turning down weekend beds,
Watching for lights that never come
Because we weren't expected.

Shall I reassure you?
My cheeks are rosier now
Than ever they were before,
Rich with borrowed blood.

The damaged platelets will not show,
None of your friends will know.
The errant cells won't spill
On Persian Carpet Floors
To prove what you have heard.

I don't want your pity,
Your long-drawn inward sigh
You were waiting long enough
To let me live.
Wait for me to die.

Mari Buckman Snell
August, 1973

EDITOR'S NOTE:

After Mari found out she had cancer, she wrote this poem to her mother, Madeline Steward Buckman. Mari died August 10, 1977, in Nashville, Tennessee at the age of 41, having fought a long and difficult four-year battle with chronic leukemia. She was the mother of two sons, Marq and Jon Snell.

V. "SIGNIFICANT OTHERS..."

A LOVE LETTER TO MY WIFE

"My love,"

When I look at the possibility of death there are many thoughts and feelings that go through me. I can remember when I had my heart attack. (Dec. 1985) I didn't fear death but the main thought was of you. 'Not yet, Becky has too long a road!" I can remember Wilford Hall – the Air Force Hospital in San Antonio, Texas in August 1976. I was a very weak Christian and you lay on death's bed. I was bitter and mad with Jesus for allowing it to appear that our world (together) was only going to be slightly more than five years. I spent the night telling Him how wrong he was and if he loved me the way everyone said, he wouldn't do me this way.

It was the time for Him to let me know that love is disciplined and not cast out (just) anywhere. Although I was mad and bitter, he used this time to show his love for me, us and you. Our walk is JOY and no matter how many more steps we have (I prayed) 'Just let it be, Lord, Let it be!'

Love,
Jim (your love)

MY REFLECTION on Jim's letter to me:

This is Jim's 'love letter' written to me after we had both survived 'near death' experiences. My first near death experience walked in on me when I was thirty-six, after the birth of our last child. At that time, we had a 2 yr. old and two teenagers, under fifteen.

If I had died, this would have been the second time Jim would have been left alone, to raise a family of children without their

Mother. The bitterness from losing his first wife had not been thoroughly removed from his mind, when this happened to me. *Now, even more anger and bitterness almost drowned him* - but GOD stepped in and kept him from thinking only of himself.

Jim's *first near-death experience* came when he had his heart attack at 55. Death came knocking on his door many more times before 'his last call' on June 16, 2007. He knew he was ready to leave the anguish of a broken body and spirit. . .ready to 'take flight' to a life of peace and rest! When that time came, I loved him enough to let him go, yet all the while wishing I could have walked hand in hand with him across the River Jordan!

Becky Williams Buckman

V. "SIGNIFICANT OTHERS..."

MY RECIPE FOR ETERNAL LOVE

Gather these ingredients into your heart:

    One lifetime of unconditional, Godly love
    One lifetime of abundant patience
    One heart 'full' and overflowing with forgiveness

YOU are ready to begin:

Select clean and proper tools for mixing
Add good humor every time the batter gets lumpy or stiff
Keep a clean cloth nearby to wipe up the 'spills' of tears
Do not allow any 'spattering' of the mix - keep it contained
Keep your eyes focused on the 'mix'
Keep your ears open for any 'bursting bubbles'
Stir ingredients diligently, until the mix is very smooth
Taste the warmth and joy of the mixture of above ingredients before baking
Pour contents into the proper 'atmosphere' for baking
Bake at the temperature that is 'best' for your mixture
Keep the temperature even so that nothing burns!

When all is done, you will find that *your eternal love* is tasty and will last a lifetime!

                                            Becky Williams Buckman
                                            September 2013

***This recipe is *'tried and true'* as our marriage of thirty-six years proved. It does require the 'two to tango' method!

PROMISE SONG
(A Wedding Song)

Lyrics: Heidi Ruska Krone
Score: Tim Buckman

Here I am on a day I never thought would be
I'm standing here face to face in the eyes of my Lord
This is a special day when I tell you, I will, yes,
I'll tell you I will, and do promise my life to you

Thank you Lord for everything and the one I love most
I promise you to be true to him all the days of my life.
No matter what storms lie ahead or the rain that will fall from the storms
It never can change that I will be a wife that serves You faithfully.

The Lord is great for giving me the perfect mate
When we met He knew we would be forever one.
As this day we'll grow in one,
We will serve Him faithfully through our lives
We will share His love as a family

Thank you Lord, for everything and the one I love most
I promise you to be true to him all the days of my life.
No matter what storms lie ahead or the rain that will fall from the storms
It can never change that I will be a wife that serves You faithfully

Thank you Lord for the peace I have found in the love of my life
We promise You to be true to You all the days of our lives

V. "SIGNIFICANT OTHERS..."

No matter what storms lie ahead
We will be a family, a family that serves our Lord.

EDITOR'S NOTE: This was written as a 'wedding song' by Heidi for her brother, Hans Ruska. It was 'scored' by Timothy Buckman and was sung at the wedding of Tim's brother, James F. Buckman, II on October 13, 2001.

SMILING ALL THE WHILE

Smile and the world smiles with you. A frown is just a 'lost' smile that turns your world, and that of others, upside down. *Smile. You are on candid camera.* In our society, truer words were never spoken. You are being watched by cameras every place you go! When we see ourselves on camera or in photos, it is a bit scary to see how others see us - *how we really look.*

I was waiting to board the church van for an upcoming trip. I walked up to a group of gals to join the conversation. One of them spoke to me, asking how my day was going. Smiling, I said *'just great.'* I'll never forget her response to me:

> "You are always smiling. You seem so happy all the time…" 'I am' was my response. I have a lot to smile about – a lot about which to be happy. I have enough wrinkles as it is." (As a child I sang: *"When you are happy and you know it your face will surely show it!"*)

Last Halloween I went to a College Choir Concert. The Choir Director said there would be a 'treat' for those who came dressed up. Well, I wouldn't dare have missed that chance. I have always *dressed up on Halloween*. I'm no spring chicken but I can spring anywhere in a costume, or without it, if I have to!

My husband might have said that I always went pretty much *'in character'*. That night I was a Witch! I had on a witch's hat, a mask and a black cape; too bad I forgot the broom! Only my mouth and chin were showing. When I walked in, one friend rolled in the aisles saying: "You can't fool me, I'd know you anywhere." My 'mouth' usually gives me away, but I had not said one word. (some would find that hard to believe!) I asked 'how could you possibly know?' She said, "I know you by your smile."

V. "SIGNIFICANT OTHERS..."

Those were two of the best compliments I could have been given. I'm still flying high, just not on my broom. I'm smiling even more, just knowing that *I can 'never' disguise who I really am*, underneath any costume or mask I put on! I've never been a good actress...I'm just ME, 24/7.

I don't take the credit for *'smiling all the while.'* I owe it to my Mother. My mother was always smiling. She was happy, inside and out - and it always showed. Maybe I was just born happy. How could I not be? My mother's smile was the first thing I saw! She had delivered me late in life - I was a surprise baby! A healthy nine pounder, no less, and she had delivered me naturally, without problems like she had had with the third baby. That was cause enough for Mom to smile for days...and years to come!

Through the years many people have told me I was just like my mother, so *'thanks, Mom,' for passing on the smile!* You taught me well so I'm passing it on, one smile at a time.

Becky Williams Buckman
November, 2013

***My parents owned Williams Food Store in Woodstock. As part of their many advertisements, they had *fans* printed to give to customers (the *hand-held* card board fans, used before air conditioning was normal). On the back were these words:

"Smile a while, and while you smile, Another smiles, And soon there are miles of smiles, and life is worth while because you smile!"

DOWN THE LINE

WORDS TO LIVE BY

As a young child I always knew the *Bible was a special book,* knowing it held the key to an abundant life, even before I really knew what abundant life meant! My mother was the daughter of a Methodist Minister, as well as the granddaughter of a Methodist Minister. Both had served churches in Georgia in the middle 1800's and early 1900's. I was *born into the faith* but I still had to claim it as my own. And, this I did, in early adolescence. Through the years I have grown closer in my walk with our Lord, as I have studied the Scriptures, and stayed in the fellowship of the Church. I've been blessed with strong Christian leaders, and committed Christians who mentored me, and showed me the way to *walk the walk.*

I was given my first Bible when I was very young, even before I could read. My Mother read to me each night before bedtime, and she taught me my first prayer. Her last words to me every night were: *'Read your Bible and don't forget to say your prayers.'*

I have every Bible that was ever given to me except the one that *one was stolen* during our travel from Japan back to the states. It had been the most expensive, and the most comprehensive *study Bible* I had ever owned. I had made many special notations in it. Significant verses were highlighted. It was a great loss, but my only prayer was that whoever took it found what they were looking for! Maybe they needed to 'hear' what it had been saying to me.

Through the years, as I have grown in wisdom and statue, there are verses that are glued to my inner being. Some I had been required to memorize, but some were just 'there' because I had lived with their truths daily. They are there in my heart and

V. "SIGNIFICANT OTHERS..."

mind, to call upon, in the good times and in the hard times. Some of them are:

> "Thy word is a lamp unto my feet, and a light unto my path."
> *Psalm 119:105*

> "I have hidden your word in my heart that I might not sin against you."
> *Psalm 119:11*

> "The Lord is my Shepherd, I shall not want. . .He leadeth me in green pastures.
> *Psalm 23*

> "Wait for the Lord; be strong and take heart and wait for the Lord."
> *Psalm 27:14*

> "The Lord is my light and salvation - whom shall I fear? The Lord is the stronghold of my life - of whom shall I be afraid?"
> *Psalm 27:1-2*

> "No temptation has seized you except what is common to man; and God is faithful. He will not let you be tempted beyond what you can bear. But when you are tempted, he will also provide a way out so that you can stand up under it."
> *I Corinthians 10:13*

> "For this reason, make every effort to add to your faith goodness, and to goodness, knowledge, and to knowledge, self-control, and to self-control, perseverance, and to perseverance, godliness, and to godliness, brotherly kindness, and to brotherly kindness, love."
> *II Peter 1:5-7*

"Cast all your anxiety on him because he cares for you."
I Peter 5:7

"Love your neighbor as yourself."
Mark 12:31

"...slow to anger, abounding in love. . .
Joel 2:13

"Now abideth faith, hope and love, but the greatest of these is love."
I Corinthians 13:13

"I am the Resurrection and the Life, no man cometh unto the Father but by me."
John 11:25

"Weeping may linger for the night but joy cometh in the morning."
Psalm 30:5

"I no longer call you servants. Instead, I have called you friends. You did not choose me, but I chose you and appointed you to go and bear fruit - fruit that will last."
John 15:15*

*On New Year's Day, 1978, Jim and I were delegates at the Congress on Evangelism, in Miami, Florida. Instead of going to the BOWL GAME with some ministers that night, he chose to go to worship with me. It was during that sermon that his relationship with his Lord took on an entirely new direction. It was this scripture that gave him a 'peace' that

V. "SIGNIFICANT OTHERS..."

he had not known the majority of his life; he knew he was chosen, and loved beyond all comprehension. That being so, our marriage relationship took on a new depth: his love for me, and our family was deeper than ever before. From there, we left the convention to 'bear fruit that would last' - to give our lives to the world-wide Marriage Encounter ministry.

OUR SONGS

My husband, Jim, had a phenomenal ability to memorize poetry, as well as any thing else he needed to 'store' in his intriguing and brilliant mind! He knew the words of thousands of poems and songs; he would sing to me (in *his own unique 'pitch' - more like a monotone!*) but I was never bored with his 'pitch.' We sang, and recited poetry to each other; it was our entertainment as we traveled across the USA. We were *'harmonizing'* in our own unique way. As long as we enjoyed ourselves, it didn't really matter if we were actually on key or not! We sang to the top of our voices and even in *his last days,* we sang Josh Turner's country music hit, *'YOUR MAN,'* as we went back and forth to physical therapy.

Here are the lyrics. I cling to those words, knowing that Jim was 'my man' and he knew he was *'my man';* it had been that way from 'day one' of our love affair!

YOUR MAN
Lyrics: Josh Turner

Baby lock the door and turn the lights down low
Put some music on that's soft and slow
Baby we ain't got no place to go
I hope you understand

I've been thinking 'bout this all day long
Never felt a feeling quite this strong
I can't believe how much it turns me on
Just to be your man.

There's no hurry
Don' t you worry

V. "SIGNIFICANT OTHERS…"

We can take our time
Come a little closer
Let's go over
What I had in mind.

Baby lock the door and turn the lights down low
Put some music on that's soft and slow
Baby we ain't got no place to go
I hope you understand.

I've been thinking 'bout this all day long
Never felt a feeling quite so strong
I can't believe how much it turns me on
Just to be your Man

Ain't no body ever love nobody
The way that I love you
We're alone now
You don't know how
Long I've wanted to

Lock the door and turn the lights down low
Put some music on that's soft and slow
Baby we ain't got no place to go
I hope you understand

I've been thinking 'bout this all day long
Never felt a feeling quite this strong
I can't believe how much it turns me on
Just to be your man
I can't believe how much it turns me on
Just to be your man!

MAMA, HE'S CRAZY
The Judds

When I was still 'wet behind the ears' someone came along who was crazy over me; well, i. e., someone other than my parents and relatives! Since there hadn't been a baby born in our extended family in 18 years, I was sort of a novelty. Now, don't get me wrong, not that I was more special than any other 'newborn' but I did get too much attention. In other words, I was a bit spoiled.

But at 17, in the height of my teen years, a *grown man* asked me out on a date! WOW – now that was a surprise to me. Was he crazy? He was such a handsome young man and I was so flattered, I didn't dare say NO.

My brainwaves were thinking *"Mama, I found someone like I never knew before..."* He was crazy over me, and I was crazy over him. Many years down the road, after we'd been married over thirty years, the JUDDS sang a song that summed up what happened to Jim and me. It is not unique to us, but it is just what happens when couples fall in love.

I sing the lyrics of this song every day, even now, years after 'my love' left this world; they still ring true for our eternal love. Here are the lyrics:

> *Mama, I've found someone like you said would come along*
> *He's a sight so unlike any man I've known.*
> *I was afraid to let him in 'cause I'm not the trusting kind,*
> *But now I'm convinced that he's heaven sent*
> *And must be out of his mind.*

V. "SIGNIFICANT OTHERS..."

Mama, he's crazy, crazy over me And in my life is where
He says He always wants to be. I've never been so in love
He beats all I've ever seen, Mama, he's crazy, he's crazy over me.

And Mama, you've always said 'better look before you leap'
Maybe so, but here I go lettin' my heart lead me.
He thinks I hung the moon and stars, I think he's a livin' dream
Well there are men but ones like him are few and far between.

Mama, he's crazy, crazy over me. And in my life is where he says
He always wants to be. I've never been so in love
He beats all I've ever seen. Mama, he's crazy, he's crazy over me
And Mama, he's crazy, he's crazy over me.

That 'feeling' of being so in love was the thread that bound our two hearts, to make them 'one.' It is the cord that wrapped up our marriage and brought joy into our home. I guess we both were *crazy!* But that's OK, by me!

OUR TWENTY-FIFTH WEDDING ANNIVERSARY SONG - 1996
("Look At Us")

I recall that day in June, 1996, with so much joy. Friends and family had come from miles to celebrate with us, the twenty-five years of being "Mr. and Mrs. James Buckman." Around that time Vince Gill had become one of our favorite country musicians. We weren't living very far from Nashville, Tennessee, at the time and we'd had occasion to see him at the Grand Old Opry. This song, *Look At Us,* by Vince Gill, was just 'what we felt about each other' all the time. If we had been fortunate enough to have celebrated our fiftieth anniversary, we would still have been singing this song to each other!

DOWN THE LINE

'Look at us after all these years together,
Look at us after all we've been through
Look at us still leaning on each other.

If you want to see how true love should be
Then just look at us.

Look at you, still pretty as a picture
Look at me, still crazy over you.
Look at us, still believing in forever

In a hundred years from now
I know without a doubt
They'll all look back and wonder how
We made it all work out.
Chances are we'll go down in history
When they want to see how true love should be
They'll just look at us.'

My Jim always said if any *one thing* had changed in each of our lives, things would not have turned out they way they did! As we walked through life together, there were many things that we did not understand at the time, but looking back, we made it all work out. No, *not just the two of us* by ourselves, but with God's hand gently guiding us day by day, moment by moment.

Becky Williams Buckman
June 19, 2008

V. "SIGNIFICANT OTHERS..."

"Look at us, after all these years together. . .still pretty as a picture"
November 22, 2006, celebrating Jim's 76th birthday

DOWN THE LINE

THERE'S A NEW WORLD SOMEWHERE
Tom Springfield

There's a new world somewhere
They call the promised land
And I'll be there someday
If you will hold my hand
I still need you here beside me
No matter what I do
For I know I'll never find another you.

There is always someone
For each of us they say
And you'll be my someone
Forever and a day
I could search the whole world over
But I know I'll never find another you.

It's a long long journey
So stay by my side
When I walk through a storm
You'll always be my guide,
Always be my guide.

If they gave me a fortune
My treasure would be small
I could lose it all tomorrow
And never mind at all
But if I should lose your love dear,
I don't know what I'll do
For I know I'll never find another you!

EDITOR'S NOTE: This was the theme song for Marriage Encounter Weekends. We went on our first weekend in Atlanta,

V. "SIGNIFICANT OTHERS..."

in May 1978, and *'found each other'* in a new and wonderful way. Our love was deepened in all three areas: *filia, eros, and agape'* love all bloomed wide open that weekend! We did not know that we could grow more in love than we had been when we married, until we spent forty-eight hours with each other, without any interruptions of daily living! No telephones, no television, no yard work, no dirty dishes, no car-pools, no babies needing a bottle... just the two of us, *focusing on each other, and our needs.*

Each of us became a 'new person.' We found out things about ourselves and each other that we had not known before! Our commitment to God and his Church led us down new paths on our marital journey. Our family life changed completely; our children saw a *'marked difference'* in our lives -our new love relationship impacted their lives in a significant way!

From that time on, *we gave our lives to the ministry* of helping married couples renew and strengthen their love life, their friendship with each other, and to find out where God would have them serve in the Church and in their community.

The blessing of *'watching a rose bud come to full bloom'* was something that deepened our own love each time a couple became 'encountered.' We saw hundreds of couples 'walk away' from their Marriage Encounter Weekend singing this song, knowing they would *'never find another you!'*

TAPS

I had heard TAPS played perhaps one hundred times but I did not know the 'story' of its beginning, its composition until after my husband died.

My husband was retired Air Force. He and I had discussed his funeral plans a few years before his death. He chose the scriptures that were close to his heart, the hymns that touched him, and together we agreed on some other details. We both knew that TAPS would bring finality to his service.

Perhaps Jim knew the story of Taps, but *I did not*. Tears have always flowed when I heard it. I knew it signified a dignified closing to all military funeral services. Below I quote an article that tells the story:

> "Reportedly, it all began in 1862 during the Civil War, when the Union Army Captain Robert Elicombeli was with his men near Harrison's Landing in Virginia. The Confederate Army was on the other side of the narrow strip of land.
>
> During the night, Captain Eli heard the moan of a soldier who lay mortally wounded on the field. Not knowing if it was a Union or Confederate soldier, the Captain decided to risk his life and bring the striken man back for medical attention. Crawling on his stomach through gunfire, the Captain reached the striken soldier and began pulling him toward his encampment.
>
> When the Captain finally reached his own lines, he discovered it was actually a Confederate soldier, but the soldier was dead. The Captain lit a lantern and suddenly

V. "SIGNIFICANT OTHERS..."

caught his breath and went numb with shock. In the dim light, he saw the face of the soldier. It was his own son. The boy had been studying music in the South when the war broke out. Without telling his father, the boy enlisted in the Confederate Army.

The following morning, heartbroken, the father asked permission of his superiors to give his son a full military burial, despite his enemy status. His request was only partially granted. The Captain had asked if he could have a group of Army members play a funeral dirge for his son at the funeral. The request was turned down since the soldier was a Confederate. But, out of respect for the father, they did say they could give him only one musician.

The Captain chose a bugler. He asked the bugler to play a series of musical notes he had found on a piece of paper in the pocket of the dead son's uniform. The haunting melody, we now know as 'Taps,' was born and is used at all military funerals. The words are:

"Day is done, Gone the sun, From the lakes, From the hills, From the sky. All is well. Safely rest. God is nigh. Fading light, Dims the sight, And a star, Gems the sky, Gleaming bright.
From afar, Drawing nigh, Falls the night.

Then goodnight, Peaceful night, Till the light of the dawn, Shineth bright;
God is near, Do not fear, Friend, Goodnight."

* I will never 'hear' TAPS with the same *'ear'* again!

THINGS ARE HARD RIGHT NOW
by Caludia McCants

*** Trust in yourself to make a NEW beginning

Sometimes life leads you in a new direction. And even when you don't feel prepared or when you don't want to change, you are forced to start over.

Life is like that...there are no guarantees. It makes you feel scared, anxious, or sad. But after you've shed your last tear, just when you think everything is out of your hands, you take a deep breath and finally realize that you have complete control. Survival is about reclaiming your 'self.' It is about learning to love who you are. Survival is about making wise choices, setting goals, and finding what really makes you happy. It's about rediscovering those things you always wanted to do. Happiness is something that has to come from within. Nobody can provide it for you.

You are a beautiful, caring, wonderful person! You are worthy of all good things. *Life is hard right* now but please know that people are there for you. And...look at this as your new beginning.

V. "SIGNIFICANT OTHERS..."

THE DANCE OF A LIFETIME

I was never given dance lessons. It just seemed to come naturally! As did my love and inclination to the world of music. In my lifetime, the two belong together. Even if my body is not on the dance floor, my spirit is dancing before the first note is played!

Life is a dance, you learn as you go, just as you take that first step, as a toddler, you soon begin to walk, then run, then dance through the myriad scenarios that life dishes out. It is not uncommon to miss a step, or trip over your own two feet, maybe even landing on your face! The music of life will soon put you upright again. That is how it has been with me. I plan to be 'dancing with the stars' throughout eternity.

Below are some thoughts about DANCING that are indelibly printed on my mind; they have kept me from 'going under' more often than not!

Without MUSIC life would B "flat"

Author Unknown

Life without DANCING would B too "sharp" - nothing more than a monotone!

Becky Williams Buckman

LIFE isn't about how to survive the storm but how to DANCE through it.

Author Unknown

DOWN THE LINE

DANCE like no one is watching,
Sing like no one is listening,
Love like you've never been hurt.

Author Unknown

HOPE is the ability to hear the music of the future
Faith is the courage to DANCE to it today.

Author Unknown

LIFE is short, break the rules, forgive sooner, love with true love, laugh without control, and always keep smiling. Maybe life is not the party that we were expecting, but in the meantime, we are here, and we can still DANCE!

Author Unknown

Life is too short to DANCE with ugly men.*

Maxine

I vote this one 'number one!'

V. "SIGNIFICANT OTHERS..."

NUMBERS. . . .DOWN *'OUR'* LINE

There was a time when 'genetics', genealogy and history did not intrigue me. Not so anymore! My father had been 'into' it and had compiled a booklet which sparked my interest when I was in mid-life. A cousin on the other side of the family had also gathered much of our history. When I began to plow through them, I found such phenomenal facts. Amazing trends!

A while back, Cherokee County, Georgia was compiling a history of its families. As I was working to update our family line for an entry to be put in the book, I found many unique things, on both sides of my heritage. And now, years later, I see trends, patterns continuing 'down the line,' in my Johnson-Williams line, as well as in the Williams-Buckman line. It makes me wonder how much of this is 'on an accident', as my children used to say, or foreordained?

Here's one set of numbers that jumped out at me one day when I was scrap booking. This 'fact' comes from the JOHNSON line of my heritage regarding seven girls who were born eighteen years apart, beginning in 1901 and continuing until 1995. Never once was a boy born!

This might be 'meat' for the mix that proves "GIRLS RULE" in our family!

(1) EIGHTEEN YEARS APART:

1901 - My Aunt Cliffie Johnson was born
1919 - Her niece, and my cousin, Martha Johnson was born

1922 – My sister, Ruth Williams Pyle, was born
1940 - I was born, Carolyn Rebecca (Becky) Williams Buckman

1958 – My niece, Anne Pyle Atkins, was born; the daughter of my sister, Ruth Pyle

1976 – My daughter, Apryll Buckman Gill was born

1995 – My niece's daughter, Hannah Faith Atkins,* was born, daughter of Anne Pyle Atkins

*At this printing, Hannah is the last-born girl in the JOHNSON line.

(2) THE BIG FORTY

There is another pattern that stands out in our ancestry lines: many marriages began when one of the couple was forty, and usually a wide age-difference between them.

My grandfather, Joseph Washington Williams, married my grandmother, Margaret Anne Jefferson when he was forty, and she was twenty-two.

I married my husband, Jim, when he was forty, and I was thirty-one at the time; our daughter, Apryll, married David Gill, when she was thirty-one.

Our son, Jim Buckman, II, married his wife, Shawn Ouzts, when he was forty. Our daughter Robin re-married her former husband, Dan Elsner, when she was forty.

My sister, Ruth Williams Pyle, married Bernard A. Pyle, when she was thirty-four; Their daughter, Anne Pyle, married Gary Atkins when she was thirty-four. Gary was forty when they married.

* * *All of this confirms that women in our family marry later in life, marry older men, and have their children later in life.

V. "SIGNIFICANT OTHERS..."

Does it make you wonder about *the 'similarities' in your own family?*
Check out your family history. See what patterns you find!

Becky Williams-Buckman
August, 2013

TO MY PARENTS

Thank you for the way you've loved me
unconditionally through the years...

For eyes insightful enough to see I needed
    help when I didn't want to ask -
For ears attuned to hear what I was
    saying...and to what I could not say -
For hands ready to guide and give,
    and to help and heal -
For feet strong and sturdy to take a
    stand when necessary -
For arms always open...warm,
    comforting and gentle -
For mouths giving forth words of
    wisdom and encouragement -
For hearts full of love and care
    and prayer for me -

                                Nancy Legat

COPYRIGHT
Columbia, SC

EDITOR'S NOTE: These words are on a plaque that hangs just inside my front door. It is *'my tribute'* to my parents, John Gordon and Leila Mae Johnson Williams.

V. "SIGNIFICANT OTHERS..."

WHEN I'M AN OLD LADY

.....I'll live with each kid, and bring so much happiness just as they did. I want to pay back all the joy they've provided. Returning each deed. Oh, they'll be so excited...when I'm an old lady!

.....I'll write on the wall with red, white and blue crayons, and I'll bounce on the furniture, wearing my shoes. I'll drink from the carton and then leave it out. I'll stuff all the toilets and oh, how they'll shout!

.....When they are on the phone and just out of reach, I'll get into things like sugar and bleach. They'll snap their fingers and then shake their head, and when that is done, I'll hide under the bed *if I'm able!*

.....When they cook dinner and call me to eat, I'll not eat my green beans, salad or meat. I'll gag on my okra, spill milk on the table, and when they get angry, *I'll run, IF I'm able!*

.....I'll sit close to the TV, through channels I'll click, and I'll cross both eyes just to see if they stick! I'll take off my socks and throw ONE away! And play in the mud till the end of the day.

.....And later in bed, I'll lay back and sigh. I'll thank God in prayer and close my eyes. My kids will look down with a smile slowly creeping on their face, and then say, with a groan: "she's so sweet when she's asleep."

Author Unknown

DOWN THE LINE

BEAUTIFUL HANDS
A Tribute to Mothers Everywhere

"My mother had beautiful hands. That seems like an exaggerated compliment. Physically, her hands were not so lovely in her latter years. She had large knuckles, rough with scars and arthritic lumps, crooked little fingers and nails that always showed signs of toil. What made her hands beautiful was the things she did with them.

They held brooms and mops, needles, scissors, and thread; they scrubbed clothes on an old washboard, and hung them out to dry on the clothesline, even on cold and windy days. They pulled weeds from the garden and gathered vegetables for us to eat. Those hands cooked many meals - three square meals a day. At 6 a. m., 12 noon and 6 p. m. as sure as the clock struck the hour! Those same hands washed dishes "by hand." She never owned a dishwasher. Those knotty knuckles still played the piano, occasionally missing a note on the keyboard, but she sang along and never was off key! Her voice was strong, her discipline was firm and her hands conveyed a loving touch on the shoulder when she had something to say to me.

Those same hands had held her babies when they were born. She had smoothed their hair, wiped away many tears, and bandaged up our hands and legs when we scraped them. They waved good-bye when those same children left home; and those hands reached out to welcome them back home when they returned.

Her hands were gifts from God. They had character. They were made so beautiful by serving her family and her friends. I'll never forget them…a beauty likened to no other."

Author Unknown

V. "SIGNIFICANT OTHERS..."

EDITOR'S NOTE:

I save almost everything! From church bulletins to clippings from the newspapers, cartoons to obituaries. As I've put my own book together, I have come across many "good things" other people have written. Most say "author unknown." *This is one clipping that I treasure so much!* It stays in the front of my Bible to remind me daily of the "treasure" given to me at birth - My Mother!

Becky Williams Buckman
Mother's Day, 2011

FOOTPRINTS

One night a man had a dream. He dreamed he was walking along the beach with the LORD. Across the sky flashed scenes from his life. For each scene, he noticed two sets of footprints in the sand: one belonging to him and the other to the LORD.

When the last scene of his life flashed before him, he looked back at the footprints in the sand. He noticed that many times along the path of his life there was only one set of footprints. He also noticed that it happened at the very lowest and saddest times in his life.

This really bothered him and he questioned the LORD about it. "LORD, you said that once I decided to follow you, you'd walk with me all the way. But I have noticed that during the most troublesome times in my life, there is only one set of footprints. I don't understand why when I needed you the most you would leave me."

The LORD replied, "My son, My precious child, I love you and I would never leave you. During your times of trial and suffering, when you see only one set of footprints, it was then that I carried you."

Author Unknown

V. "SIGNIFICANT OTHERS..."

EDITOR'S NOTE:

In 1982, our daughter, Robin, gave us a plaque with these words; it has hung on a wall, in every home we owned, as a constant reminder that "we never walk alone."

DOWN THE LINE

FOR MOMS AND GRANDMAS

Before I was a Mom,
I slept as late as I wanted and never worried about how late I got into bed
Before I was a Mom, I cleaned my house each day.
I never tripped over toys or forgot words to a lullaby
I didn't worry whether or not my plants were poisonous
I never thought about immunizations.

Before I was a Mom,,
I'd never been puked on, pooped on, chewed on, or peed on!
I had complete control of my mind and thoughts. I slept all night.

Before I was a Mom
I never held down a screaming child so the doctors could do tests or give shots.
I never looked into teary eyes and cried.
I never got gloriously happy over a simple grin.
I never sat up late hours at night watching a baby sleep.

Before I was a Mom,
I never held a sleeping baby just because I didn't want to put it down.
I never felt my heart break into a million pieces when I couldn't stop the hurt.
I never knew that something so small could affect my life so much
I never knew that I could love someone so much
I never knew I would love being a Mom.

Before I was a Mom,
I didn't know the feeling of having my heart outside my body

V. "SIGNIFICANT OTHERS..."

I didn't know how special it could feel to feed a hungry baby
I didn't know that bond between a mother and a child.
I didn't know that something so small could make me feel so important and happy.

Before I was a Mom
I had never gotten up in the middle of the night every ten minutes to make sure all was okay.
I had never known the warmth, the joy, the love, the heartache, the wonderment or the satisfaction of being a Mom.
I didn't know I was capable of feeling so much before I was a Mom.
And before I was a GRANDMA I didn't know that all those MOM feelings more than doubled, when I saw that little bundle being held by MY BABY!

Author Unknown

DOWN THE LINE

WHAT IF. . .*

What if today were the very last day
That on earth we were permitted to live,
That before the break of another dawn
An account of our lives we have to give.

Would we live today as we did yesterday,
Never giving our very best,
Just doing those things we were forced to do
Leaving undone all the rest.

The weary, the faint, the lowly oppressed -
We leave them to do the best they can,
While we are engrossed with our selfishness
Not taking time to lend a helping hand.

But remember though, the dawn will break tomorrow -
That today is somebody's last.
Leave nothing undone at the close of the day.
To your purpose in life, *hold steadfast.*

> Melvin T. Haynes
> Dec. 21, 1941

EDITOR'S NOTE:

* This poem was found among Martha's poems, written by Melvin Haynes, the *'love of her life.'*

Melvin Haynes was a young man who grew up in Clermont, Georgia, and was in ministry in the North Georgia Conference of the Methodist Church. He was active in youth and young adult activities. There, he met my cousin, Martha Johnson and fell madly in love with her. Theirs was a long courtship, lasting

V. "SIGNIFICANT OTHERS..."

ten years or more. They never married but that was *her* choice *not his!*

Martha's mother, Mae Smith Johnson, had died within days of Martha's birth so her Grandparents and her Aunt Cliffie Johnson raised her. She always felt responsible for taking care of her 'Granny Johnson,' giving *that* as her reason not to marry Melvin. He died very early in life from chronic illnesses. When she was asked what was the cause of his death, Martha always said, with tears in her eyes, *"he died of a broken heart!"*

I often wonder if Martha's death came with '*a broken heart,*' as well.

DOWN THE LINE

WHEN YOU THOUGHT I WASN'T LOOKING

When you thought I wasn't looking, I saw you hang my first painting on the refrigerator, and I wanted to paint another.

When you thought I wasn't looking, I saw you feed a stray cat, and I thought it was good to be kind to animals.

When you thought I wasn't looking, I saw you make my favorite cake just for me, and I knew that little things are special things.

When you thought I wasn't looking, I heard you say a prayer, and I believed there is a God I could always talk to.

When you thought I wasn't looking, I felt you kiss me goodnight, and I felt loved.

When you thought I wasn't looking, I saw tears come from your eyes, and I learned that sometimes things hurt, but it's OK to cry.

When you thought I wasn't looking, I saw that you cared, and I wanted to be everything that I could be.

When you thought I wasn't looking, I looked - and want to say thanks for all the things I saw when you thought I wasn't looking.

Author Unknown

Printed in Ann Landers column, 1998.

V. "SIGNIFICANT OTHERS..."

ON DEATH AND DYING

The following quote comes from *Pamela Jekel's book* titled RIVER WITHOUT END:

An Indian was speaking to a very young boy as he watched his 'old' grandmother dying slowly. The boy could not understand what was happening or why. The old Indian put it this way:

> *"Dying is no different from 'sleeping', boy! Anyway, it is only more of it. We each die a little each night, when our souls fly out of our bodies in our dreams. The old ones sleep more and more as their time nears an end. And if you ask them, they will tell you that they come to prefer their dreams to their waking hours. That is how it is with death. Unless it comes to us by surprise we are often quite ready to welcome it."*

EDITOR'S REFLECTION:

The older I get, and the more people I observe 'growing old,' the more I can understand this concept. I've heard many older people say, *"just let me go, I'm ready;"* meanwhile relatives panic and hurry to brush aside the wishes of their loved one. Their immediate response to their loved one appears to be a *scolding one* by saying: *"don't say that!"* In doing so, they are denying the honesty and integrity of their loved one, thereby not respecting their wishes. The dying patient has dealt with the reality, and finality of his/her own death, but the relatives are refusing to accept that.

They are not ready to 'let go' of their loved one, and let God take them on home. It is the *selfishness of man* that wants to cling to their loved one, and keep them here on earth. Man looks at his *own void,* rather than allowing their loved one to find the joy of being 'released' from the pain and suffering. If we were in the position of the one who was suffering, more than likely we too, would want relief!

Death is as sure as life. It cannot be escaped, avoided, or ignored! Neither can birth. They are real. Both will happen in your lifetime. When we are born, we do not feel the pain of birth. The mother experiences that pain. But, *when we are dying, we do feel that pain, so very vividly!*

If somehow, family members could learn how to 'let go' they could assist us in our dying, letting us move over into eternity with greater joy! Their holding on to us, not letting us go, only multiplies the grief process for everyone. Not only that, it leaves the dying patient feeling guilty, thinking they should not their family 'alone.'

Let's wake up and live each day to the fullest…but with the *reality* of knowing that we are *dying* daily! It was meant to be that way…God ordained it. Why do we try to deny it?

When I say "I'm ready to go," I trust my loved ones will respect my feelings and *'let me go, lovingly.'* I might be going on a big trip but I do not plan for my baggage to include any guilt feelings for leaving them behind. Actually, they will probably be glad to help me pack my bags! I imagine if Jim were here helping me pack, he might send me off in *'my private plane'* without any clothes at all, like he did when we flew to Texas in 1976!

But, not to worry, from what I gather about heaven *'one size fits all.'* So I'll leave it up to God to take care my clothes! The kind that won't have to be ironed. . .

Becky Williams Buckman
June 22, 2012

V. "SIGNIFICANT OTHERS..."

SOMETHING MEANINGFUL

You, like I, have a quiet reverence for life
and all living things.

We share a silent thrill at the breathtaking view
of a distant landscape or a nearby valley
where birds fly free and wildlife rambles unmolested.

This common bond, our appreciation of
nature's breathing world, keeps our minds
and hearts together in a spiritual closeness.

When you're with me and I'm with you we
share deeply each other's sensitivities,
delicate feelings and love of life.

The pure and simple beauty of our relationship
is something meaningful beyond words.

Author: J. Carie Sexton

EDITOR'S NOTE: These beautiful words are on a plaque given to me by my husband in 1975. It has hung in our home since 1975 as a reminder of *our common bond!*

DOWN THE LINE

WE BURIED HER BENEATH THE WILLOWS

One day an Angel came down from Heaven
An envoy of our God above.
From this great world to choose a token
That on his throne in Heaven, would love!

He winged his way down to this earth
He picked our girl, her soul, her voice.
Today our treasure sings in heaven.
God praised the angel for his choice!

We buried her beneath the willows
With heads bowed low, we walked away.
God needed someone to sing in Heaven…
We'll meet again on that GREAT DAY!

Through all her pain, she sang and smiled
A lovely smile of Heavenly birth.
And when God's angel called her homeward,
She gently smiled farewell to earth.

Heaven retaineth now our lovely treasure.
This lowly earth her casket keeps.
But still, the sunbeams, they love to linger
Above the grave where Linda sleeps.

Author Unknown

EDITOR'S NOTE:

In going through stacks of writings I had stored away in my attic, I found this poem. I believe it was written about a dear cousin of mine: *Linda Bowen - my best friend.*

V. "SIGNIFICANT OTHERS..."

Linda died in March, 1960, a few months before her wedding day. A life cut short by sudden illness. Linda was truly a blessing to all she met! She was beautiful in every way, and had the voice of an angel. . . her life was given in service to her Lord each day that she lived among us.

***I dedicate this poem to her memory having been blessed by the twenty years of life we shared together.

GROWING OLD

"Lord, thou knowest better than I know myself that I am growing older, and will some day be old. Keep me from getting talkative, and particularly from the fatal habit of thinking I must say something on every subject and on every occasion. Release me from craving to straighten out everybody's affairs. Keep my mind free from the recital of endless details - give me wings to get to the point. I ask for grace enough to listen to the tales of others' pains. Help me to endure them with patience. But seal my lips on my own aches and pains - they are increasing and my love of rehearsing them is becoming sweeter as the years go by. Teach me the glorious lesson that occasionally it is possible that I may be mistaken. Keep me reasonably sweet: I do not want to be a saint - some of them are so hard to live with - but a sour old woman is one of the crowning works of the devil. Make me thoughtful but not moody; helpful, but not bossy. With my vast store of wisdom, it seems a pity not to use it all - but thou knowest, Lord, that I want a few friends at the end. AMEN

Author Unknown

EDITOR'S NOTE: This was written by a Mother Superior. It is pasted in the front of my Bible - I read it often to remind me to take her advice!

V. "SIGNIFICANT OTHERS..."

WHAT IS LIFE ABOUT ?

When I woke up this morning I asked, *"What is Life about?"* I found the answer in my room. I looked around and these are things I saw that spoke to me:

The FAN: *be cool.*
The ROOF: *aim high.*
The WINDOW: *See my world.*
The CLOCK: *time is precious.*
The MIRROR: *reflect before you act.*
The CALENDAR: *be up to date.*
The DOOR: *push hard for goals.*
The FLOOR: *kneel down and pray.*

EDITOR'S NOTE: from a 'post' on FACE BOOK.
(August 2011)

DOWN THE LINE

MOVING FORWARD

WHAT ARE SOME OF THE FEELINGS I'm having that indicate I am moving forward in the grieving process? And...HDMAMMF? (how does my answer make me feel?)

I am feeling more like the "old me," the one who sees light and rejoices, the one who finds some little happiness in each day, over and above *the tears that still 'wash my face'* when I least expect to be 'washed.'

I am finding joy in "teaching" children and adults again; I am finding others who need a friend - others who recently lost their spouse. I have begun playing the piano every day - it connects me to GOD and to my dear Jim!

I feel a bit like an amputee might feel …part of ME is missing! No artificial limb or part can be added to my being to make me whole again…the loss is still there and SO REAL. The adjustment of functioning without the part of me that was "bound in and for eternity" is a minute-by-minute struggle; the disfigurement of being without my soul-mate leaves me hurting. The loneliness still hovers over me, painfully. It strikes me daily!

Yet, I am moving on. My answer makes me feel like the "battle is being won…." one step at a time!

Becky Williams-Buckman
May 2008

* *Previously published:* August, 2008 issue of BRIDGES, a national newsletter for grieving spouses by United Marriage Encounter.

V. "SIGNIFICANT OTHERS…"

GOD SAW YOU

God saw you were getting tired
and a cure was not to be,
so He put his arms around you
And whispered, "Come to me."
With tearful eyes we watched you
And saw you pass away and
although we loved you dearly,
we could not make you stay.
A golden heart stopped beating,
Hard working hands at rest.
God broke our hearts to prove to us
He only takes the best.

Author Unknown

RELAX

"This is the day which the Lord has made; we will rejoice and be glad in it." Psalms 118:24

I don't know about you, but I tend to live my life as though my sole purpose is somehow to get *everything done before I die!* Does this sound familiar? We get up early, stay up late, avoid doing things we really enjoy, thinking we can finish our 'list' today.

We convince ourselves that this is only a temporary issue. "Once the crisis of the moment is over, we'll have lots of time to do what we enjoy." But, when one crisis ends, another always begins. When one of our daughter's was young, she asked why so many bad things were happening to us. I told her that 'things will get better,' trying to persuade her, as well as to convince my self! Her response: *'well, as soon as we get over this hump, I know there will be another.'* In her young innocence, she was right! Over the years, our family life proved that to be true. So, if life is one 'hump after another' how do we move ahead with our list?

The nature of an "in-basket" is that it is meant to have items in it to be completed; it is not supposed to be empty. In fact, a full "in-basket" just means that you are successful and that your time is in demand. God wants us *to be led, not driven;* to have purpose, peace and happiness, and to enjoy the blessings he gives to us.

In reality, almost everything can wait. Very little in our lives truly falls into the "emergency" category. The truth is, if we stay balanced, we will accomplish everything we need to do. The purpose of the journey is not to get it all done before the clock runs out. *It is to become all that God intends us to be and enjoy the journey with Him.*

V. "SIGNIFICANT OTHERS..."

I have to remind myself that when I die there will still be things to do. I simply need to look at my 'in basket' and determine my priorities. Someone else will do the things that I left undone.

So RELAX, let GOD guide your choices. Then you can *rejoice, and be glad in the day the Lord has made for you!*

****adapted from an old church bulletin:*

Becky Williams Buckman
January 5, 2011

SIGN LANGUAGE...

at my house!

Becky Williams Buckman

"Love is the Garden of My Soul"

SIGN LANGUAGE

Bare walls bore me. One of the first things I do when I move into my new abode is find the tool box, get the hammer and nails. Of course, the more basic things, like my 'necessities' and some food, have to be number one priority. After that, I open the box with all my signs and wall decorations, and begin designing the layout: the perfect place for that 'perfect' sign or picture.

Once some of them are hung, I sleep better. Plus when the first visitor arrives they soon know a little about who I am and my philosophy of life. That is why I am glad you have visited with me today. If you have time, I'd like to show you the 'sign language' around my new home. Let's start at the front door:

"The Only Way to Have a Friend is to Be One"

I saw this truth played out in my home as I grew up. I do not recall anytime when as a child, there were not friends coming and going in and out our doors. My genetic make up requires *people*. People who need people are the luckiest people in the world. . . I get my energy from people; they keep my motor running!

I've been fortunate enough to make friends wherever we have lived. I have a 'best friend' in ever port. . .all the way from Georgia to the west coast as well as in Japan and England so you can imagine the different accents I hear. Even so, I've lived in the South so long that I'm easily identified as a *'southerner.'* But that is fine by me!

I don't ever meet a stranger. . .if I do it is simply a friend whom I have not met before! I'm thankful for *every friend*. I am now a part of all whom I have met!

"Dull Women Have Immaculate Houses"

This one makes me feel good because I never have an immaculate house! I just hope I'm not as 'dull' as the dirt on my floors, or the dust on my tables. Many years ago when I was stressing out over the 'housecleaning' that I'd left undone, a friend gave me the best advice: "find the level of *Clean* that your husband will accept; do that and no more! Then you can 'enjoy' life more. . ."

My husband never complained about a messy house but I did much more than *he* expected; as I have gotten older and now live alone, I have lowered my expectations of myself. So if I can live with the 'dirt devil' why should I bother breaking my back to be immaculate?

I've come a long way, baby! I've even learned not to apologize for the mess. Life is short, right?

"Keep Smiling"

I got to work one day and found this 'sign' cross-stitched and framed lying on my desk. I have no clue who did this, or why, but it is a constant reminder that a smile will take you farther in life than any frown, and there is 'no pain.' It keeps you from looking at life up-side down. . . .after all a smile is simply an upside down frown!

Our family has had its ups and downs, like everyone else, and smiling through those hard times is not the easiest cake to slice, but a sense of humor will turn those hairpin curves in life into a smoother ride. It's worth a try, right?

"To Love and Be Loved is the greatest Joy on Earth"

Being born into a Christian family was the first blessing I felt once I 'hit ground.' The love that wrapped me so warmly that

VI. SIGN LANGUAGE. . .

day has continued to run through my veins every moment of my life. My friends continue to keep me *'pumped up'* with love, thereby causing it to spill over to all with whom I encounter daily. It seems the more I 'empty' my tank, the quicker it is refilled! What a blessing!

Because I was loved by my family, and by God's grace, I could love myself, even with all of the 'zits and kinks' of growing up. To love others, as God loves them, is not always easy, but that is our goal. Once we know the unfailing love of God and family *we are free to love unconditionally,* without any effort. There is no greater Joy!

"Drink Coffee - Do Stupid Thing faster with more enthusiasm"

After I open my sleepy eyes, and hit the floor, I go to the Coffee Pot, and hit the 'on' button. It was 'ready' and waiting for me to get up so it could do its job! It is 'readied' the night before; if I didn't I might put sugar in the filter instead of the coffee - a stupid thing for sure!

While it is still perking I begin doing some *'stupid'* things. . .like going straight to the computer! (even before I get dressed!) That indicates how addicted I am to the two C's: *'coffee and computer!'* If I had partaken of either of these things in college, I'm sure I would have been late to class!

Once the coffee is done I start drinking. . .it only takes one cup, and actually what I drink is basically *colored water with a lot of sugar.* I feel sure my *enthusiasm* comes from a 'high' on sugar, more than from the caffeine! I guess I took Julie Andrew's advice: *a spoon full of sugar makes the medicine go down.*

The next stupid thing I do is forget to take my medicine, but when you have a bunch to take and they are like 'horse pills' who wouldn't forget, even if you aren't senile? Beyond that, I often burn the toast, while trying to do three or four other things at once. Another indication of my ADHD condition. . .I try to juggle too much too fast. Another attempt to make the toast, and I succeed, then swig down a half cup of colored water, and I'm off to work, running faster than a three legged dog going for his dinner! That really is not too fast. . .

I've been known to do a lot of *stupid things* in my life but so far I'm still here, with a lot of *enthusiasm* for life, so maybe they weren't too stupid after all! I will admit however, that one morning instead of putting the milk back in the refrigerator I left it out, and I put the empty coffee pot in the fridge. Reckon I should drink more coffee and less sugar?

> "Grandma's Kitchen: Tasters Welcome, Everything Made with Love and an Extra spoon of sugar."

Well, by now you know that I am one for 'sweets.' Sweet Tea is tops, of course. It always was even before I moved to Summerville, SC, the *'home of Sweet Tea.'* Most people tell me it is more like syrup than sweet tea. . .funny thing, however, is the number of people who guzzle it down like it was their 'nite cap!' At my house it disappears in thin air!

When our son's Band practiced at our house, Chris, the drummer came in the door asking for a glass of my sweet tea. During their breaks, he came back for a refill, and had another before he left that night. The guys knew I'd have plenty of that, as well as brownies to keep them *'rocking the night away.'* The clerks at Kroger always seemed to know when the Band was going to be practicing at our house because my order had more bags of sugar, brownie mix and tea bags than I normally bought!

VI. SIGN LANGUAGE. . .

When Chris married, it didn't take me long to decide what their wedding gift would be. I bought a lovely crystal Tea Pitcher, a 5 pound bag of Sugar, a box of family sized Tea Bags, and included my recipe for Sweet Tea! It was *a hit.*

I always loved to cook and bake, even before I became a *Grandma,* and for sure I 'tasted' everything before it went on the table! Well, let me back up: one time I didn't, and it could have cost me some marital problems!

When Jim and I married, we began our family with his two elementary-aged children. Being a new bride and 'mom' I was so eager to do everything just right. I was making spaghetti one night and it should have been a snap since I'd done that many times when I had roommates.

This particular night when I was cooking, I think 'honeymoon-itus' was still working on my brain because somehow, I really goofed up! However, I had no idea I had done anything wrong until my husband commented on the meal. He was a man of few words and had never criticized me before, so I was devastated when he said: "this spaghetti is not good; what did you do to it?" Sputtering, with moistened eyes, reeling with insecurity, I said: "what is wrong?" I assured him I had measured everything very carefully, just as the recipe said. He quickly said, "well something is wrong with the recipe. Maybe you had better find another one!"

I had the correct amount of noodles, salt and had boiled the water as I should have. After all was said and done, I realized I had put the right amount of noodles and salt into the boiling water, but I had not put enough water in the stewer! *Result?* BAD DINNER. . . Too salty!

The 'proof in the pudding' that night was that the children did not complain. Maybe they were being kind to this 'new mom' and didn't want to hurt her feelings, perhaps they didn't notice, or were so hungry it didn't matter! I prefer to think it was the former. They ate their meal - cleaned their plates, and went to their rooms! Lucky for us all, the spaghetti didn't make them sick!

After the children left the room I cried like a baby; I had a lot of explaining and apologizing to do to my husband. I had to promise to be a *better cook:* like being sure I measured everything correctly, and like *tasting the food* before I served it to 'anyone. ' The good news is that Jim stayed with me thirty-six years and the children kept coming to the table at every meal!

"Grandchildren are God's Reward for Growing Old"

As of now, I have four and would welcome more. . .because I just love kids! They are like the 'touch of an angel' on my shoulder.

I'll never forget when we found out that we would become grandparents. The most difficult part of the news was that *the first grandchild* would be born in North Dakota, and we were in Georgia, miles away. Thank God for airplanes!

We couldn't wait to share the news with our friends, many of whom were already grandparents. Once we told them, they began pulling out photos of their 'grandchildren' and we knew we'd soon be doing the same thing. That's just one of the things grandparents do!

The time came for the baby's arrival. We had two young children still in elementary school and saw no way we could afford for me to go, but our daughter had called and wanted "Mom"

VI. SIGN LANGUAGE. . .

to come be there when she got home from the hospital. Still, we couldn't see how that could work, i. e. until late one afternoon our doorbell rang. Jim answered the door and a dear couple who were close friends stood there with an envelope in hand. We invited them in, but they insisted they couldn't stay but they wanted us to open the envelope before they left.

By this time, our minds were bombed out with anxiety, wondering what this was all about! Inside the envelope was sufficient money for my airplane ticket to Grand Forks, N. D. With a note inside that read:

"Dear Jim and Becky,

Here is a little love gift for you from people who love you, and want you to be there to hold your first grandchild when your daughter brings him home from the hospital. Just rock him and love him with all your heart, just like we love you!"

All our Love,
Your Friends

No one ever admitted they contributed to the gift (about $400.00) but we had an idea it was from our 'encountered' friends! It was a 'pay it forward' *miracle!* Once they left, we stood there, in tears, holding each other in *unbelief.* It didn't seem real. What had we done to deserve such a gift? We thanked God for such *a surprise blessing - not just the money but for those kinds of friends.*

We bought my plane ticket and within 3 days I was on my way to North Dakota, *wearing a new hat*: now I was 'Grandma Buckman.' I flew out on April 29th, 1983 and celebrated my forty-third birthday that night rocking our first grandchild, Josh, to sleep.

I'll never forget that feeling. Now that grandchild is in his thirties, and I'm older than dirt but the 'grandparent' in me will never die!

"Kindly Control Yourself"

People who know me will perhaps tell you that I still have not learned to do this. No, I don't think I do harmful things, *I just get excited very easily!* Like when I see a friend whom I haven't seen in years, or when I see a Cardinal pecking away at my bird feeder! Or when my piano students go 'over the top' at their Recital, or when my grandchildren come for a visit. And when I see an elderly couple *hugging up* like newlyweds, or when a new father takes a first glimpse of his baby. . .a miracle on the horizon! My heart is so full of joy - with tears of happiness as I see life unfolding before me. That's excitable stuff!

Or, when I'm at a concert that is stellar! And when the Choir sings one of my favorite gospel songs, and when I travel and discover a *'new world'* somewhere in the USA. The first flowers of spring bring me into a state of ecstasy, to see the tips of a rosebud just waiting for its petals to spread open, or to smell the aroma of confederate jasmine when I open my back door; to find a special package in the mail from my pen pal of sixty-three years! Who could contain themselves when 'showered' with so many blessings? Not me, that's for sure!

When there is a Dance Band playing, and there's an open space on the dance floor, that is when I have the most difficulty controlling myself! Just ask my girlfriends, or my kids. . .they know I will be 'all over the place' with excitement, rocking and rolling with the rhythm. Yes, *I am over 70*, and have four titanium joints, but that doesn't stop me from dancing for all I'm worth.

VI. SIGN LANGUAGE. . .

No, I cannot keep pace with the jet-set, but not to worry, that doesn't slow me down a bit! I'll keep on. . . maybe it will have to be in a wheelchair someday, but life is too short to be 'in control' all the time, right?

"Blessed Is The Man"

> For whom a good woman lives,
> To whom his work is a pleasure,
> By whom his friends are encouraged
> With whom all are comfortable
> To whom a clear conscience abides, and
> Through whom his children see God!

It's been said that behind every successful man is a a good woman. I must add that behind every good woman there is a man who loves her unconditionally, just as God loves her. I was abundantly blessed to have that kind of man. I'm sure there were times we each failed to love each other with unconditional love - usually when we put *our own needs* above the needs of our partner. That is where forgiveness had to come into play!

Jim's work as an electronics technician was stellar. For thirty-five years he served his country, was conscientious and went above and beyond the call of duty, both in the USA and overseas during the Korean and Vietnam Wars.

His children saw God through his life. Late in life he found a new and deeper relationship with his Lord and began to serve Him in ways that surprised us all. He was basically a shy person and when he volunteered to teach the Gospel of John in our Sunday School Class, we all 'wondered' what would come next! He was a 'hit' for sure, and so was the study.

He'd always loved children but had never volunteered to teach Sunday School until there was a need for a teacher in the fourth grade class. After several months parents asked him what was he doing to inspire their children to do homework for Sunday School? Their children had *never had homework* assigned by a Sunday School Teacher. As a new Christian, there were many questions the children would ask, and he had no clue how to answer them! His theory: *"well, none of us know the answer, so between now and next week, we'll all do some research, and pool our knowledge. . .and see who comes up with the right answer!"* He was a 'hit' with the kids, and it even spilled over onto the parents: they found themselves studying the Bible with their children during the week. A win-win deal! God is so good!

"Love is the Garden of My Soul"

When I see this sign each day, I am reminded of the 13th Chapter of I Corinthians. We have heard it time and again, but the message is more clear each time I read it: *without love, I am nothing.*

I cannot wrap my mind around the idea of a baby coming into the world without it being wrapped in a blanket of love; from the moment of conception, this *'person-to-be'* is loved completely. It is a child of God, not simply a fetus, not something to be cast aside!

When I was born, I came into the world wrapped in a blanket of love, even though I was not 'planned!' The love of my parents surrounded me constantly. When I met and fell in love with Jim, I had the warmest blanket of all, for over half of my life! Then, from the moment we knew I was pregnant, we loved that child with all our heart and soul.

VI. SIGN LANGUAGE...

No matter where we have lived we found ourselves and our souls in *the garden of love*. When that is the case, blooming where you are planted just comes naturally! My prayer is that I bloom with love wherever I go, whatever I do, and *to God be the glory*, for the things he has done in my life.

"Friendship"

A Friend knows the song in your heart
And can sing it back to you
When you have forgotten the words.

Since I made my first childhood friend, this has been true. I'm fortunate that I still have many of those kinds of friendships. I'm not the *'one-friend'* kind of person. *The more the merrier* is my philosophy.

I have made a 'best friend' in every city where I have lived. Every one is unique, each one adding a different ingredient to the cake, making each bite rich and delightful. I am always making new friends, but I keep the old: *one is silver and the other gold.*

Distance never separates true friends. Years can pass but the connections remain strong. It only takes a Christmas letter or a phone call to 'go back in time' - to pick up where you left off. The GOLDEN GIRLS of Cherokee High School, Class of 1958 are a prime example. We were a close-knit group back then; years passed before we were able to re-connect, but when we did, the bond became even stronger. Every year since 1995, we have taken a trip together. It is nothing more than our old 'spend the night' parties revisited, but *the joy juice* we get from it lasts until the next trip!

When Jim died, the 'girls' came to his Memorial Service, filling up an entire church pew. Their support was like steel beams holding me up. They have continued doing it now for seven years. . .being the sunlight on dark days, and showering me with moonlight on the blackened nights. They know me inside and out, just as I do them! What a comfort it is to have those kind of friends in 'every port.' *I'll never walk alone*: they are beside me all the way, and God is our guide. That's for sure!

"Dancing"

Dance like no one is watching
Sing like no one is listening
Love like you have never been hurt

I had rather dance than eat when I'm hungry. There's just something about hitting the floor and swaying to the music that sets me on fire. I think I must have come out of the womb dancing, and never stopped!

Jim and I were 'dancers' from day one. Not that we were professionals, by any means, but it was our all-time favorite entertainment. Even now that I'm alone I find myself dancing in the living room to our favorite songs! I'm still holding him in my heart, as if he were holding me in his arms. I feel sure he knows I'm still dancing. . .just as he is dancing with the angels in heaven. I'm hoping he is waiting for me to 'cut in!'

I can be found singing along with the music wherever I am. The stereo is always on full blast, at home or in the car. So far the Housing Association has not 'written me up' for disturbing the peace. I guess the 'noise ordinance' in my neighborhood isn't too rigid. . .or else the other *old folks* who live out here are too hard of hearing to notice!

VI. SIGN LANGUAGE. . .

GAMES PEOPLE PLAY

I have always loved to party so Jim and I entertained a lot. It didn't have to be a holiday for us to throw a whopper of a party. My brain went into overdrive and stayed in cruise control for weeks in advance. Instead of sleeping, I dreamed up 'games' - and just hoped the group wouldn't walk out on me before prizes were given out!

So here goes. Grab a pencil and let's PLAY and see who is smarter than a fifth grader. OK?

"WHY DO FOOLS FALL IN LOVE"

DIRECTIONS for the game:

Give everyone a sheet with these lyrics on it and a pencil. Each person underlines the song titles they recognize. Have each person count the titles underlined. The person with the highest number of correct answers wins a "lovers" prize!

"...because what the world needs now is love. It is something stupid to dream the impossible dream but dream along with me while we listen to music to watch girls by.

...because love makes the world go around with fascination. I see those Spanish Eyes of Alice Blue Gown cruising down the river. She gave me heartaches by the numbers and told me "anytime" you send me paper roses I'll send you pennies from heaven.

...because roses are red I only have eyes for you, and the melody of love makes my happiness, and your kiss of fire makes love a many splendored thing.

DOWN THE LINE

...because in the days of wine and roses, when I was young and foolish my secret love for you, you, you, showed that little things mean a lot when you bought me those red roses for a blue lady.

...because behind closed doors it must be him, saying "goodnight sweetheart" making me the happiest girl in the USA.

...because you needed me but you always hurt the one you love. Only you want to release me, so I'll never fall in love again. You've said "goodnight, Irene, goodnight". I now see the red sails in the sunset and my future just passed, so I'll say "goodnight sweetheart - it's time to go."

...because til I waltz again with you, somewhere my love, what's forever for?"

HOW MANY SONG TITLES did you find?
***You should have 43 to score 100!

***Created by: *Becky Williams Buckman*

VI. SIGN LANGUAGE...

MUSIC MANIA: Songs of Yesteryear

1. Songs with *STATES* in them:

   * Moonlight in _____

   * Yellow Rose of _____

   * _____ on my Mind

   * _____ Waltz

   * My Old _____ Home

   * Carry me back to Old _____

   * _____ Wedding Song

   * Deep in the Heart of _____

2. Songs with *COUNTRIES or AREAS* in them:

   * _____ Eyes are Smiling

   * I wish I was in the land of _____

   * Springtime in the _____

   * _____ the Beautiful

   * _____ (country of a famous musical)

3. Songs with *CITIES or PLACES* in them:

   * By the time I get to _____

   * M_____ R_____

   * _____ Choo Choo

   * _____ PTA

   * I left my heart in _____

   * R _____ R _____ Valley

   * _____ Rose

4. Songs with *COLORS* in them:

   * _____ Roses for a _____ Lady

   * _____ Christmas

   * _____ Moon

   * _____ Rose of Texas

   *Deep_____

   *Don't it maky my _____ eyes _____

   *Honkey Tonk_____

   * _____ Christmas

   * _____ is the color of my true love's hair

VI. SIGN LANGUAGE...

* When my _____ moon turns to _____

* By the Light of the _____ Moon

* _____ (Leann Rimes sings this)

5. Songs with *NAMES* in them: (hint: starts with the letter given)

   * E_____

   * C_____ C_____

   * L_____

   * L_____

   * D_____ D_____

   * R_____ R_____

   * Wait til the Sun Shines_____

   * Old_____ Tucker

   * F_____ and J_____

   * _____ Be Good

   * _____ by Starlight

   * A_____ B_____ G_____

   * _____ B_____, won't you please come home

* _____ o' my H_____

* M_____ L_____

* _____ the Knife

* _____ Don't Take Your Love to Town

6. Songs with *SUN, MOON, EARTH or WATER* in them:

* You are my _____

* _____ Serenade

* _____ River

* Beyond the _____

* _____ becomes you

* When my blue _____ turns to Gold

* By the Light of the Silvery _____

* Wait til the _____ Shines Nellie

* _____ by Starlight

7. Songs that have *FOOD, FLOWERS or MONEY* in them:

* _____ from Heaven

* Days of _____ and _____

* Paper _____

VI. SIGN LANGUAGE...

* I never promised you a _____ Garden

* _____ Hill

* Mexicali _____

* When you wore a _____

* _____ JULEP.

SCORING: Out of 66 songs:

if you get 63 or more = BEST OF THE BUNCH
if you get 56 or more = SUPER GOOD
if you get 46 or more = GOOD
if you get 45 or less = You need to **LISTEN TO MORE OLD SONGS!**

*** *CREATED BY: Jim and Becky Buckman*

DOWN THE LINE

ST. PATRICK'S DAY GAME

***FILL IN THE BLANKS

1. _____Apples

2. _____Stew

3. _____Beans

4. _____Grass

5. _____with envy

6. Fried_____tomatoes

7. _____peas

8. _____land

9. _____beret

10. _____thumb

11. When_____eyes are smiling

12. _____Boy

13. _____Day Parade - New York

14. _____of the Irish

15. St. Patrick was a _____Missionary

VI. SIGN LANGUAGE. . .

16. Who died March 17, 461?_____

17. _____ME, I'm Irish!

18. _____Clovers

19. What color is a Shamrock?

                MY SCORE: _____out of 19

***CREATED BY: Becky Williams Buckman

DOWN THE LINE

THE CANDY CRAZE

1. A famous swashbuckling trio of old_____

2. Indian burial grounds_____

3. Galaxy_____

4. Red planet_____

5. Home of the movie stars_____

6. Not laughing out loud_____

7. A famous author_____

8. Famous baseball player_____

9. Famous New York Street_____

10. Twin Letters_____

11. Superman's other identity_____

12. A sweet sign of affection_____

13. Favorite day for working people_____

14. What bees make_____

15. Nut happiness_____

16. Pleasingly plump_____

VI. SIGN LANGUAGE. . .

17. Two female pronouns put together_____

18. A feline_____

19. Single women look for him_____

20. Round flotation devices_____

21. Sun explosion_____

22. Bite with crackling noise_____

23. Dry Cow_____

24. Children of the Cane_____

MY SCORE_____ of 24. ***

*** ***CREATED BY:*** Becky Williams Buckman

DOWN THE LINE

ANSWERS FOR THE FOLLOWING GAMES:

I. WHY DO FOOLS FALL IN LOVE?

Because, What The World Needs Now, Something Stupid, Dream The Impossible Dream, Dream Along With Me, Music To Watch Girls By, Love Makes the World Go Round, Fascination, Spanish Eyes, Alice Blue Gown, Cruising Down the River, Heartaches By the Number, Anytime, Paper Roses, Pennies from Heaven. Roses are Red, I Only have Eyes for You, Melody of Love, My Happiness, Kiss of Fire, Love is A Many Splendored Thing, Days of Wine and Rose, Young and Foolish, My Secret Love, You/You/You, Little Things Mean A Lot, Red Roses for A Blue Lady, Behind Closed Doors, It Must Be Him, Goodnight Sweetheart, The Happiest Girl in the USA, You Needed Me, You Always Hurt the One You Love, Only You, Release Me, I'll Never Fall in Love Again, Goodnight Irene Goodnight, Red Sails in the Sunset, My Future Just Passed, Til I Waltz Again with You, Somewhere My Love, What's Forever For.

II. MUSIC MANIA: Oldies for the Goldies

1. *STATES:* Vermont, Texas, Georgia, Tennessee, Kentucky, Virginia, Hawaiian, Texas

2. *COUNTRIES/AREAS:* Irish, Dixie, Rockies, America, Austria

3. *CITIES/PLACES:* Phoenix, Moulin Rouge, Chattanooga, Harper Valley, San Francisco, Red River Valley, Mexicali

4. *COLORS:* Red/Blue, White, Blue, Yellow, Purple, Brown/Blue, Blues, Blue, Black, Blue/Gold, Silvery, Blue

VI. SIGN LANGUAGE...

5. *NAMES:* Elvira, Corrina/Corrina, Lorena, Laura, Delta Dawn, Rocking Robin, Nellie, Dan, Frankie/Johnny, Johnny, Stella, Corina/Corina, Alice Blue Gown, Bill Bailey, Peg, Mona Lisa, Jack, Ruby

6. *SUN/MOON/EARTH:* Sunshine, Moonlight, Moon, Sunset, Moonlight, Moon, Moon, Sun, Stella

7. *FOOD/FLOWERS/MONEY:* Pennies, Wine/Roses, Roses, Rose, Blueberry, Rose, Tulip, Mint,

III. ST. PATRICK'S DAY:

Green, Irish, Green for the next 8 answers, Irish, Danny, St. Patrick's, Luck,
Christian, St. Patrick, Kiss, 4-leaf, Green

IV. THE CANDY CRAZE:

3 Musketeers, Mound, Milky Way, Mars, Hollywood, Snickers, O'Henry, Babe Ruth, 5th Avenue, M&M's, Clark, Kisses, Payday, Bit O Honey, Almond Joy, Chunky, Hershey, Kit Kat, Millionaire, Life Savers, Sunburst, Krackle, Milk Duds, Sugar Babies

THIS and 'That. . .'

'Spinning some yarn, from 'days gone by!'

FROM DAYS GONE BY

My sister, Ruth, is eighteen years older than me, and has memories of her childhood back in the 1920's and 1930's. I love to hear her recite some of the sayings she heard at our home and at my Granny's house. When I asked her to write them down for me she didn't hesitate a moment. Now in her early nineties she still has a remarkable memory, just like our mother had. Our Mother also lived to be ninety-five, so longevity is passed *down the line*. I'm counting on being around a long time too! *(I think my children might be a bit worried over that fact!)*

Some of these ditties I recall from my childhood, but a few were 'foreign' to me – but nevertheless, fun to know! I wonder how many children in today's generation have ever heard *'any'* of them! Have you?

A PRAYER FOR KIDS

Lord, bless us and bind us,
Tie our hands behind us
And throw us where the
Boogey Man can't find us!

A PRAYER FOR FORGIVENSSS

Lord have mercy on my soul
How many chickens have I stole?
One last night and the night before
I'm going back tonight to steal two more!

LISTEN, MY FRIEND

My gentle friend as you pass by
As You are now so once was I

As I am now, you soon shall be
Prepare for death, and follow me.

AN IRISH BLESSING

May neighbors respect you
Trouble neglect you
Angels protect you and
Heaven accept you.

PEAS PORRIDGE HOT

Peas, porridge hot,
Peas, porridge cold,
Peas, porridge in the pot nine days old
I asked my Mom for 15 cents
To see the elephant jump the fence
He jumped so high
He touched the sky
And never got back til the Fourth of July.

Tossed my head
Broke my comb
That's all right
Till I get home.

I'll tell my Mom
The boys won't let
The boys won't let
My curls alone

VII. THIS AND 'THAT...'

WONDERFUL WORDS

***It doesn't matter where I go, what I read or with whom I share conversation, there are *'wonderful words of life'* that bathe me, they wrap around me like my warmest robe, and inspire me to sing, day and night! With so much 'muck' floating around in our world today, selective hearing is a must; if you choose otherwise you will choke on the grit and the grainy substances. Your body, mind and soul will be devoured by the poisons that roam freely. It is *your choice!*

Below are some truths that I hold on to: Breathe them into your being, one at a time. *ENJOY!*

Becky Williams Buckman

"Live each day like it is your last, 'cause one day you are gonna' be right!"

Ray Charles

"Life began with waking up and LOVING my mother's face."

George Eliot

"*Yesterday* is a canceled check; *tomorrow* is a promissory note; *today* is the only cash you have. Spend it wisely.

Kay Lyons

DOWN THE LINE

Life is too short. Grudges are a waste of perfect happiness. Laugh when you can. Apologize when you should, and let go of what you cannot change!

Author Unknown

"A wise old owl sat in an oak. The more he saw, the less he spoke. The less he spoke, the more he heard." *Why can't we all be like that wise old bird?*

An Old Proverb

'Music propels the dancer to keep moving.'

Anonymous

"All Music is folk music. I ain't never heard no horse sing a song."

Louis Armstrong
(1901-1971)

"Love is always bestowed as a gift, freely, willingly and without expectation. We don't love to *'be'* loved. We *'love'* to love."

Leo Buscaglia

Is prayer your steering wheel or your spare tire?

Corrie Ten Boon

EPILOGUE

As we conclude our walk together through the sunlight and moonlight of my journey in life I trust that you will have experienced the goodness and the greatness of your own life. . .*the miracle* of it all!

Many of you will have recognized yourselves along the way. You have been part and parcel of who I have become! It has been my joy to walk along beside you. Thanks for sharing your precious time with me!

And, if we just met for the 'first time' may this not be our last.

I hope that what I have learned along my journey can somehow be a beacon to you - to help you see where you are in your own journey, as well as see your pathway becoming more illuminated with God's wisdom and guidance with every step you take.

Becky Williams Buckman
March, 2014

CONTRIBUTING AUTHORS

James (Jim) F. Buckman (1930-2007)

Born Nov. 22, 1930 to Floyd Merriman and Madeline Steward Buckman, in DeKoven, Kentucky. Retired Tech. Sgt., U. S. Air Force, 1950-1970; Retired Civil Service, 1972-1987, Electronic Technician/Precision Measurement Equipment/Radar. He served during the Vietnam and Korean Wars.

He and his wife, Becky Williams Buckman were co-founders of United Marriage Encounter ministry in Okinawa, Japan in 1985. They were members of the National Board of United Marriage Encounter for two years. He was active in the United Methodist Church.

Timothy Merriman Buckman (1973 -)

Born December 15, 1973 in Warner Robins, Ga., the son of James F. and Becky Williams Buckman. Dr. Buckman is a composer, songwriter, and guitarist who holds degrees in guitar and composition from GIT, Hollywood, CA., from Western Kentucky University, Bowling Green, Kentucky. He received his Doctor of Musical Arts from University of Colorado, Boulder, Co. in 2009.

His compositions and songs have won awards from the Music Teacher's National Association, New Miami Music Festival, BMI, and the Cecil Effinger award for composition from the University of Colorado, at Boulder; he has received commissions from artists such as Gilmar Goulart, Gina Raz'on and the Mountain Music Ensemble.

He has written scores for more than a dozen independent films, had his music placed in various music libraries through the

United States, and can be heard on cable TV networks such a E! And Oxygen Network.

Timothy resides in Denver, Colorado where he owns 'Buktruk' Music Company.

Martha Mae Johnson (1919 - 1998)

Born Feb. 19, 1919 to Glen L. and Mae Hawkins Johnson in Cherokee County, Georgia. She was a native of Woodstock. Martha was raised in a Methodist parsonage by her grandparents, The Rev. and Mrs. R.I. Johnson. Martha's mother had died from complications within days eight days of her birth, in 1919. Physically, she had many handicaps but never allowed them to hinder her desire or ability to achieve.

Martha was active in the Methodist Church, not only locally, but across North Georgia, serving in many capacities of leadership with youth and adults. During her life she was employed by the United States Postal Service, Co-owner of Williams Food Store, and Office Manager for Boddy Medical Clinic in Woodstock, Ga.

Serving the needs of people was her passion; her motto came from the hymn *"Others:" Lord help me live from day to day...for others!* She felt that she took on the 'mantle' of her grandfather, Rev. R. I. Johnson, a minister who served in the North Georgia Conference of the Methodist Church. In 1966, she passed that 'mantle' on to her niece, Becky Williams Buckman, for whom she was a mentor.

The Reverend Robert Ithamar Johnson (1870 - 1934)

He was born May 4, 1870 to William Jefferson and Mary Penny Carmichael Johnson in Cherokee County, Georgia; he died on

Dec. 21. 1934, after having conducted three services of worship that day.

Rev. Johnson was husband to Amanda Mae Hawkins Johnson, and the father of four children: Bertha Mae, Glen, Leila Mae, and 'Cliffie'. He received the 'call to ministry' from Woodstock Methodist Church, in Cherokee County, Georgia. He was licensed to preach in 1908, and ordained deacon Nov. 24, 1909. His first 'circuit' had seven churches in the Canton area.

During his twenty-five years in ministry, he served sixty-four churches, as a Circuit Rider, on horseback, with a saddle bag full of sermons, notes and his Bible.

He was ordained Elder in the Methodist Episcopal Church, South, November, 1916. In 1928 he was admitted to the North Georgia Conference in full connection .

It was said of him that "*he knew little of the text of psychology in the art of fishing for men, yet he met the test as a successful fisherman throughout his ministry. He was one of the wise men of his generation, He was not versed in the methods of the seminary, he was not learned after the fashion of schools, but he was an efficient and fruitful winner of souls.... He may not have known grammar, but he knew God.*"

Becky Williams Buckman (1940 -)

Carolyn Rebecca (Becky) Williams Buckman was born to John Gordon and Leila Mae Johnson Williams, April 29, 1940, in Atlanta, Georgia but grew up in Woodstock, Georgia. The wife of James F. Buckman, and mother of James F. Buckman, II, Robin D. Elsner, Apryll D. Gill, and Timothy M. Buckman, Becky's career field of Christian education has led her into many avenues of employment and volunteer service across the southeast and Japan.

ABOUT THE AUTHOR AND EDITOR

Becky Williams Buckman served in United Methodist Churches across Georgia as a Certified Director of Christian Education and later, as a Teacher and Director of a private Lutheran School in Kentucky. After her retirement in the field of Christian education, she was employed by the City of Bowling Green, Kentucky.

Her undergraduate degrees were from Reinhardt and LaGrange Colleges in Georgia. She received her Master's in Christian Education at Candler School of Theology, Emory University, Atlanta, Georgia.

After she married, her full-time career became a homemaker, but she continued to give her time and talents to her church and community.

Her love of journalism and music have been dominant *'notes'* that came *'down the line'* from both sides of her family heritage. In her golden years she began playing those *'notes'* full time, as a freelancer, and owner of *Ms. B's Music Biz* teaching piano in the Charleston, South Carolina area. *Down The Line* is her first book.

She and her husband were active in United Marriage Encounter ministry in the USA and Japan for twenty-five years, and served on the National Board. In 2011 the National Board honored Ms. Buckman (and Jim) with the *'Ham and Eggs'* Award for her untiring service in the establishment of the ministry in South Carolina.

In her free time she can be found at concerts of all genres, in her flower garden, or scrap booking. She is an avid reader and enjoys traveling with friends and family. Ms. Buckman is a member of Summerville Writer's Guild, and Bethany United Methodist Church. She resides in Summerville, South Carolina, the *'home of sweet tea.'*

WHAT OTHERS SAY

"Each poem evokes a combination of feelings, though one feeling seems paramount to others. Becky's readers might feel spiritual. . .encouraging. . .romantic. . .loving."

                        Ellen E. Hyatt

"I have known the author for almost sixty years. . .she enjoys life as much as anyone I know, and the poetry and essays she writes reflect this. . .they let me into her heart."

                        Ann Rutledge

"Heartwarming, sensitive, yet powerful, this writer has the innate talent to turn the ordinary into extraordinary, enthralling the reader from beginning to end. Her writings are genuine, and intertwined with love, humor and unexpected treasures."

                        Martha Jean McClellan

"Please keep writing. You are creative, with a wonderful touch. . . You are a marvel."

                        Dr. G. Ross Freeman
                        Author

"Becky has a way with words which is a talent."

                        Brenda Whitfield

"Truly you have a gift for writing."

                                            Dale and Sharon Bradley

"Everyone has a story to tell. . .from the past and the present, unfolding from all the memories. Becky's writings are real - they deal with humor, inspiration and other attributes. Her stories are penned for readers of all ages."

                                              Jessie Hayden
                                              Author

"I have read your writings over and over. . .they give me a big jolt of warmth and love feelings all the way down to my toes."

                                            Margaret Rhodes

Made in the USA
Charleston, SC
15 December 2014